MACHO MAN

MACHO MAN

The Untamed, Unbelievable Life of

RANDY SAVAGE

JON FINKEL

Published by ECW Press
665 Gerrard Street East
Toronto, Ontario, Canada M4M 1Y2
416-694-3348 / info@ecwpress.com

Editor for the Press: Michael Holmes
Copy editor: David Marsh
Cover design: Jessica Albert
Cover photograph © George Napolitano

PRINTED AND BOUND IN CANADA

LIBRARY AND ARCHIVES CANADA CATALOGUING
IN PUBLICATION

Title: Macho Man : the untamed, unbelievable life of
Randy Savage / Jon Finkel.

Names: Finkel, Jon, author.

Identifiers: Canadiana (print) 20230587089 | Canadiana
(ebook) 20230587119

ISBN 978-1-77041-758-8 (softcover)
ISBN 978-1-77852-285-7 (ePub)
ISBN 978-1-77852-286-4 (PDF)

Subjects: LCSH: Savage, Randy. | LCSH: Wrestlers—
United States—Biography. | LCSH: World Wrestling
Entertainment, Inc. | LCGFT: Biographies.

Classification: LCC GV1196.S28 F56 2024 | DDC
796.812092—dc23

PRINTING: FRIESENS   5   4   3   2   1

For Lanny

CONTENTS

PART III: The Macho Man Cometh

INTRODUCTION

When I was three-quarters of the way through writing this book, Randy Savage's brother, Lanny Poffo, passed away suddenly. He was sixty-eight years old. It was a tragic loss for his family, his friends (he had many around the world) and the wrestling community as a whole. Since Randy's passing in 2011, Lanny had become the torch-bearer for the Poffo wrestling dynasty, which began over seventy years ago when his dad, Angelo, first stepped foot in a wrestling gym.

Lanny was a human encyclopedia on his father and brother and much of the history of pro wrestling in the last half of the 20th century. He was well read, curious, sharp and loved the family business. With his passing, all of the Poffos featured in this book are now gone: Angelo, Judy, Randy and Lanny.

I've wanted to write the definitive biography of the Macho Man since I first wanted to be an author, at maybe thirteen or fifteen years old. When I finally got to a place in my career where I felt confident enough to tackle a project of this size, I put the full book proposal together with one internal catch: I wouldn't go ahead with the book unless I knew Lanny was on board and that I'd be able to talk to him.

I couldn't imagine doing a book on Macho without interviewing his brother. They were best friends. They were tag team partners back in the day. They grew up in wrestling together, from the small territories to the ICW to the WWE, and they grew old together. They had a wonderful relationship with each other and with their parents until the very end.

As the proposal was being reviewed, I exhausted several avenues to get in touch with Lanny, which was tough because he spent much of the year in Ecuador and largely stayed off social media, save for Facebook posts and the select few blogs he worked with.

In an incredible coincidence, someone I interviewed for a previous book, *1996: A Biography*, knew Lanny well and my buddy helped me finally get in touch with him, essentially vouching for me.

By this time, the proposal had been sitting around for over a year, with my own green light hinging on access to Lanny. If he was against the idea or didn't want to be interviewed for the book, I wasn't going to do it. From a personal and journalistic perspective, it wouldn't feel right.

When we finally spoke, his first question was, "Are you related to the great Howard Finkel?"

Howard Finkel was a legendary WWE ring announcer who was on hand for many of Macho's biggest career moments and knew Lanny and Randy well.

I told Lanny that while all Finkels have an inherent interest in wrestling, Howard and I weren't related, sadly. I told him that my dad's name is Harvey, and that he had the same initials as Howard, if that counted for anything.

Lanny got a kick out of that. He liked clever coincidences.

After some small talk I laid out my vision for this book, why I wanted to write it and, more importantly, why I felt I *should* be the one to write it. I explained what Macho meant to me and my own brother as kids and why it was so important to me to be able to interview him, Lanny specifically, about his family and brother.

Lanny then asked me a bunch of rapid-fire questions about Macho — a test of sorts. I guess I passed because we spoke for over two hours after that.

He was funny and gracious and lit up when talking about his parents and his brother's life and career. I had pages of questions ready to go and we plowed through them all and then some, culminating with him saying he was glad I was writing the book. (Man, that felt good.)

He also offered to help clarify anything or answer any questions as I worked on the manuscript. Lanny was always available and as I wrote, I kept a running list of small details and questions that I wanted to ask him next time we spoke.

I called them "Lanny Q's."

When I got the email about his passing, I had the list of questions open on my desk. The notebook is next to me now as I write this.

Life happens fast.

I'd venture to say that nobody has spent more time studying and researching Randy and the Poffos over the course of the last two years than me.

Lanny was a fun-loving guy, but he took his and his family's legacy seriously. I'm proud that he was comfortable with me being the one to document that legacy seriously with this biography.

But not too seriously. Because as Lanny told me, wrestling is sports *and* entertainment — with emphasis on entertainment.

I hope you enjoy reading this book as much as I did writing it.

Ooohhhh yeeahhhhh.

PART I

Randy Poffo

CHAPTER 1

Angelo

Blood seeped through the raw skin on Angelo Poffo's back, smearing the mat below him. The soft flesh along his lower lat muscles had long since been scraped and chafed away. Blood trickled from his abdomen too, running down past his belly button, mixing with sweat.

He ignored the pain and kept pace, his torso pounding up and down like a jackhammer. On his quest to break the Navy's record for consecutive sit-ups, he'd been averaging twenty-four reps per minute since he started.

That was three hours ago.

Up. Down. Up. Down. Up. Down. Nonstop.

2,997 . . . 2,998 . . . 2,999 . . .

He'd just passed three thousand.

The blood was a concern for sure. So was death. The last man before Angelo to try for the record died at this very moment, rupturing an aortic vessel, tearing his heart wall from the repeated strain.

But there was no turning back. This was the twenty-year-old's second shot at glory and he would not be denied.

In his first attempt he completed 5,003 sit-ups, thought the title was his, then discovered he'd used the wrong form. *Poof.* Disqualified. It gnawed at him.

This time he would leave no doubt.

For his venue he chose the U.S. Naval Repair Base Gym in San Diego, California. For the date, a holiday: July 4, 1945. And for his goal, he aimed beyond the Navy record this time to the world record of 5,900.

He also enlisted a crew of support staff to monitor the attempt and his health. Along with a half-dozen witnesses were four German prisoners of war assigned to hold down his legs, several timekeepers, a physician, and an official to ensure that every rep counted as a regulation sit-up.

According to the rules of the day, a regulation sit-up was legal only when "the legs were straight and flat on the ground, the hands were clasped in the back of the neck, then upon rising and bending forward, the right elbow must touch the left knee and vice versa."

Brutal.

If any of these points were not followed on any given rep, the timekeeper declared it a "fault" like in tennis. No exceptions.

And so on the way to 3,000 and beyond, Angelo performed a few dozen extra that never made it into the record books; tiny setbacks on the way to greatness.

3,471 . . . 3,472 . . . 3,473 . . .

Poffo was a Pharmacist's Mate Third Class. Used to be skinny. Scrawny, even. But all that changed once he discovered two things about life on a naval destroyer base:

One, he had a lot of time on his hands.

Two, he had open access to barbells and dumbbells.

"I thought I was in heaven," he said.

In the gym he quickly discovered that his body responded well to whatever physical punishment he threw at it. While his shipmates took leave off the base, he often stayed for solo sessions in what became his personal iron paradise.

The more weight he lifted, the larger he became, transforming himself from a six-foot-tall kid who wore medium-sized T-shirts to a musclebound man with a thick chest, veiny arms and a six-pack.

Soon he was over 200 pounds and in search of an outlet for all that brawn — a North Star, a goal to show off and show himself what his new physique was capable of. He scoured the Navy's logs for a record that piqued his interest and he zeroed in on the mark for consecutive sit-ups in the fastest time.

4,885 . . . 4,886 . . . 4,887 . . .

The room buzzed as Angelo passed 5,004 sit-ups, his unofficial personal best to that point. His neck ached and his hands cramped from being clasped behind his head for over two hundred minutes. The German prisoners of war were exhausted, rotating in and out to keep Angelo's ankles pinned to the ground so his massive body could piston up and down.

The physician worried about dehydration, cramping, bleeding, strains, sprains and a possible heart attack. He'd never witnessed physical exertion on this level. He kneeled next to Angelo, feeding him water and candy bars at various intervals for fuel.

5,897 . . . 5,898 . . . 5,899 . . .

Just before the four-hour mark, Angelo captured the world record with 5,900 consecutive sit-ups. But he pressed on. He secretly had his sights set on 6,000.

With the crowd in awe, his midsection glistening with sweat and blood, he hit number 6,000 at four hours and eight minutes. Then he gutted out 33 more (one for each year of Jesus Christ's life, he'd later say) to land on 6,033 consecutive sit-ups in a total time of four hours and ten minutes.

The record was his. Finally.

As the crowd cheered, Angelo lay flat on the ground, watching his abdominal muscles vibrate, twitch and contract involuntarily. He tried to remove his arms from behind his head but they were frozen in place from the restricted blood flow. Assistants had to help him slowly and painfully lower his limbs to his sides, and when he tried to stand, he couldn't.

Not wanting the young man to die on his watch, the physician rushed Angelo to the hospital, where he received a full evaluation. Other than wear and tear and fatigue, he was fine. A few hours later he was released: a new local celebrity.

Earl R. Gibson, a lieutenant on hand to witness the event and an athletic officer on base, dubbed Angelo "The Sit-up Champ" and officially put it in the record books. A short time later, *Ripley's Believe It or Not* featured him in a newspaper column and sent him a sit-up champion belt to commemorate the feat.

The centerpiece of the gold plate on the belt was an image of Angelo doing a sit-up in his Speedo-like trunks. Underneath, it read:

ANGELO POFFO
DID 6,033 CONSECUTIVE SIT-UPS
A NEW RECORD
DOWNERS GROVE, IL. — JULY 4, 1945

Within days he was the most popular man on base — a bona fide world record holder.

"I won't try to break that record again, that's for sure," he said in the aftermath. "I just want to get my BS in physical education and after that, well, I really don't know."

But why the hell did he do it in the first place?

"I did it for my own satisfaction," he said. "I felt good after getting the record and I could have done a lot more because I didn't feel too tired."

The man's hands were stuck behind his head.

He was bleeding from his stomach and back.

He couldn't stand up.

Not too tired?

What a showman.

This, ladies and gentleman, is the future father of the "Macho Man" Randy Savage and Leapin' Lanny Poffo.

CHAPTER 2

The Poffos

Angelo Poffo steadied himself against the door. Upside down. His head pressed into the ground as he tried to push his back up against the top panel and straighten his legs. His neck strained while his arms splayed and tried to keep his body from tipping over.

His friends looked on, wondering if their buddy could pull off the headstand he was confident he could perform. He was close. His legs were nearly straight, his neck was braced for the weight and his body seemed to be evenly distributed, but he hadn't accounted for the one thing that would make his headstand impossible: the door opening.

Whoosh.

Just as Angelo removed his arms from the floor, the handle twisted and the door swung back. He spotted the cute girl who'd opened the door a mere moment before crashing down on top of her.

This was one story of how Angelo Poffo met Judy Sverdin, the woman he'd quickly date, fall for and ultimately stay married to for over fifty years until his death.

"Mom opened the door, they collapsed into one another and it was love," Lanny Poffo said.

Let's call that one Version A: The Headstand Story. This is the story told in Judy's obituary in the *Tampa Bay Times* after she passed away in 2017 at the age of ninety, and it's the one her son Lanny remembers hearing as a kid.

But there's a different version that's been shared as well. We'll call this one Version B: The Kick Story.

This telling of their Hollywood-style first meeting takes place in a gym, of course. As the story is told, Angelo was working out hard on the parallel bars and while doing a rep he slipped and his leg swung out, kicking the shoulder of a good-looking girl walking by.

"So, that was it," Angelo joked when retelling this version in 2001. "I had to marry her."

The common denominator in the two stories is that their relationship began with a collision, which is fitting for one of wrestling's most famous families.

Regardless of whether either story is 100 percent true or was embellished over decades of family lore, there are several facts we know for sure.

Whatever activity Angelo was doing when the future couple bumped into each other, it was most certainly on the campus of DePaul University, where he'd enrolled after returning home from the Navy to pursue his physical education studies.

Angelo also walked onto the DePaul University baseball team and made the squad as a catcher.

"My catching was good, and everything, but my hitting was bad. So I had to give it up," he said.

He played baseball for the DePaul Blue Demons in 1948 and 1949, and to be fair to Angelo, his hitting didn't start off poorly. For a brief period during his junior year he thought he had a shot at the minor leagues, but after getting beaned in the head with a fastball during his final college season, he never felt comfortable in the batter's box again. His last game for DePaul was the last game of his baseball career.

Outside of the baseball diamond, Angelo worked out regularly in the gym and was a member of the chess team. He also had an early run-in with a legend, occasionally playing pick-up ball with the 6'10" future NBA superstar George Mikan.

All his other free time, it seems, was spent with Judy.

Judy was born January 28, 1927, and grew up in Naperville, Illinois, a suburb about thirty miles west of Chicago. She was two years younger than Angelo but because of his time in the service, she was a sophomore and he was a freshman when they met.

While Angelo had to claw his way onto the baseball roster, Judy excelled at aquatic sports and attended DePaul on a diving scholarship, competing in everything from races to swim meets to synchronized swimming. She was lean and athletic, with dark hair and a broad, friendly smile. Like Angelo, she majored in physical education.

The couple began dating immediately after they met and cruised to their wedding in 1949 — with the exception of one major snag.

Angelo Poffo and the Poffo family were devout Catholics.

Judy Sverdin and her family were Jewish.

Judy's parents were immigrants from Lithuania and Belarus and the idea of their daughter marrying an Italian Catholic did not sit well with them.

A Jew marrying a Catholic? In 1949? Who does such things?

Unfortunately, the only people more upset with the marriage were Angelo's parents, who still mostly spoke Italian and could hardly put into words their disappointment that their only son was marrying out of the religion.

Scratch that, they did put their feelings into words — during the wedding.

"At the reception, all the Jewish people were sitting on one side of the room, and all the Catholics were on the other," Judy said. "And his mother said to him in Italian, 'What have you done?'"

Tell us how you really feel, Mrs. Poffo.

Despite their families' shock at the interfaith wedding, Judy Sverdin became Judy Poffo and the couple persevered without the approval of their parents.

After graduation, Judy found work teaching physical education for the Chicago Park Department, and initially, Angelo was going to follow her into teaching. That is, until he had a life-altering, future-of-wrestling-changing conversation with a fellow student and friend, Carl Engstrom.

CHAPTER 3

The Man from Mars

Born in Sweden, Carl Engstrom was a thick-fisted heavyweight boxer on DePaul's varsity squad who spent time moonlighting as an amateur wrestler. Though just under two hundred pounds at the time, he had giant shoulders, a back like a highway billboard, ropy traps, a powerful chest and a ripped midsection. In later years he'd bulk up and roam the ring like a graceful grizzly bear, but in his early twenties, he looked like a modern-day middleweight.

Though not an elite boxer, he competed in DePaul's first Catholic Youth Sports tournament and battled his way to the finals. Unfortunately, the match went to the judges and a "questionable round" on one scorecard doomed him. That was the closest he came to winning a title.

When Engstrom wasn't punching men in the face, he was pinning them to the mat. With a natural taste for hand-to-hand combat, he built a minor league wrestling career around his boxing schedule, fitting in training and tournaments on the fly. His biggest success came when he won the Illinois YMCA wrestling tournament at 191 pounds.

In 1948, he turned his attention to pro wrestling, left school and toured from Seattle to Portland with Pacific Northwest Wrestling to perform and earn money. It was during this stint that he came up with one of the truly bizarre gimmicks in the history of the sport.

Like most wrestlers, Engstrom desperately wanted to get over with the fans, and to do that, he racked his brain to develop something that would stand out.

Some wrestlers opt for a prop, others for wild outfits or crazy names or a distinct dialect, or maybe they adopt the characteristics of a certain stereotype or region of the United States or another country entirely. Engstrom thought that was small boy stuff and turned it up a notch, adopting a whole new planet and creating the masked character named:

Zuma: The Man from Mars.

Trying to capitalize on a growing interest in space travel, aliens and Mars in the 1940s, Engstrom went all-in with Zuma.

His costume was part sci-fi movie, part fourth grade science project. His helmet had a pointed spire on top that jutted up about two feet from his head. The spire was tipped with a beacon and there were small, medium and large circular saucers that looked like UFOs spread evenly down the point, like a hat with different-sized Frisbees on it.

The headpiece itself resembled an early leather football helmet with clear goggles in front that looked like they may have been stolen from a welder. Underneath he added a chinstrap to hold the entire beautiful structure in place.

On his back he wore a massive, flowing cape that draped all the way to the ground. He wore no shirt, only large trunks that rode high on his thighs and up over his belly button, and a pair of shiny wrestling boots with straps up to his knees.

The centerpiece of the costume, the one touch that really tied it all together, was a giant Z emblazoned on a circular shield held tight to his chest with straps that wrapped around his back.

Engstrom debuted his Zuma creation at a wrestling match in Chicago in 1950. Even though it was his hometown, nobody recognized him, for obvious reasons. Many of the matches were broadcast on local TV and wrestling fans all over the Windy City were wondering, "Who is this masked Martian man?"

It was only after several matches that a local reporter, Ed Pazdur, who covered the DePaul boxing beat, recognized the former pugilist as the current pro wrestler. Rather than being upset about having his cover blown, Engstrom embraced it and decided that he may have milked the Martian motif for all it was worth by that point.

"I believed that a character such as Zuma would arouse the imagination of the sports fans and give me the publicity I would not have under the name of Carl Engstrom," he told Pazdur in *The DePaulian*. "It has achieved its objective and I believe that the asset of the name Zuma is now going to help me immensely in going back to my right name."

For the next twenty-three years, spanning over seven hundred matches, Engstrom wrestled under his own name until he retired in 1973.

This was the half-man/half-Martian who introduced Randy Savage's father to wrestling and, in a ripple effect neither could have anticipated at the time, sowed the generational seeds for there to one day be a Macho Man.

And it all started with four simple words:

"I can help you."

This is what Engstrom said to his friend on the DePaul campus after Angelo lamented that he didn't know what to do with his life now that school was ending and baseball was almost over. Sure, he could become a physical education teacher, but that just sounded . . . boring.

Engstrom didn't hesitate.

He knew Angelo well. He knew his buddy was a natural athlete and lived in the weight room. He knew about his sit-up record and brush with fame and his inner desire to take on big challenges. And he also knew that Angelo enjoyed the spotlight and was blessed with the natural charisma of a performer.

Before college, Engstrom had spent time as a member of a dance troupe. He had the entertainment bug and he could spot it a mile away. Angelo had it, plain and simple, and to Engstrom's mind, inviting his pal to the wrestling gym was a no-brainer.

"He helped me a lot," Angelo said, reflecting on that conversation.

In the summer of 1949, Angelo Poffo found himself walking through the door at 3142 South Halsted Street in Chicago, where Engstrom planned to introduce him to the great Karl Pojello.

The building, located just south of 31st Street and a few blocks northwest of what is now the home ballpark of the Chicago White Sox, was the headquarters for Pojello's Midwest Wrestling Enterprises. Pojello billed himself in ads as an "advisor for leading international independent wrestlers."

Pojello was built like a sculpted tree stump, standing 5'8" but weighing 190 pounds. Born in Steigviliai, Russia (now Lithuania), in 1893, Pojello became one of the best wrestlers in all of Eastern Europe by the time he was eighteen years old and won his first international wrestling competition when he was twenty. This led to a tour in the early 1920s that took him around the globe, from Europe to China, Japan and the United States and ultimately Chicago.

Along the way he collected wrestling trophies like most tourists collect postcards. He won the National Mongolian Championship in 1920, followed by the International Championship in Manchuria in 1921. He was the International Tournament Champion in Beijing, China, in 1922 and then became Jiu Jitsu Champion in Yokohama, Japan, in August of 1923 before traveling stateside.

"He was, as I recall, a wonderful physical specimen," wrote E.J. Harrison in his book *Lithuania Past and Present*. "With his black hair, rosy cheeks, retroussé nose and ever-ready smile, Pojello was one of the most naturally gifted mat-men I have ever seen. He was absolutely tireless and his good nature and high spirits never flagged."

Once in North America, Pojello took on all comers, flattening and crushing the competition, occasionally in record time. He beat the Canadian wrestling champion, Carl Van Wurden, who wrestled while wearing a mask and calling himself The Green Asp, in three minutes. His next major victory came against the Light Heavyweight Champion of the World, Johnny Mayers, and his famous "stopper hold."

With Mayers and Van Wurden in his rearview mirror, Pojello suddenly was not only an undefeated world champion, but also the most famous wrestler in America. Promoters called him "The World's Greatest Wrestler," and to capitalize, he traveled the United States and then headed back to Europe, where he remained champion until returning to Chicago to open his school at the start of World War II.

This is the man who taught the father of the Macho Man how to wrestle.

By the time Angelo and Engstrom walked into Midwest Wrestling Enterprises, Pojello was an old man of fifty-seven and despite his storied history as a champion, he was no longer the most recognized man in his own training facility.

That honor belonged to Ruffy Silverstein.

"It wasn't a fantastic gym or anything," Poffo recalled years later. "But Ruffy Silverstein was there."

Silverstein was the Brock Lesnar of the 1930s, turning a brilliant collegiate wrestling career into fame on the professional circuit.

Born Ralph Silverstein in Chicago on March 20, 1914, the powerful young man started wrestling as a kid on playgrounds and never stopped. He made his first appearance in a wrestling tournament final match at just nine years old and he punished the competition at Crane Technical Prep High School.

"He had a very low center of gravity and tremendous strength in his upper body," teammate Ralph Gradman said. "There wasn't anybody he couldn't take down from the standing position."

With offers to wrestle in colleges all over the region, Ruffy chose to stay close to home and wrestle at the University of Illinois in 1931, moving up a few weight classes and becoming unstoppable.

With forearms like steam pipes, an Igloo cooler–sized chest and a head like a Rottweiler, Ruffy didn't lose a single match in his three-year varsity career for the Fighting Illini. He was an NCAA Champion and All-American at 175 pounds in 1935, while also winning the Big Ten championship. In 1936 he won the Heavyweight Championship and led Illinois to the Big Ten title.

The only feat left for him to accomplish in amateur wrestling was to win an Olympic gold medal, something that was well within reach after he finished second at the 1936 Olympic trials to make the team. However, after being selected, Silverstein, who was Jewish, chose to boycott the games being hosted by Nazi Germany.

With his prospects for an Olympic title dashed, he quickly became the top prospect among pro wrestling promoters in the Midwest.

Longtime wrestling manager Ed White signed Ruffy in 1937 and wrote a letter to a promoter describing him as, "Not a clown, but one who has natural showmanship and a certain appeal to the public. We have that man in Ruffy Silverstein."

During the late 1930s and very early 1940s, Ruffy tried to live up to White's hype, touring the Midwest and nearly winning a title in St. Louis. His run was interrupted by World War II, where he served under General Douglas MacArthur in the Pacific Theater.

Following the war, during which he picked up judo and kendo in Okinawa and the Philippines, Ruffy continued his pro wrestling career, perfecting his signature move — the falling arm drag — and winning two American Wrestling Association titles.

To make extra cash and to put his badassery to good use, Karl Pojello hired him as a one-man hell week, giving him the job of either breaking, or breaking in, new recruits.

"On Sundays, our day off, he would bring in Ruffy Silverstein, who would kind of run us through the mill," said Rip Hawk, a fellow wrestler. "He would come down and literally beat the hell out of us. I wrestled Ruffy Silverstein several times and I still feel it."

Another wrestler, Buddy Rogers, described working with Ruffy this way:

"I tried to teach him showmanship but this guy was not a broomstick you sweep around; he was a crowbar. He was the best wrestler I ever worked with . . . And probably the greatest Jewish wrestler that ever lived . . . After he almost broke my arm the fourth time, I said . . . You want a piece of my gates? Then stop murdering me!"

Silverstein wrestled on and off for the next decade before retiring and settling in as a high school gym teacher, wrestling coach and swimming coach. But despite his illustrious achievements on the mat, the most important footnote to his career as far as we're concerned is that after showing Angelo Poffo the ropes in Karl Pojello's gym, Ruffy volunteered to be his opponent in the first match of Poffo's career in Benoit, Wisconsin, towards the end of 1949.

Pojello to Silverstein to Engstrom to Poffo.

This is the genetic through line of early and mid-20th-century wrestling royalty that formed the foundation of the Macho Man, instilling in his bones the DNA of what it takes to make it: the tools, tactics, style, presence, charisma and knowledge to get over and stay over with fans, plus the business know-how to earn a living.

CHAPTER 4

Universally Disliked

With the number 6,033 etched into the butt of his wrestling trunks as a nod to his sit-up record, Angelo Poffo, with Judy at his side, set out on the slow, scattered and occasionally seedy path to grinding out a living as a new professional wrestler.

He performed at carnivals, high schools and fairs. He wrestled veterans and newcomers. He'd wrestle twice a day. He'd wrestle four nights in five days. He'd wrestle, drive and wrestle again. Big venues. Small venues. Places that barely qualified as venues. Chicago, Fort Wayne, Milwaukee, Madison, Detroit, Green Bay — they roamed the entire territory. On profitable weeks he'd make $300 for his troubles. On slow weeks he'd make $100.

"Before we got married I'd never left Illinois," Judy said. "I thought it was terrific to go state to state."

With Chicago being one of three markets to embrace wrestling, and with matches often aired on the DuMont Television Network (back when there were less than a half-dozen stations total), in a matter of months Poffo became somewhat of a local celebrity.

Not that he was opening car washes or franchising restaurants just yet, but if you owned a deli or grocery store or were a mom-and-pop business in the early 1950s near the Windy City, you might just have found yourself putting in a request to have Poffo show up for a meet-and-greet.

Case in point: only eight months after getting married and only one week after his graduation day at DePaul, Angelo Poffo got his first taste of being a hometown hero with an appearance at Cloverleaf Dairy and Wally's and Ed's Food Mart in Lemont, Illinois, just ten miles south of where he grew up in Downers Grove. And he got the full "prodigal son returns" treatment.

The headline and write-up that announced the twenty-four-year-old's event in the *Lemont Herald* on February 16, 1950, says it all:

ANGELO POFFO TO VISIT
HERE ON SATURDAY

Owners of Wally's and Ed's and of the Cloverfield Dairy have arranged to have Poffo give balloons to the Lemont children. Television and sports announcers have hailed Poffo as one of the most outstanding young wrestlers of the day, and those watching the young Downers Grove resident on TV have been greatly thrilled over his appearances because of his clean sportsmanship and great ability.

Poffo has attracted widespread publicity. Feature writers have used him as a subject for material for numerous articles published in sports magazines and in sports sections of metropolitan papers. *Body Builder Magazine* devoted two pages to an article entitled, "The Story of Angelo Poffo."

The *Body Builder Magazine* profile was not surprising. It was inevitable for the future father of the Macho Man.

As much as Poffo was getting over with the fans with his style and ever-evolving in-ring persona in 1950 and 1951, one specific trait separated him from all of his colleagues and it had nothing to do with wrestling. It was his physique.

If there was one thing Poffo took pride in above all else, it was taking care of his body. Amidst all the performing and traveling and crappy lodging and long drives on the road, his two constant companions were Judy and exercise.

"My dad always insisted on light weights," Lanny said. "He thought heavy lifters would hurt themselves. He preached calisthenics. Sit-ups. Push-ups. Air squats."

These were movements he could do anywhere with no equipment: locker rooms, motel rooms, changing rooms. Didn't matter. Angelo always found time to train and the regimen worked.

Wherever Poffo performed, spectators marveled at his muscle. Whenever journalists described him, they began with his body. Writers often mentioned his sex appeal, adopting an Austin Powers "women want him, men want to be him" mentality, almost like they had to let readers know how magnetic this man was.

One description in a newspaper piece, hyping up a match in central Pennsylvania, reads like a dating profile.

"His hobbies are body building and sports of all kinds. Poffo, a six-footer who pushes down the Fairbanks [weight scale] to the extent of 200 pounds, is a handsome man, and he has a great following among both the feminine and masculine mat fans ... Little wonder is it that a fellow who would go to all this trouble to improve his body is being called one of the greatest comers in wrestling. Just watch him in the next few years."

One reason for such a strong focus on Angelo's Michelangelo-level sculpted frame is because he stood in stark contrast to many of his contemporaries.

Keep in mind, the wrestlers of the mid-20th century weren't modern reality TV stars, Instagram influencers or dudes who grew up never skipping leg day or taking selfies at 24-Hour Fitness or training at trendy CrossFit gyms. The men who became career wrestlers in the 1930s, '40s and '50s were capital-letters M.E.N. They were nearly all veterans of World War II. Most saw combat. Many were college wrestlers or college football players back in the days when leather helmets were standard and concussions were for wimps.

Other than a few men who had gimmicks based on their good looks, many of the men were sasquatches who smoked cigarettes and cigars and who drank beer and had hairy chests and concrete chins.

They were old-time tough guys who took on cartoonish names to match their dispositions. They were men like William Fritz Afflis, better known by his ring name, Dick the Bruiser.

The Bruiser played college football at Purdue and four seasons as a lineman for the Green Bay Packers before turning to wrestling. He was a 6'1", 261-pound tank of a human — a gigantic man with neck muscles resembling cables on a suspension bridge and traps the size of baby anacondas.

He was also a fifteen-time world champion who won the AWA World Heavyweight Championship, the WWA World Heavyweight Championship and twenty tag team titles. And he did it all with his trademark buzzed head, crunched eyes, cockeyed snarl and a stogie jutting out of his mouth.

Then there were guys like Verne Gagne, who has one of the manliest pre-wrestling resumes of anybody in the sport. Before World War II, he played football at the University of Minnesota and made the All–Big Ten Team. Then he joined the war effort and became a member of the Navy's elite Underwater Demolition Team (a precursor to the Navy SEALs). And then *after* the war, he went back to school, switched to wrestling and became a two-time NCAA wrestling champion.

Total stud.

By the time he became a pro wrestler, he was a stocky 5'11", 215 pounds. And unlike Angelo, whose skin seemed to be made out of pristine marble, Gagne, an outstanding athlete to be sure, had a muscled body that was a little less defined and a lot hairier than Poffo's.

Dick Hutton, who was a three-time NCAA wrestling champion at Oklahoma A&M, with his only loss in the finals coming at the hands of Verne Gagne, was a 5'10", 235-pound star whose body was as stout and sturdy as an oak cabinet.

The "Nature Boy" Buddy Rogers, an outstanding swimmer and high school athlete before joining the Navy, stood 6' and weighed 235 pounds. He was long-limbed, with a mammoth chest, burly midsection and none of the perfect proportion Poffo had.

Gorgeous George, who revolutionized the sport and blazed the trail for everyone from Hulk Hogan to Ric Flair, Macho Man and The Rock, was not a physical specimen. Despite calling himself the "Beautiful

Bicep," George was only 5'9" and weighed over 215 pounds, with a body that resembled a former high school athlete who now played beer league softball.

Killer Kowalski was 6'7", 275 pounds and in a league of his own size-wise.

Poffo tangled with dozens of others in the ring during his era, and yes, a few had comparable musculature, but of the men who crisscrossed the country and dominated the sport in the 1940s and 1950s, he paid the most attention to his health and fitness, and it paid off. He rarely drank more than the occasional glass of wine. He didn't swear. He didn't overindulge with food. Didn't use drugs. This is why even though he was Italian through and through, he was often referred to in the press as looking like the Greek god Adonis.

Knowing how audiences felt about him gave Poffo an edge when it came to getting a crowd reaction. And he leaned into it. Hard. Rather than using his looks to try to become a fan favorite ("babyface") he took a page out of the playbook of famous "bad guy" Professor Roy Shire and turned heel in late 1950.

Shire's gimmick was to play an elite, Ivy League–looking professor who sneered at the audience and his opponents. He'd strut into the ring wearing a big black gown and graduation cap and do everything in his power to piss off the paying customers.

"I was probably the worst bad guy you could find," he once said. "I was always that way. To be a good wrestler, you have to be kind of sadistic, whether you're a good guy or bad guy."

And as the saying goes, it was good to be bad for the Professor.

In his heyday he sold out Madison Square Garden as a headliner, packing the famous arena with twenty thousand furious fans. He wrestled A-lister Gorgeous George regularly, and at a time when most performers were struggling to make enough money to cover crappy motels and late night diner food, Shire pulled down $1,000 a week with his appearances.

This is the man Angelo Poffo chose to emulate: a wrestler whose gimmick was built on acting like a preening, pompous ass.

It worked brilliantly.

"The wrestling match doesn't start at the bell," Poffo said. "It starts when the dressing room opens and the crowd first sees you."

During a typical entrance, Angelo would slowly stroll towards the ring and through the ropes wearing a large flowing robe. His dark hair was slicked back and he had full, Elvis-style sideburns. As soon as the in-ring announcer called his name, boos would rain down and he'd barely acknowledge them.

Once the wrestlers went to their corners, the real performance began, with Poffo disrobing at a slow, deliberate, maddening pace. The slower he'd go, the louder the booing would get.

First he'd grab the robe's garment bag and carefully hang it on the top rope of the ring.

Booooo.

Then he'd slide off the robe and take his time putting it on a hanger. The moment he exposed his upper body, catcalls and whistles would come from all over the arena in Chicago, Columbus, Lansing or wherever he was performing.

Booooooooooo.

As he slid off his warm-up trunks (yes, he wore a pair of trunks over his wrestling trunks to the ring), the whistles and jeering would grow louder, until he'd take off the trunks, fold them, place them in the bag with his robe and hand his robe to one of his early managers.

Meanwhile, the wrestler in the other corner would be waiting, egging the crowd on.

Booooooooooooooooo.

After the whole process was done, and he'd milked every last ounce of patience from his opponent and the crowd, he'd do a quick chest stretch in his corner of the ring and come out fighting.

Like Professor Shire, he'd peacock around the ring, brushing off his opponent's moves with arrogance and disrespect. He learned early on how to sell a hard hit to the mat, earning a reputation as a solid bump-man. He also developed his own finisher, which he called an Italian Neckbreaker hold.

"It was a front face lock, then I turned them around, jumped up in the air and dropped them," he explained. "Both of us would go down, but I'd cover."

If Poffo won the match, he'd raise his right arm triumphantly and stare off into the crowd as they shouted him down and yelled their disapproval.

In footage from a match against Bobby Managoff restored by the Chicago Film Archives, we get a glimpse into what the TV audience in the middle of the 1950s experienced: a heavy dose of Poffo complaining to the refs, taking cheap shots, pretending to quit matches, having tantrums like a three-year-old, almost leaving the ring, being a poor sport and doing everything he could to rile up a chorus of boos.

"I've never known a man to be so universally disliked," broadcaster Russ Davis commented during the match. "And he is, believe me."

All in a night's work.

Unfortunately, those nights were taking their toll on Poffo and his young wife. The pay was often low. The schedule was always hard. To make more cash, Poffo became a driver for wrestling headliners or big-name stars involved with the promotions.

While making one such trip, Poffo found himself cruising through Minnesota with the Brown Bomber himself, former heavyweight boxing champion Joe Louis, as his passenger. Louis, whose last match was his sad, infamous loss by TKO to Rocky Marciano on October 26, 1951, ended his boxing career with a staggering amount of debt due to unpaid taxes, poor investments and untrustworthy financial advisors and schemers. Desperate to make money any way that he could, he traded on his fame with jobs and appearances, including a regular gig as a wrestling guest referee.

During this particular long drive, Poffo stopped to grab a bite to eat with Louis but the restaurant they pulled into wouldn't serve the champ because he was Black. Poffo was outraged and bought both of them meals and they ate in the car together.

The routine of wrestling and driving went on and on as Poffo tried to build his name in the business. Aside from the performances, it was a daunting, occasionally dreary existence. There was no financial consistency. No stability with schedule. No home base to stay in for very long. Over time, Poffo began questioning whether this really was the life he wanted — not only for himself, but for his wife as well.

After all, they were both college educated. They could both easily find steady, decent jobs at high schools or universities to put down their roots and build a life as physical education teachers or coaches.

On the long nights driving between towns like Des Plaines and Naperville or Grand Rapids and Youngstown at 11:30 p.m., when the moon hung low and the highway lines stretched out for miles under the cold sky, we can imagine Poffo wondering to himself, *How long do I want to do this?*

Then, as is often the case, life intervened and forced the issue.

Early in the spring of 1952 Angelo discovered that Judy was pregnant with their first child. Suddenly, a family was imminent. The prudent thing to do may have been to hang up his trunks, grab a salaried job and opt for a reliable, stay-in-one-place type of career.

"The double paychecks of my mom and him would have been a good life and safer life," Lanny said.

And for a while, Angelo leaned that way.

"In the fall of 1952, my father was the designated driver for Gorgeous George, working for Al Haft in Columbus, Ohio," Lanny continued. "My brother was about to be born. My father told Gorgeous George that he was thinking of quitting the business."

This is a scene you have to take a moment to picture.

Angelo, at the wheel of his car, driving on Interstate 33 along the Scioto River in central Ohio, telling Gorgeous George, a man with flowing platinum blond hair held in place with gold-plated bobby pins, a man who entered the ring with a valet named Jeffries carrying a silver mirror in front of him who dropped rose petals at his feet, a man who had the ring sprayed with perfume before he'd wrestle . . . Angelo told *this* man that he thought if he and his wife could both earn paychecks together at a school that it would be a better, safer life, and he was considering going that route.

Gorgeous George, whose most famous saying was "win if you can, lose if you must, but always cheat," would have none of it.

"You're out of your mind," he said. "You have charisma. You can make it in this business. You haven't given yourself a chance."

Over the next few days Angelo considers George's words. Talks things over with Judy. Decides he's not quite ready to stake his claim in the suburbs just yet.

He has unfinished business in the ring.

Consider the ramifications of this conversation. In an alternate universe, Angelo Poffo wraps up his wrestling career in the winter of 1952, right around the time his first son is born.

That son, Randall Mario Poffo, never sees his dad wrestle. Never attends live wrestling matches. Never sees the reaction his dad gets from a crowd. Never hangs backstage with headliners, babyfaces and heels. Never falls in love with the performance and pageantry and pain of it all.

The seed of wrestling is never implanted in his psyche. It's not transferred to his brother Lanny, either. Maybe they follow the sport like every other kid growing up, but the idea of becoming a wrestler, of making a life in the ring, never enters their mind.

In this scenario, we only get Randy Poffo. We don't get Randy Savage and we certainly don't get the Macho Man.

Fortunately, that's not the timeline we live in. And it's all because a man who signed his portraits "Gorgeously Yours, Gorgeous George" believed in Angelo Poffo and told him so.

It should also be mentioned here that when it comes to giving advice about careers, Gorgeous George was a bit of a savant.

Not only did he keep Angelo Poffo in wrestling, but when a nineteen-year-old boxer asked him for advice on showmanship and selling a performance after a show, George told him, "A lot of people will pay to see someone shut your mouth. So keep on bragging, keep on sassing and always be outrageous."

That young boxer he gave the advice to?

Muhammad Ali.

Years later, after Gorgeous George retired, he spiraled into alcoholism and depression. Despite reportedly earning over $9 million during his seven peak years of fame, he blew it all. In turn, it broke him. He eventually died of a heart attack, nearly penniless, in 1963. When Angelo heard the news, he reached out and paid for the funeral.

"The reason I did it," Angelo said, "was because if it wasn't for Gorgeous George, I would have quit the business."

CHAPTER 5

The Macho Kid

"**Y**our dad sucks."

"Stop it."

"How come he always loses?"

"Shut up!"

"He's the worst wrestler."

"You're dead!"

With that, seven-year-old Randy Poffo leaps out of his third grade classroom seat and decks the snooty kid two seats over. Other kids jump in, wildly swinging and pulling and tugging. They rip each other's shirts, yank on their ties, smash each other into their desks and chairs before a teacher enters the scrum to separate the kids.

"Break it up!" the teacher shouts. "Now! Everyone back to their desks."

Staring daggers at the other boys, Randy picks up his chair, half-heartedly fixes his clothes and sits back down.

"What is going on?" the teacher asks. "Randall? What happened?"

"They were making fun of my family," Randy says, upset.

Just another day in class.

"Randy would come home from school with his tie off to the side, and his hair a mess, and I knew he'd been fighting," Judy said. "He couldn't take anyone saying a bad word about his dad if he'd lose a match. Lanny was calmer. He'd walk away. But not Randy."

"Of course, kids were always saying things, but I just let it go in one ear and out the other," Lanny said. "But not Randy. Randy was the kind of kid to start fights over it."

These fights weren't unique to any particular school because they happened in every school Randy attended as a kid. And he attended a bunch.

After Angelo's pivotal conversation with Gorgeous George, he and Judy decided to commit to the wrestling life with family in tow.

Randall Mario Poffo was born November 15, 1952.

Their second son, Lanny Mark Poffo, was born December 28, 1954.

While the young married couple juggled the demands of newborns and toddlers and sippy cups and never-ending snacks in the backseat of their car, Angelo continued to build his wrestling career.

For most of the boys' early years, Angelo made a living traveling the country as part of a tag team or the quintessential mid-level heel, never moving to the top spot in billed matches but always playing the critical role of foil to the more popular babyfaces and draws that the promoters built their events around.

As a result, Angelo and family were on the road constantly, transferring the kids in and out of schools multiple times a year.

They'd get to a territory, enroll the kids in a parochial school with a standard curriculum and then they'd move on and do it again. And again. And again.

"We went from place to place," Judy said. "Our kids went to lots of schools . . . Traveling all over and all that kind of stuff, every couple of months moving."

By the mid-1950s, Angelo became one of the first wrestlers to embrace the idea of having a manager when he teamed up with Bronco Lubich.

Lubich was a Hungarian-born Canadian who would have competed in the 1948 Olympics for the Great White North as a wrestler if not for a broken arm. As he approached his thirties, he was working in a factory, trying to support his family, when a couple wrestlers he met while lifting weights at the Montreal YMCA suggested he give pro wrestling a shot.

Standing 6' tall and weighing 175 pounds, Lubich had jet black hair, piercing dark eyes, and a mustache that made him look like every dad you'd see in a bowling alley in 1960. In nearly every existing photo, he stands glaring at the camera, with his shoulders pulled back, his chest flexed and his belly clearly sucked in.

While a decent wrestler, Lubich truly thrived once he teamed up with Angelo to be his valet/manager. Together, they doubled down on pissing off audiences with their dirty tricks, whining and perceived cheating against the "good guys" in every match.

"My dad's idea was to make the babyface look as good as he could," Lanny said. "He was one of the first people that had a manager, and he knew how to use him. During their matches, they'd give the babyface nearly the whole match. Then when it looked like the babyface was going to win, Bronco would interfere with one small thing and give my dad the win. The crowd would lose it."

Their scheme worked to perfection.

One famous newspaper clipping in the *Terre Haute Tribune* described how they worked together against the 6'4", 240-pound mauler Hans Schmidt. Nicknamed the Teuton Terror for his brutal in-ring style, Schmidt played the role of "German bad guy" with enthusiasm. And yet audiences still rooted against Poffo.

"Poffo is always accompanied to the ringside by his manager-adviser Bronco Lubich, who appears in a tuxedo and carrying a cane," the paper reads. "He coaches his protégé from a ringside location. Lubich was once a wrestler and a rough one and for that reason he urges Poffo to become as unruly as his opponent when the occasion calls for it."

The article then describes Poffo's finishing move with a flourish.

"Poffo has created an Italian neckbreaker hold that is devastating and if clamped on properly can be a grueling grip to the opponent. In fact, if Poffo's hold is used on Hans and the latter does not concede the fall in short order, Schmidt will be in danger of being hospitalized."

All part of the plan.

Hans Schmidt. Buddy Rogers. Wilbur Snyder.

Didn't matter who the opponent was, they ran the same script to perfection.

"I'd go out there to wrestle, and the guy was dumping me all over the place," Angelo explained. "Then at the end of the match, Bronco would pull his leg and I'd beat him and I created a riot. It's that simple."

Simple for Angelo, that is — fairly complex for his kids to grasp.

Imagine you're four years old. Or six. Or eight.

You worship your dad. He's a big, strong, strapping guy. He's your hero. You drive with him and your mom to a packed arena and you hang with him in the dressing room as he goes through a transformation.

He ditches his regular day clothes and puts on his work clothes. But unlike other dads, he's not putting on a stuffy suit and tie. No way. Your dad removes his shirt to reveal a tan, carved body. His muscles ripple in front of you.

Then he puts on tight wrestling trunks and boots up to his knees and wraps a shiny, billowing robe around his neck. He slicks his hair back and stretches, warming up for his match.

You're maybe three or four feet tall. He's twice your height. You look up at him in awe. He's magnificent. A God.

Then a promoter's assistant rushes over and says, "You'll be on in two."

You head through the bowels of the arena, down a corridor towards a door that leads to the ring. You pass a half-dozen other big, bare-chested men dressed kind of like your dad. It's a land of giants.

You wait by the door with your dad as the assistant comes over and counts down the time to the entrance.

5...4...3...2...1...

The assistant opens the door and the loud buzz of the audience blasts through. Your father gives you a wink, takes a deep breath and crosses the threshold into the arena. You are beaming with pride.

Look at him. He's glorious!

Then, suddenly . . .

BOOOOOOOO!!!!!

The moment the fans lay eyes on your dad a crescendo of boos shower down towards you. Obscenities are shouted. Threats are made. It's an avalanche of anger.

They hate him.

Your dad has already explained to you that they are *supposed* to hate him. That it's his job to make the crowd angry with him.

But he's your dad. And while you heard his words about the mean jeers being a *good* thing, you don't like them. You want the audience to cheer for your dad. You want them to know he's a good guy. The best guy.

It's almost too confusing for a little kid's brain to understand.

Then there's the match itself.

While your mom and dad have assured you that "daddy isn't really getting hurt," it sure looks like he's getting his butt kicked. The slams. The clotheslines. The slaps and pokes and backbreakers and pushes and punches and suplexes. All of it looks and sounds real.

But it isn't "real," you're told. It's fake.

But not fake fake.

Just kinda fake.

Because if there's one thing you've learned even as a little kid, it's that you don't tell a professional wrestler, especially your dad, that wrestling is fake.

It's just not really real.

Got it?

And so night after night, you watch your dad get booed (meaning he's doing a great job) and get beat up (but not actually getting hurt) and then be friends afterwards with the guy who slapped him around the ring and pinned him to the mat.

It's a lot to process.

But eventually, you get it. You learn to love the crowd hating on your dad. You feel the power of how he can manipulate thousands of people into thinking and behaving a certain way — almost as if he's controlling them like puppets on a string. You grasp that what he's doing is more than a job. It's a performance. Even beyond that. It's an art.

And your dad's an artist with a talent you take great pride in, so much so that you fall in love with his craft. And deep down, you want to do it yourself.

"When your father's a wrestler, you just don't know any other way," Lanny said. "I was the youngest in the family, so I didn't know it was different. Then, as I grew up, I realized it was a little strange, what my dad did. But I thought it was very appealing."

"Wrestling was always my first love," Randy often said. "Because my dad was a wrestler."

But while most grade school kids who get the wrestling bug limit their fandom to mimicking their favorite finishing moves on friends and siblings and dropping high-flying elbows on their beds, Randy and Lanny took it to the next level.

Yes, they smashed into the dressers in their bedrooms and body-slammed each other on couches and put each other into sleeper holds, but they didn't just love the wrestling side of the business. They loved the whole profession; even the promos.

"The boys always wanted to be part of wrestling," Judy said. "They used to practice as if they were being interviewed on TV when they were kids."

What a scene.

Angelo Poffo comes home from an actual wrestling match and he's got his sons in elementary school, the future "Macho Man" Randy Savage and Leapin' Lanny Poffo, wrapping a balled-up sock on top of an old wooden spoon to form a makeshift microphone and then asking each other questions about the "title fight" they just pretended to have in the kitchen.

Wild.

As the kids got deeper into grade school, Angelo took them on the road more and more. They'd drive eight hours to the then-famous Kiel Auditorium in St. Louis, Missouri, where the ex-NBA Hawks used to play. The massive brick building resembled either a fortified armory or a branch of the treasury department and sat 9,300 people. During the 1950s, the only wrestling venue more famous in the United States was Madison Square Garden, and in its heyday, the arena was one of the most popular hosts for National Wrestling Alliance events. The Poffos were regulars.

If not on a road trip to Kiel, the boys might be driven three hours to the old Indianapolis Coliseum to watch their dad wrestle Cowboy Bob Ellis, a 6'2", 240-pound Texan who spent time racing horses before he turned to wrestling. Then they might loop back and watch Angelo wrestle at the Chicago International Amphitheatre.

Keep in mind this was long before the days of GPS. No smartphones. No Google Maps. No Waze. The Poffos were often driving along some tiny interstate in the dead of winter, looking at an unfolded map under the dashboard lights, trying to figure out where the hell they were going.

If they missed a turn, it could cost them miles and, more importantly, gas. Angelo Poffo was renowned for his frugal ways on the road. He saved as much money as he could. He didn't blow his fees on booze or drugs or women. In fact, one of the first places he looked for on the road was a financial advisor's office to talk about index funds and investing.

"When they'd go on to the next city, they'd like to get there really early to relax, read the paper, eat . . . sometimes they'd catch a movie," Bronco Lubich's daughter, Kathy Lupsity, said. "But the biggest thing that he and Angelo used to do is go down to the Merrill Lynch office and talk to the guys about investments."

Wrestling historian and photographer Dr. Mike Lano said it wasn't uncommon for the other wrestlers in the locker room or changing room to bust Angelo's chops about being a cheapskate.

"The boys made fun of people who didn't go out and blow their money and party," Lano said. "But they ended up being jealous. Angelo was one of the few who not only provided for his kids and put them through college, but had something to show for himself."

So a wrong turn meant more miles, and more miles meant wasted gas, and wasted gas meant wasted money, and there was nothing on earth Angelo hated more than wasting money.

Ricky Morton, one half of the world-famous Rock N' Roll Express tag team with Robert Gibson, remembers how crazy Angelo could get about searching for the best gas prices.

"Back when we wrestled with the Poffos, gas wasn't anything," Morton said. "Sixty or seventy cents a gallon. But Angelo would find out that a gas station was three cents cheaper twenty miles down the road, and he would drive there with gas cans and fill them up to save three cents on the dollar. I couldn't believe it and I'm someone who once had an Acura that had 500,000 miles on it."

Now picture being a kid and it's getting close to show time and your dad can't find the venue in the middle of Evansville or Bloomington or

Terre Haute. Though Angelo was steadfast against swearing, he was not above getting furious.

"I remember my dad would get lost sometimes if we were looking for a new place and he'd get so angry," Lanny said.

Another throwback to a different era was the prevalence of smoking. Though Angelo didn't have a nicotine habit, to the kids it seemed like the rest of the world did. Every arena they entered felt like getting punched in the face with an ashtray.

"That was one thing I hated about back then," Lanny said. "Man, everyone was smoking. You couldn't breathe in some of those venues. Especially as a kid."

Road rage. Gas hunts. Second-hand smoke. Cramming into motels. Handling money. Dealing with fans. Meals on the go.

Randy and Lanny received a crash course in life as a pro wrestler when they were still teenagers. But before they graduated from their dad's de facto seminar Life as a Traveling Heel 101, and just before Judy decided it was time to settle down and give the boys some solid roots for their childhood, they were about to experience the highlight of Angelo's career.

After a decade spent as the bad guy and a tag team partner and a quality villain for the big stars, it was time for Angelo to reach the mountaintop.

On December 27, 1958, after a yearlong buildup of their rivalry, Angelo Poffo defeated 6'2", 235-pound former football player Wilbur Snyder to win the National Wrestling Alliance Championships belt in Chicago. The belt, which was the top wrestling prize in the Midwest at the time, and was promoted as such on the popular Sunday morning wrestling broadcasts, vaulted Poffo into stardom.

Suddenly, he wasn't being introduced as "the villain" or "the despised" Angelo Poffo. He was "Heavyweight Champion" Angelo Poffo. And for most of 1959, Poffo went back-and-forth with Snyder as the headliner for every show they entered, giving Angelo an extended run at the top of the bill that he'd never enjoyed before.

The crowds loved it.

Poffo vs. Snyder showdowns drew ten thousand fans wherever they'd clash. Terre Haute. Detroit. Cincinnati. Dayton. Columbus.

It didn't matter. Poffo had done such a great job as a heel that the fans *could not stand* that he was champ. They watched just as much for him to lose as for Wilbur to win. But every time Angelo strolled to the ring with the belt, his boys loved it.

Our dad is the champ!

And back in the 1950s, the number one way to promote a fight was through the newspapers. Columns. Interviews. Ads. Features. They used all the classic phrases to drum up the showdowns:

> Angelo Poffo and Wilbur Snyder get together again in a stipulated free-for-all for the U. S. Heavyweight Championship currently held by Poffo.
>
> The feature bout will match Wilbur Snyder, 231-pound grappler from San Anita, Calif., and Angelo Poffo of Chicago, who weighs 228 pounds. The match has been billed by the National Wrestling Alliance as a grudge battle for the heavyweight championship title.
>
> Angelo Poffo and Wilbur Snyder will headline the first 1959 outdoor wrestling card of the season in Dayton. Poffo and Snyder drew a turnout of 11,000 in Cincinnati at the Gardens last month.

Grudge battles. Free-for-alls. Massive crowds. Angelo and Wilbur had found a sweet spot. Much like in boxing, styles make fights in professional wrestling. Snyder's style included many of his old football moves like bull rushes, tackles and blocks, which meshed well with Angelo's hit-and-run form and his natural talent for taking bumps. Add in how Snyder's "good guy" popularity clashed directly with Poffo's antics and Bronco Lubich's dirty tricks and cheating, and the matches were, well, matches made in wrestling heaven.

For much of the first half of 1959, life on top was good for Angelo and he experienced a well-deserved taste of hearing a new level of jeering reserved for champions.

Wrote Pat Harmon, sports editor of the *Cincinnati Post*:

> Wrestling is back. Attendance was 10,633 and gross receipts were $20,327 for the latest show.
>
> Jim Barnett of Chicago, the promoter, had another gate of $23,000 at Indianapolis, $11,000 at Cleveland and $9,600 at Fort Wayne.
>
> The wrestlers are the enduring formula — good guys vs. bad guys . . .
>
> In the main event Friday, the principals were Wilbur Snyder (cheers!) and Angelo Poffo (boos!). Poffo brought a silver belt, engraved with "U.S. Television Wrestling Champion." Snyder was challenging him.
>
> The bout opened with Poffo kicking, kneeing, elbowing and gouging. He won the first fall and the wild hatred of 10,633 witnesses.
>
> The crowd called on Snyder to reply with illegal kind. He doubled up his fist, swung at Poffo, and the audience cheered. Poffo went down and was counted out for the second fall.
> The third was the same as the second, Snyder threw a fist and Poffo went down. Before the referee could count over Poffo, Bronco Lubich leaped into the ring and pushed Snyder. The referee announced he was awarding the belt to Snyder, but Poffo keeps the belt. Under the rules, the belt can't change hands on a disqualification.

On and on this went as winter changed to spring in the Midwest. Boos. Cheating. Cheers. Disqualifications. Poffo keeps the belt.

Unfortunately, you can only keep an audience's emotion pent-up for so long before it needs a release. And in this case, a release meant Snyder's revenge against Angelo.

After a string of rematches throughout the territory, milking the duo's drawing power and headlines for all they were worth, Snyder took the belt back for good in the late spring and Poffo never won another singles title again.

With the run over and the boys getting older, Judy and Angelo decided it was time to put down some roots and give the kids some much-needed stability with school, friends and sports.

"When Lanny was in second grade and Randy was in fourth, we finally had our house built and we settled down in Downers Grove, Illinois," Judy said.

CHAPTER 6

3909 Venard Road

Thirty-five years had passed between Angelo Poffo's birth in Downers Grove and his return as a husband and father of two sons. Sitting roughly twenty miles west of Chicago, the suburb had a population of two thousand people in the 1920s but had watched its number of residents explode tenfold, to almost twenty thousand, by the time it became the childhood home of the Macho Man.

For Angelo, who famously invested a majority of his wrestling earnings in safe, solid AT&T shares, Downers Grove represented a physical embodiment of the blue chip stock in the 1960s. The town was a rock: no crime, good schools, a strong community, close proximity to Chicago, excellent sports facilities and room to grow.

Downers Grove was exactly what the Poffos needed: a welcoming Midwest suburb with warm people who took pride in their neighborhood and looked out for each other.

The village also had a sense of humor.

Named after Vermont farmer and founder Pierce Downer, the town was officially incorporated in 1873 but was somehow registered officially with a grammatical error — the possessive apostrophe after Downer (Downer's) wasn't used. Why or how this happened remains an enigma to this day, but the mishap gave the citizens an unusual slogan to rally around ever since: "Apostrophe-free since '73."

Editorial excitement aside, for many residents in 1960, especially young boys into sports, the most unique and interesting thing in town was the new kids who just moved in whose dad was a wrestler and whose house was like a sports complex.

The home, built at 3909 Venard Road, about two miles north of the town's main commercial street, Ogden Avenue, was a veritable Dave & Buster's for the kids lucky enough to become friends with the boys.

John Guarnaccia, one of Randy's childhood best friends and a future fourth-round Major League Baseball draft pick and minor leaguer, had strong ties with the Poffos.

"Angelo and my dad went to high school together at Downers Grove in the 1940s," he said. "They became friends because of their Italian descent and connections to the old country. They were good buds. My dad went into the Navy and Mr. Poffo went into the Navy and they lost touch for a while. Then they reconnected again after Angelo moved back to Downers Grove."

Once introduced, Guarnaccia bonded with Randy and Lanny over their shared love of sports and in no time "Johnny G" became a regular at the Poffos' house. They played everything. Baseball. Basketball. Football. They even made up their own backyard sports when that wasn't enough.

"They had a very nice house for Downers Grove," Guarnaccia said. "They had a pool table. And they had an in-ground pool with a diving board, which was rare. We'd play this baseball type of game in the pool, where one of us would pitch a ball from the shallow end and we'd hit the ball with the kickboard off the diving board. Then we'd swim to each corner of the pool as a base. Actually, their mom taught me to swim."

Dave Buehrer, who would one day grow to be a lanky, 6'1", 190-pound right-handed pitcher for the University of Nebraska, was another staple in the revolving door of middle school athletes looking for pickup games, snacks and good times over the summer and after school.

The Buehrers lived a few houses over from the Poffos and Dave played on Randy's Little League team, the Moose. After games and practices it was commonplace that he and some of his teammates would head on over to his buddy's place to relax and goof off.

"After working out we'd get to swim," Buehrer said. "They had this big patio around the pool and we'd eat on the deck. We'd never go home without eating. They were very hospitable people. It was like a 'my house is your house' kind of deal."

But the Poffos' house wasn't like any other house in Downers Grove. Or Illinois.

Or your neighborhood, for that matter.

"They had a full wrestling ring in their basement," Buehrer said. "I would go down there and mess around. They'd practice their moves and flips. Lanny was very acrobatic back then."

As the boys got older, Angelo added a weight set and other equipment to lift.

"They did bench, curls, lots of ab workouts and leg workouts," Buehrer said. "I had my own small Sears block weight bench at home. Mainly because I was so embarrassed to lift with them because they were so strong."

The entire vibe of the Poffo house was just as much a 24-Hour Fitness as it was a family's place to live. They had the equipment. They had the workout routines. They even had the health food and nutritional mindset that wouldn't be widely accepted by athletes and trainers for decades.

Tom Bruno, another regular friend and teammate of Randy's who had a short Major League Baseball career with the Royals, Cardinals and Blue Jays, remembers the house fondly.

"We played baseball, we swam," he said. "It was real health conscious. They had a blender and they'd make drinks with all kinds of blueberries and raspberries and strawberries. Nobody called them smoothies back then. They were health drinks. They were into that stuff. When we worked out we did stretching exercises with rubber bands and inner tubes so that we'd get resistance in our throwing motion. They were way ahead of their time."

The main reason for the focus on throwing and core strength was because young Randy Poffo was completely, totally and utterly obsessed with America's pastime. Like, posters on the wall, watch every game, collect baseball cards and stickers and helmets obsessed.

"My first love was baseball," Randy said later. "My dad played at DePaul. He was a catcher so I wanted to be a catcher."

Fittingly, Randy's first favorite player was Johnny Bench, the Cincinnati Reds Hall of Fame catcher.

"He also loved Pete Rose for his hustle," Lanny said. "And he loved the Reds."

But like most kids, Randy dabbled with a few favorite teams and players.

"He definitely loved Johnny Bench," Guarnaccia said. "But I know he loved the St. Louis Cardinals for a while too. He had Cardinals paraphernalia everywhere. I'm not exactly sure why, but he even had a Cardinals helmet and he'd talk about Bob Gibson and Lou Brock all the time."

According to Tom Bruno, there was also a third team in the mix — the hometown Chicago Cubs.

"We watched the Cubs a lot," he said. "Because of Chicago's WGN television network, the Cubs were always on TV, so we watched them most of the time. We weren't like fans of the Cubs. It was more like we wanted to *be* Cubs. We wanted to play in the majors."

When Randy wasn't watching one of his three favorite teams or ten favorite players or studying Bench behind the plate for the Reds or Tim McCarver for the Cardinals or Randy Hundley for the Cubs, there was a 100 percent chance he was outside playing baseball.

"Randy played ball from the time he got up in the morning until he was forced to go to sleep at night," childhood friend John Comforte said. "He was exceptional. But it was earned. Randy was not a natural athlete. He was a well-practiced athlete. We were both Little League players. We had something in common: a burning desire to achieve. Of course his was stronger than mine."

Proof of Randy's baseball obsession could be traced, literally, by the path he wore out from the backyard of his house to the baseball field behind it. In fact, there was no path until the Poffo boys made one. This was another reason 3909 Venard became the crown jewel of fun for so many kids: its proximity to the Downers Grove North American Legion baseball field.

If you were standing on home plate at the field, you'd have a parking lot and the American Legion building off to your right on the first base side, while Saratoga Avenue runs behind the right field wall, begging for kids to hit bombs onto the side street. Center field is deep enough and wide enough to be a cow pasture and the entire left-center fence butts up against the side yard of a house on the street behind the Poffos.

The dugout on the third base side is at the bottom of a small hill. If you walk off the top step of the dugout, turn left and walk up the hill away from the field, you'll encounter a small wooded area loaded with maple, birch and oak trees. Wind your way up through a small path of beaten-down brush and grass about three hundred feet and you'll be standing directly in the Poffos' backyard.

That's how close the field was — a dream scenario for a kid who could recite the entire Reds starting lineup, pitching rotation, batting averages and ERAs.

"All spring and summer we'd be on that field," Dave Buehrer recalled. "He'd practice his infield throws. Our dads would pitch to us. Randy would practice switch-hitting. Even Judy would go out and shag fly balls."

But this is Chicago we're talking about. Not West Palm Beach. You could only count on enjoyable baseball weather, touching sixty degrees during the day, for about five months. The rest of the year you're in for nights in the thirties and daily highs that require multiple layers and gloves to leave the house. It's hard to work on your throwing motion when you're dressed like Ralphie's little brother in *A Christmas Story*.

And even if you were willing to brave the cold to work on your swing (Randy and his friends definitely were) there was the little matter of snow and ice on the field from November to late April.

No worries. Dad to the rescue.

"You're putting a batting cage where?" Judy asked.

"On the side of the house," Angelo said.

"Yessss!" Randy said.

Where others saw an obstacle (limited baseball practice in the winter) Angelo saw an opportunity to get better than the competition (a winterized batting cage). All they had to do was clear space away from an area of the yard dedicated to another of the elder Poffo's hobbies, viticulture. Randy's grandfather, who lived next door, tended to the grapes.

"They had these grape fields on the side of the house," Buehrer said.

"They made their own wine. We just cleared out a giant space in the middle of his personal vineyard."

Once committed to the idea, Angelo enlisted Dave's dad to be his co-foreman and they had an unlimited supply of local kids to act as labor. Then they got to work deciding the size and scope of the cage they wanted.

Now, you might be thinking, *A batting cage in your yard sounds cool. What did they do? Clear out a nice little twenty-by-twenty space with enough room for a makeshift tee and a hitting net?*

Hell. No.

If the Poffos' house was going to be home to a batting cage, it was going to be home to a full-sized, big league–level, badass batting cage. With an eye towards a future in pro ball, they mapped out a massive seventy-foot-by-thirty-foot patch of grass that could comfortably fit the official sixty-foot, six-inch pitching distance between the mound and home plate required by Major League Baseball.

"Angelo said, 'tear it all down,'" Buehrer remembered. "Me, Lanny, Randy, Angelo, my dad and maybe a few other kids went to work."

And so with shovels, shears, hoes, rakes and saws, the ragtag crew set about ripping apart the yard, limb by limb, to put a batting and pitching setup the same size as Wrigley Field's on their side yard.

Through sun and sweating and sawing and endless splinters, the group leveled the area, leaving a big, empty rectangle to construct their masterpiece.

"We wanted to have a mound and everything, so we made sure the ceiling was high," Buehrer said. "It was probably the height of a basketball hoop. Maybe nine or ten feet tall."

The dads bought a few pallets of two-by-fours and went about framing the area over the dirt ground, with studs measured evenly across the seventy feet. Instead of using heavy fencing, they used chicken wire to wrap around the frame to keep it light and easy to replace. Once the structure was completed, they went about making it look exactly like it would in a game.

"We had a pitching mound and a home plate," Buehrer said. "We got chalk to draw in batter's boxes. They even put up extra lights on the side of the house so we could play at night."

Then, for the finishing touches, Angelo spared no expense. He went out and bought a pitching machine so they didn't have to blow their arms out for batting practice and so the boys could crank up the speed of the fastballs as they got older.

The pitching machine was one of the old one-armed bandit setups, either a distant cousin of the modern Louisville Slugger Blue Flame machine or an old Remco Bat Away model. Then the dads stocked the cage with a dozen batting gloves and buckets filled to the rim with balls. There were hundreds of balls in there at a given time.

The coup de grâce, though, was the bats.

Each kid had their favorite model and Dave Buehrer remembers to this day the sizes and weights of their preferred bats.

"Once we got older, Randy was much stronger than me," he said. "He was using a 36" × 34" Louisville Slugger. I used a 34" × 32" and Lanny used a 34" × 34". We tried all the different bats. Randy liked Rod Carew's bat. Nellie Fox had a bat with no handle. It was all tapered and you'd always choke up on it. Carl Yastrzemski's bat was popular with all of us. There were no metal bats. We'd splinter the wooden ones and break them all the time. We probably went through dozens of bats every year."

Even though Mr. Poffo and Mr. Buehrer were both standout baseball players in high school, they made the boys read Stan Musial's book on hitting and they used it to improve their swing and stance.

"We'd be out there three or four hours a day in the summer," Buehrer said.

Then, in October, they'd cover the whole thing with a giant tarp so the boys could keep swinging away in the winter.

Pool. Pool table. Wrestling ring. Weight room. Indoor/outdoor batting cage.

Add it all up and Judy and Angelo's home became a living, breathing monument to the Poffo lifestyle and ethos; a testament to family, fitness and sports. As a direct result, by the time Randy became a preteen, he was the best Little Leaguer in town.

He was so good, in fact, he often intentionally swung at outside pitches that were ball fours just so he wouldn't walk, keeping his at-bat alive.

"I remember pitching against him one time and he was ahead in the count 3-0," Guarnaccia said. "I couldn't throw a strike, but he swung at my awful fourth pitch so I had to keep pitching. Then on the next pitch he hit it out."

"He absolutely dominated Little League and Pony League," Tim Gunn, who played against Randy, said. "He was a strong, athletic kid. He'd always talk about how he was going to be better than Johnny Bench. He was a phenomenal hitter. Even when we were kids, he had these shoulders like an adult. He was doing all these sit-up and push-ups and pull-ups while we were all at home eating Pop-Tarts."

It's hard, from a modern perspective, to fully appreciate the eventual physical transformation that Randy Poffo would make to become the Macho Man. The only way to do it justice is to get a good snapshot of where his body began in adolescence as a baseline.

To start, Macho was not born of marble like Bo Jackson, with muscles rippling on a jacked frame without even lifting. He wasn't gifted with the natural foot speed of one of his heroes, Pete Rose, who was once clocked running to first in 3.5 seconds in the minor leagues and earned the nickname Scooter. He wasn't blessed with soaring height like his future rival Terry Bollea (Hulk Hogan), who was 6'2", 250 pounds early in high school on the way to 6'7".

With this in mind, forget the WWF-billed 6'2", 240-pound Macho Man you typically picture in your mind's eye, the one decked out from head to toe in neon colors and cowboy hats and tassels who seems to fill every television frame he's ever in.

Remove this image from your brain because the junior high school version of Randy is essentially the opposite of that. He was not physically imposing or impressive. He was sinewy and strong, yes, but would he stand out in a crowd?

No.

Entering high school he was about 5'7", 150 pounds. Skinny. He could hit the hell out of a baseball, but he was a mediocre running back on the football team and an average guard on the basketball team. Though there was a hint, even in those days, of the future savage mentality he'd take into the ring.

"When we were sophomores playing basketball, we had a competitive team," Tim Gunn said. "He and I were guarding each other during practice. He didn't like my hand checks. Didn't like my tough defense. But he was very physical right back. After practice, he came into the locker room and said, 'Where's Gunn?' I turned and he just leveled me. He punched me in the face and knocked me to the floor. I got up and went after him and then we were separated by the team and coaches."

In another instance, Randy used his aggression for good, defending a fellow student who was getting bullied. John Comforte described the scene:

> We heard one of the greasers walked up to a special-needs child and poured milk on his head. So Randy and I decided we were going to get them. The following day, I say to one of them, "I heard you poured milk on [the boy's] head?" He said, "Yeah, what are you going to do about it?" I look at Randy and — pop. I hit this guy. Randy does a double-leg takedown of the other guy. We beat the heck out of them. Savage hated bullies. Strange, isn't it? His hatred for bullies, I believe, is what made him portray a bully in his persona.

And for the record, his first wrestling uniform wasn't a pair of tights or a "Macho Man" shirt, it was a standard-issue, purple-and-white Downers Grove singlet. He was a middleweight, wrestling in the 145 or 152 weight class. Coaches and friends say he was nothing special, and in an even bigger contrast to his later in-ring persona, he was barely noticeable.

"He was very smart, but very quiet," said Bruce Ritter, Randy's wrestling coach at Downers Grove. "He didn't have the personality that he created in the wrestling world. And he was lanky. He didn't have any of that bulk."

Tom Bruno, who was on the wrestling team with both Randy and Lanny, said there was no way you'd have ever predicted that Randy would become an acrobatic, charismatic and iconic wrestler. Same with Lanny, for that matter.

The wrestling team practiced up on the second-floor loft of the gymnasium at Downers Grove North. Every day after school, Randy, Tom and their teammates would pull the rollaway bleachers off the gym floor and grab the mats off the balcony to set up the practice area. All the mats were adorned with the school's mascot, a Trojan.

"I was a wrestling fan, so I knew who their dad was from television. I watched him every Sunday morning," Bruno said. "I remember they'd get teased a lot by the other kids, who would always say that their dad's wrestling was all fake. They'd say he wasn't a real wrestler like they were.

"Looking back, it was probably hurtful. Aside from that, nobody would have guessed what they were destined for. They were just two average high school wrestlers whose dad was a professional wrestler. But their dad stood out."

Even though Angelo was a pro wrestler and had a college baseball background, and he'd once played hoops regularly with the great George Mikan, he never interfered with practices. He'd simply show up to watch and support his sons, which was a completely normal thing to do — lots of dads watched practices when they could.

They'd roll into the gym or to the sideline of the baseball field in a boring beige or gray or navy suit with a white button-up shirt and lame matching tie. Maybe they'd unbutton the top collar and loosen the knot a bit. Or maybe they'd head home and put on jeans and a white T-shirt or Izod polo first — classic '60s and '70s dad gear.

Not Angelo.

He didn't meddle and he didn't blend, choosing to cruise around Downers Grove with all the subtlety of a slot machine in a library.

First, there was the car.

No boat-like blue Ford Galaxy. No goofy green and wood-paneled Jeep Wagoneer. No oversized Oldsmobile Cutlass Supreme. Those were for regular dads, not wrestling dads.

Angelo drove a big, audacious Cadillac with fins on the back.

"It was like an Elvis Presley car," Tom Bruno said. "He was a showman."

"It was a Cadillac convertible," Guarnaccia said. "It was fun riding in that car."

The car was just the start.

"He'd sit in the upper row of the bleachers," Bruno said. "One day he'd have blond hair. The next day he'd have black hair. Or he'd have a pinky ring on. He was there like every other parent, but he wasn't like every other parent."

That's an understatement.

When talking to Randy's childhood teammates and friends, and the subject of Angelo would come up, they'd all laugh and share a vivid memory of what he was wearing (or wasn't wearing) at a particular game or event:

> "Randy's dad would come to the ball field
> wearing a Speedo and flip-flops and no shirt.
> He'd have this dyed blond hair slicked back.
> Sometimes he'd bring other wrestlers and they'd
> all stand on the fence and watch the game.
> He was a big man."
>
> — TIM GUNN

> "We'd be playing baseball and Angelo would
> come traipsing down to the field in flip-flops
> and his short shorts and no shirt. There would
> be a hundred people at the game, and everyone
> would turn to see him. He was in great shape."
>
> — DAVE BUEHRER

> "I don't care what temperature it was at our
> games. Angelo would be there wearing his
> white Speedo and his flip-flops and he had this
> beautiful tan. And he'd stand there watching."
>
> — RUSS HOLPUCH

> "Randy's dad would always be at the games. And
> he would always be in his Speedos or tight shorts
> in the stands. And he'd have on a tank top."
>
> — JOHN GUARNACCIA

Bruce Ritter, who was in his twenties at the time and coached both Randy and Lanny in wrestling and baseball, got a heavy dose of Angelo during the boys' high school years and enjoyed his company.

"Angelo was a great guy to talk with," Ritter said. "He was very outgoing . . . We'd be at an American Legion game and a lot of the kids recognized him and knew him from being on television."

Ritter remembers fondly how Angelo would often have to toggle back and forth between being Randy and Lanny's dad and being the publicly despised wrestling heel he'd portrayed for nearly a decade. It made for some comedic moments where real life collided with the personality he'd constructed.

"We'd be talking about Randy or baseball or something and he'd spot a group of kids approaching," Ritter said. "Then he'd lean into me and say 'alright, I have to do a little playacting here now' and then he'd turn to the boys, who were expecting a villain, and he'd go into character and yell, 'What do you guys want!!' and they'd laugh and run away. Then we'd go back to talking. He was a very nice man. He and Judy were at every one of the boys' games. They were a tight-knit family and the parents really supported the kids."

There's a black-and-white photo from the Poffos' scrapbook that exemplifies the influence Angelo would ultimately have on Randy. In the picture, Angelo is about forty years old and Randy is about fifteen. Father and son are standing in the backyard of the house on Venard Road. It's summer. Both are shirtless. Both are curling dumbbells.

Randy, with a classic teenage-boy "take the picture already, Mom" face, looks at the camera. He's a few inches shorter than Angelo at this point and he's rail thin, but he's cut. Early six-pack. Defined shoulders. Budding biceps. He's wearing a plain dark Speedo.

Angelo is right next to him. He's wearing a bright, patterned Speedo. He's big, built like a powerlifter. And he's got close-cropped platinum-blond-dyed hair.

In most families, it's the teenager who's coloring his hair and wearing flashy clothes and rebelling while the dad is clean-cut and in plain clothes.

Not in the Poffos' house, because Randy hadn't embraced his dad's flash and flair and full size just yet. But the seeds had been firmly planted.

CHAPTER 7

The Prospect

The kid was obsessed.

Some high school students sit in the back row of the classroom to disappear, others to take naps or cheat on tests or pass notes or flirt with girls.

Randy Poffo sat in the back of the class to hide his baseball workouts . . . *What?*

The average major league baseball weighs between 5 and 5.25 ounces. To get stronger, some players will toss a heavier baseball in the outfield or around the diamond to build muscle. These are called weighted balls. They're the same size as regulation balls but can weigh up to 12 ounces.

Obviously, Randy wasn't going to chuck around a three-quarter-pound baseball in chemistry class, smashing beakers and Bunsen burners. Instead, Randy brought a super heavy metal baseball to school and while the teacher was lecturing on mitochondria or the Magna Carta or *Of Mice and Men*, he'd pull out the ball and get to work, trying to strengthen his fingers, grip, forearms, biceps and triceps.

"He was so focused on baseball and he had such a great work ethic," Tim Gunn said. "Randy would sit in the back of classes with a lead baseball and he'd be squeezing and then doing these arm exercises. It was the same size as a regular baseball but really heavy and he'd carry it all around school. Whenever he was in class, he'd head right to the back and he'd be doing these triceps exercises the whole time."

Obsessed.

Most kids walking around high school had one bag, a basic L.L.Bean or JanSport backpack loaded with books, pens, pencils and notebooks and all the tools needed to learn. Randy had that backpack, but he also had another bag he carried around with him with all the tools he needed to hit.

"He used to always carry his bat bag," Guarnaccia said. "All around school. He had his own bats and he always had them with him."

Did any of this look weird? Maybe. Did Randy care? Not at all.

"All of us on the baseball team had girlfriends and went out drinking and stuff, but I never saw Randy at a party," Russ Holpuch, a baseball teammate at Downers Grove, said. "It's funny because most of us weren't aware of who he hung out with. I know he was close with his family. He was kind of a loner. That's why when I learned he became the new guy, the Macho Man, later in life, it was fun and surprising. Because it was nothing like the guy we went to high school with."

Lanny said his brother certainly noticed girls and they liked him, but he didn't have time to date because he was singularly focused on baseball. All. The. Time.

"He was always working on his game," he said. "He'd come home from school and go right to practice. After practice he'd practice. I knew I wasn't good enough. My dream to play professionally was a wish. His was a goal and a plan. Some people may say he had OCD, but he was just a guy trying to make it in baseball."

Anything Randy read or heard about that might improve his skills he tried, including a unique exercise that some of his future minor league teammates would emulate: the tire drill.

"Randy hung an old tire from a tree about strike zone height and he'd stand there and hit that tire with a baseball bat over and over again," Lanny said. "*Bang! Bang! Bang!* He'd hit the tire to make his arms and forearms stronger and stronger. And it worked. He had a fantastic grip."

Even on game days Randy could be found putting in extra work, astonishing his teammates with an unquenchable desire to master his craft.

"You could see the top of the batting cage next to his house from the baseball field," Gunn said. "We'd head down there before practice or a game and you could hear the crack of the bat from the cage for thirty minutes straight."

One reason for the seemingly never-ending string of swings was because Randy was determined to turn himself into a switch-hitter like Pete Rose. A natural righty, he'd make sure he took as many, if not more, cuts from the left side of the plate to force himself to get comfortable.

Coach Ritter said he was the most disciplined kid on the team, living up to the cliché of the guy who was the first one to practice and the last one to leave.

"He was so dedicated," Ritter said. "He was very quiet, but you couldn't help but respect him. The kids all looked up to him. He lived at the field. I'd drive by on a Saturday or Sunday and he'd always have someone there pitching batting practice to him or standing on second so he could make his throws from behind the plate like Johnny Bench."

Perhaps the best evidence of Randy's desire was the detritus of his efforts, the thousands of dead balls thrown away and the endless yards of chicken wire removed and refitted on both sides of the batting cage after hundreds and hundreds of line drives had been hit into the light metal mesh.

"We tore up the left and right hand side of the cage," Buehrer said. "We had to fix and repair the chicken wire a bunch of times. The bottom of the cage was dirt and we probably went through a thousand balls. There were old torn-off covers and seams from balls all over the place."

The end result?

Randy turned himself into the greatest baseball player Downers Grove had ever seen.

After dominating Pony League and Little League and Babe Ruth League and the high school freshman team, Randy was poised to finally see how good he was against the big boys: the high school varsity squad.

Then Angelo threw the family a metaphorical curveball.

Boys, we're moving to Hawaii!

"Gentleman" Ed Francis, the famous wrestling promoter out of Hawaii who ran *50th State Big Time Wrestling*, a popular show in the islands, reached out to Angelo and offered him a hefty contract to wrestle around the Honolulu territory for a year. Francis would eventually sell his company to "High Chief" Peter Maivia, The Rock's grandfather, and he was always looking to bring big names out to the Pacific.

As Angelo and Judy weighed the offer, they saw the potential problem of having to pull Lanny and Randy out of school as a solution to a few lingering concerns.

One, by pushing back each of the boys' graduation years, it would decrease the likelihood of them getting drafted to go fight in Vietnam. Two, pulling the kids out for a year would give them an extended period to work on their baseball skills. And as an added bonus, Randy would have a competitive advantage by reentering school a year older than his classmates.

After hearing the plan to ditch high school for a year to play baseball in Hawaii, the boys only had one question:

When do we leave?

The original plan was for Judy to homeschool the boys so they wouldn't get too far behind when they returned to normal life in Downers Grove. What actually happened was that the boys read a little, wrote a little, filled out a few math worksheets and otherwise spent time at the beach and played an absurd amount of baseball.

Randy played so much ball that he signed on to catch for a small semipro team on the big island called Gouvea's Sausage Phillies.

"That time in Hawaii made Randy a different player," Lanny said. "It helped us both develop in big ways."

Eleven months later, tanned and trained, Randy returned to Downers Grove ready to make his mark on the high school diamonds of DuPage County.

It didn't take long.

In order to give his full attention to hitting and throwing, Randy dropped wrestling, basketball and football. In his mind, he was now a 24/7/365 baseball player with his eyes on one prize: getting drafted.

His play backed up his goal. Throughout Randy's entire junior year, a pitcher had a less-than-even chance of getting him out. They had a better shot at calling a random coin toss correctly.

"His junior year he was an unbelievable right-handed hitter," Coach Ritter said. "He was the leading hitter in all of Illinois. He hit .525 for the entire season."

In a sport where a batting average over .300 is good and anything over .350 is considered excellent, .525 is otherworldly. The team won the conference championship and in a surprise to no one, Randy was named Most Valuable Player.

"Watching him play ball, you thought for sure he'd make it to the big leagues," Gunn said.

Following his junior season, Randy played summer baseball with the Illinois State Baseball League's DuPage Cardinals, coached by Joe White, who'd been running the team for twelve years. The season started in early June and featured the best players in the county. Randy continued his stellar hitting, getting on base and cracking home runs along with the rest of his all-star team.

Where he separated himself was behind the plate. His years of studying Johnny Bench and Randy Hundley began to show. And the arm exercises in algebra class were paying off. With the forearms of a lumberjack, he could smoke a runner trying to steal second with the snap of his wrist. To many spectators, his footwork appeared to be damn near perfect. Pro level even.

In one of the first games of the year, a play developed that allowed the sixteen-year-old to unveil his full defensive repertoire, and thankfully, the *Bensenville Register* had a stringer on hand to describe it for posterity:

"With a man on first and one out, the Elgin Merchants put on the hit and run. The batter topped the ball toward third. The third baseman charged the ball and fired to first while the base-runner ripped around second and headed for third. Out of position, the third sacker couldn't get back to the throw.

"But Poffo streaked for the bag, dove through the air to grab Pat Doyle's throw, and put the ball on the runner sliding in."

"It was a fantastic play," Coach White said. "This kid is the best catcher I have ever seen — he gets the ball away quicker than a major league catcher."

When Randy wasn't practicing with his high school teammates, honing his swing in his batting cage or making dazzling plays with the DuPage Cardinals, he occasionally moonlit as a fill-in catcher for the Olympic Saving semipro team, run by former Chicago White Sox scout and Midwest Baseball League coach Lou Menchetti.

"When we were sixteen and seventeen they used to have these semipro summer leagues," Tom Bruno explains. "Guys in their twenties and thirties playing all across the state and they always needed pitchers and catchers. We'd be all over Illinois, even out to Wisconsin. Angelo would drive us around somewhere that he had a wrestling show. He'd wrestle in the town, then we'd play in the beer league game and drive back. We made a little money for food. It was fun. That filled in the time between American Legion games and Senior Babe Ruth games and all that."

Baseball. Baseball. More baseball.

"Baseball was Randy's entire life back then," Judy said.

MLB or bust.

This was the theme for Randy's final year in high school.

He entered his senior season as the MVP, league-leading hitter and number one catching prospect in all of Chicago.

"I was a hot property," he said, knowing that all he had to do was continue on his torrid pace and a draft spot would likely be his.

He didn't waste any time.

By the end of the first week of the 1970 spring baseball season, he established himself as the top hitter in Illinois.

"Poffo No. 1 Prep Hitter in 1st Weekly Averages," blared the headline in *Chicago Today* on Friday, May 1, 1970. Tommy Kouzmanoff, the high school beat reporter for the paper, wrote:

> Randy Poffo hopes to some day play in the big leagues. And, if the big, strong Downers Grove North High School

catcher continues to hit and throw the ball as he has recently, he may achieve his goal.

A long-ball hitter, Poffo, for whom many outfielders play against the fence, leads Chicago area prep batsmen in hitting, according to CHICAGO TODAY'S first averages of the season. Young Poffo is batting a fantastic .750.

A 6', 185-pound senior, Randy has blasted pitchers for 12 hits in 16 times at bat, four for triples and one for a home run.

Did Randy continue hitting at a .750 clip for the whole season?

No, he didn't. That would be damn near impossible. But equally astonishing is that he never fell below .500 all spring, even as he committed himself to playing the entire season as a switch-hitter.

"He hit mostly as a righty his junior year," Coach Ritter said. "Between his junior and senior years he really learned how to switch-hit and senior year he came back a full switch-hitter. He had a little more power left-handed, but he was a little more susceptible to the curve. You could strike him out from the left side. Not the right."

Looking at a string of box scores from Randy's senior year, they're so consistently great they're almost boring:

2-4, 2-4, 3-5, 3-4, 2-4, 1-3, 2-4, 2-5, 2-6

He was like a blackjack dealer who dealt twenties nonstop.

Game after game Randy would outsmart, outwork and outhustle the opposing team's pitcher. If they struck him out as a lefty he'd bat righty next time and slap a single. If he started batting righty and hit a single, he might switch to lefty and swat a home run the next at bat.

High school aces were simply overmatched — so much so that Randy didn't even like settling for singles if he could help it. Coach Ritter remembers one instance where his young star comically (and aggressively) tried to give back a single to get back into the batter's box.

The scene takes place in a league game with a runner on second. Randy is battling the pitcher, looking for something to hit to drive in the run. He gets fooled on an off-speed pitch and tries to check his swing, but makes contact with the ball.

"As Randy sprints down to first base, the ball just kind of rolled down the line," Coach Ritter said. "Randy gets to first and the ball is still trickling slowly. Finally it stopped on the white line and the umpire makes the call that it's a fair ball. He awards Randy the single . . . And Randy gets in an argument with the umpire!"

"That's gotta be foul!" he yells.

"I'm giving you the base," the umpire says, perplexed. "You're not out."

"It was a foul!" Poffo shouts. "Let me get in the batter's box!"

"You're safe!"

"I'm still up!"

"They got in this huge argument," Ritter said, laughing. "Randy is safe on the bag, but he'd rather have another shot at a double or home run or whatever than take a single. The kid loved to hit."

Randy even had his own Mickey Mantle–like moment, pounding a ball where nobody had ever hit one before.

When the Westbrook condominium complex was built in 1968 on Saratoga Avenue, the developers had to be thrilled to land such a choice location. The rows of homes were within walking distance of shops and restaurants. They were near the commuter bus to the METRA rail system. They were close to good schools.

To top it off, across from Saratoga Avenue and through a row of trees, residents had easy access to a park and the high school baseball field. At no point, standing on the balcony of one of the condos, would a developer or condo owner think they were in danger of being hit by a baseball. After all, you couldn't even see home plate. It was nearly two hundred yards away.

However, nobody took into account the left-handed power of Randy Poffo.

During the overlapping years that games were played on the baseball field and the condominiums existed, there was zero thought given to a ball even coming *close* to the buildings.

Nobody had hit one that reached the pavement on Saratoga Avenue. Nobody had even cleared the trees to bounce to the pavement on

Saratoga Avenue. Nobody thought it was possible because, for a high school kid, it wasn't.

Until it was.

"Randy hit the farthest home run I have ever seen a high schooler hit," Coach Ritter said. "He hit it left-handed and the ball soared up and out. Over the fence. Over the trees. Over the roadway. Until it finally landed on the third floor patio of the apartment complex across the street. It was an unbelievable blast. Well over 500 feet. Nobody has ever come close to that."

Major League scouts took notice.

"There were always scouts at our games," Dave Buehrer said. "There were three or four in the stands all the time. They were watching Johnny Guarnaccia, me and Randy. Between the three of us there was a lot of interest. And people came to our games. We'd have a hundred people in the stands."

Not one to enjoy divided attention, Randy chose to shine a spotlight on himself, personally setting up his own pro day and inviting as many representatives from MLB teams to one of his games as he could.

"I remember driving over with another coach and when we got to the game there were like thirty-five cars at our field," Coach Ritter said. "Somehow he'd gotten in touch with a bunch of scouts and they were all there to see him."

The Downers Grove coaches and players were pumped to have such an esteemed audience for the game and they were excited about the scouts seeing what their superstar teammate could do.

Then Randy showed up. Sweaty. Hunched over. Clammy. Green. Miserable.

"He was sick as a dog," Ritter said.

Randy had none of his usual pop and confidence. With a 102-degree fever, he could barely stand up straight, let alone swing a bat.

"He didn't have a good day," Ritter said. "He was very disappointed. A lot of the scouts left."

After that game, only a few die-hard scouts maintained a presence at the field and it was too bad. Other than the dud he put up on his exhibition day, he continued to light up the rest of the league — including in the clutch, like on the last day of his senior season when the team was fighting for first place.

Downers Grove needed to win both games of their doubleheader against Glenbard West on the final day of Randy's senior year. After they squeaked by with a 2–0 win in Game 1, he wanted to come up big in his final nine innings in a Trojan uniform. With first place riding on every at bat, he went a clean 3-3, leading the team to a 10–2 win and the first-place finish they'd battled for all year.

It was the perfect finish to a high school career that saw Poffo bat over .500 through two full seasons and establish himself as one of the best catchers under eighteen years old in the state.

In the sixteen days between Randy taking off his Downers Grove baseball hat for the last time and the 1971 MLB Draft on June 8, all he could do was wait. Sure, he had a crappy exhibition day, but he'd put together a solid two-year body of work that to everyone in his life still made him a lock to get drafted.

"He was dedicated and focused," Lanny said. "We all assumed Randy would be welcomed into professional baseball."

The draft began on Tuesday before noon. It was an unusually cold summer morning, even for Chicago, with a sunrise temperature of only fifty-four degrees. The Chicago White Sox kicked things off by selecting another catcher, Danny Goodwin from Peoria, about 150 miles away.

Randy was a strong prospect, but Goodwin was considered to be one of the best in the nation all year, and his selection as the number one overall pick was not a shock. No worries. There were plenty of rounds to go and plenty of teams who needed catchers. It was only a matter of time before one of them selected Randy.

Or was it?

As the midday temperature outside 3909 Venard rose into the high 70s, the mood in the Poffo house plunged to arctic levels. Round one passed. Nothing. Round two, three, four, five . . . nothing. Twenty rounds later, still nothing. The entire first day of the draft had passed, and all the teams had passed on Randy.

He was inconsolable.

"That was a tough day for him," Lanny said.

The next day would be worse.

Randy suffered through all forty-eight rounds over two days and at the end of it all, he was left undrafted and heartbroken. To add insult to injury, the final pick of the draft was a catcher, Don Stackpole out of Wildomar, California, to the Los Angeles Dodgers.

In total, over 60 catchers were drafted, averaging nearly three per Major League team.

And no team wanted Randy Poffo.

"They ignored him," Lanny said. "But we don't quit."

After processing the devastating turn of events, Randy joined the Chicago Orioles, an amateur baseball team that plays about 130 games a year. He was the youngest player on the team and made an impact immediately, hitting several home runs in his first few games.

He played to stay sharp because Angelo had a plan.

If the scouts weren't going to bring Randy to a Major League stadium, he'd bring the boy himself. Together, they drove 280 miles to St. Louis for a free agent tryout.

When Angelo and Randy stepped on the field of Busch Stadium, there were two hundred other undrafted hopefuls chasing their dreams with them.

Randy, summoning all the hours in his personal batting cage and all the workouts in class and all the chilly nights on the Downers Grove field, absolutely played his ass off.

Hitting. Throwing. Catching. His full repertoire was on display.

"All these kids were out there, playing as hard as they could to make the team," Lanny said. "And then Randy gets in the batter's box and he hit a hard line drive that caught everyone's attention. *Boom*. Randy had very strong wrists. He hit the ball hard over and over. When they saw that, they went, 'oh my God!'"

At the end of the tryout, 199 of the 200 dreamers left without a contract.

Only one player was signed on the spot:

Randy Poffo.

"The Cardinals signed Keith Hernandez and my brother on the same day," Lanny said. "He didn't get a signing bonus. But he got $500 per month and a chance to prove himself in the minors. That was all he needed."

When the father-son duo rolled back into Downers Grove triumphantly, news spread fast.

Randy Poffo signed with the St. Louis Cardinals!!!!

He did it!

The local paper even sent a reporter over to interview Randy.

"The Cardinals were really surprised I wasn't drafted," he said. "They felt I had unlimited potential. But it doesn't matter now. I've got my chance. You can't bring your contract to spring training, only your bat."

CHAPTER 8

Sarasota

Quiet.
    Boring.
Unassuming.

These are the most common recollections of Randy Poffo in the minor leagues by the coaches, executives and players who knew him — but there's a catch. These descriptions are all said with a headshake and smile and qualifying remark that is equal parts amazement and amusement.

Why?

Because all the interviews take place after they've seen the end of the movie, the part where Randy Poffo transforms into one of the most flamboyant, charismatic, energetic entertainers of all time: the Macho Man.

They smirk when asked "What was he like?" because back between the years of 1971 and 1974, when Randy Poffo was actually playing in the minors, *nobody gave a shit*. There were no interview requests. No media attention. Nothing.

"He seemed like such a quiet guy at the time," said Lee Thomas, the old Cardinals player development director. "He was a real nice guy. I had no idea he would end up like [Macho Man]."

Paul Faulks, who ran the farm system for the Cardinals for decades, said Poffo barely made an impression.

"He didn't have much to say to anybody," he said. "He was just one of those kids trying to make it in baseball with very little chance."

Even his appearance in the team photo is bland. There's none of his signature long hair or beard or headband or even a unique expression. He's clean-shaven. Looks kind and polite. Blends right in.

When an associate editor for the *Sporting News* was asked to do some research on Randy for the *St. Louis Dispatch*, he was underwhelmed.

"He looked like a regular goof," he said.

The perspective of opposing players and teammates, however, was a little different. They weren't evaluating him as a future talent or how he appeared to management. Instead they remember how he was in practice or in the locker room or as a roommate sharing a dumpy six-hundred-square-foot apartment in Sarasota, living off crackers and fast food.

To them, he was a hard-nosed, intense guy who was loyal and talented and liked to have fun. Even one of his idols took notice.

"Randy was a super athlete," Pete Rose, his spring-training teammate in 1974, said. "He was very limber, flexible, so it didn't surprise me he was a pretty good baseball player."

In his first season for the Single-A Sarasota Red Birds in the Gulf Coast League, he slugged .492 and hit .286 with 2 home runs and 13 RBIs. Doesn't sound like much, but in a shortened season, his average and home run totals were good enough to lead the team. He also finished the year with no errors and made the all-star team.

He followed that up with a second all-star nod in 1972, leading the team with 3 home runs and batting .274 with 26 RBI in 53 games.

During those first two seasons, a few themes began to develop around Randy's talent. One was that if there was a Major League Baseball team that exclusively rewarded heart and effort, he'd be on it. The guy flat-out hustled.

Jim Lett, who later coached Randy in Tampa, said, "The thing that stood out is, he was a good competitor. He always played hard."

"Randy was a great guy," former teammate Jim Walthour said. "A really hard worker, and a kid with a lot of pride."

"He was an intense kid," Russ Nixon, another coach, said.

"He was an aggressive player, strong, just like in the ring," said Mike Bombard, his one-time roommate and later minor league coach. "And he did love baseball."

"Randy Poffo was a very aggressive player and was well-liked on the team because of that aggressiveness," Tito Landrum, a minor league Cardinals teammate, said.

Intense. Tough. Hard-working. Aggressive. Passionate.

But . . .

That "but" is where thousands of major league dreams have gone to die.

The thing was, he *could* hit. There was no doubt about that. The doubt was about consistency over time, improvement and whether he could separate himself from the pack and move up the minor league ranks.

"He was a heck of a hitter," Tony Garofalo, a former Sarasota teammate and longtime minor league trainer, said.

Garofalo roomed with Randy for three months, splitting a $400-per-month apartment lease with four dudes on the beach. They were living on the fringes of pro baseball but were young, determined and looking to each other for camaraderie and motivation. And occasionally, honesty.

"He wasn't a five-tool baseball player," Garofolo said. "He could hit, he could field, he could run a little, but he couldn't throw very well. He had a funky throwing motion."

On this last point, Randy agreed.

"I had kind of a scatter arm," he said. "My throws to second would tail to the outfield, sometimes to right field."

The question then becomes, How long can a good (not great) hitting catcher, with so-so speed and a rough throwing motion, last in the minors?

The answer is usually until you get cut or can no longer afford to live off a meager five hundred bucks a month. But Lanny said his brother was in no danger of starving.

"Randy never needed money because he played cards with all these bonus babies," Lanny said. "He had an incredibly sharp mind. Like a razor blade. He was quick. He never cheated and he rarely bluffed. He had such a talent for it. He'd make you naked in ten minutes. He could just play cards."

The irony wasn't lost on Randy. Yes, he didn't get a signing bonus like the guys on his team who were drafted. But whether the cash came to him from the playing field or poker, what did it matter? The money was still his.

"People don't know he was in the National Honors Society," Lanny said. "He knew all the statistics. He knew all the odds of winning. He could look at what you were throwing away and guess what you had. Whatever game you were playing, he figured it out. My dad never had to send him money. Randy made a lot of money playing cards in the minors. You wouldn't believe it."

He also liked to have fun, occasionally foreshadowing his career as an entertainer.

"I can remember him setting up a ring in the locker room and wrestling with the guys," Landrum said. "He told us he was going to be a wrestler some day."

That is, if the baseball thing didn't work out.

And for a time, if he squinted *juuuuuust* hard enough, and believed enough, it looked like maybe, *maaaybe*, it could work out. All he needed to do was catch a hot streak and find a way to get past Single-A.

It almost happened.

The beginning of Randy's third season started with a slump. A bad one. So bad that after about a month he was certain he'd leave the field one day and find a dreaded cut slip in his locker.

With nothing to lose, he loosened up. He figured if he was going down, he might as well go down swinging. But the opposite happened.

Rather than hack his way out of baseball, his bat began to make contact. One hit. Then another. Then another. All of a sudden he was batting over .320 through fifteen games. At the twenty-five-game mark, he was up to .344.

The Cardinals brass took notice, promoting him to Class-A Orangeburg in the Western Carolinas league. On the surface, this was the major break Randy had been waiting for, but he quickly realized it was anything but.

Instead of being an everyday starter like he was in Sarasota, in Orangeburg he bounced in and out of the lineup, playing first base, catcher and whatever else they needed. To make matters worse, the team played in the dreaded Mirmow Field, forty-seven miles south of Columbia, in a two-thousand-seat, rickety blast furnace. Game-time temperatures in the summer were often in the low to mid-nineties. The humidity plus the giant outfield plus the pterodactyl-sized mosquitoes made the park feel like the baseball apocalypse — a place where high hopes of the big leagues were murdered. To add to the misery and general funk in the locker room, the team found itself stuck in the middle of a fifteen-game losing streak upon Randy's arrival.

Rough.

On July 7, 1973, Randy had his best game in Orangeburg against the Anderson Tigers to finally grab a much-needed *W*.

In the first inning, after three straight singles by teammates, Randy hit a sacrifice fly for the game's first score. Later, in the bottom of the sixth, he combined his hustle and his swing for a gutsy run. After hitting a laser up the middle for a double, Poffo sprinted to third on a passed ball. Then, a moment later, as the catcher again struggled with a pitch, he put his head down and busted for home, crossing the plate safe. It was the kind of one-man-gang effort that Randy was capable of, but it wasn't enough to salvage the team's season or his time with St. Louis.

The Orangeburg Cardinals finished 50–72 and Randy never got his average above .250. Aside from a nostalgic Downers Grove moment, where he faced his old pal John Guarnaccia's Spartanburg Phillies (and tipped off the 1972 fourth-round pick to a few pitches), Randy's season was miserable and kept getting worse, until it ended in a literal thud.

In one of the last games of the year, still fighting for a roster spot, still fighting for his baseball life, Randy rounded third for what he knew was going to be a close play at home. As the ball sped through the air to the catcher, Randy thundered down the line, lowering his right shoulder like a battering ram, preparing for impact.

"If there was a play at the plate, he wasn't going to slide around," teammate Jim Lett said. "There was going to be a collision."

Oh, there was a collision.

Boom!

Randy slammed into the catcher with everything he had, trying to jar the ball loose through brute force. The catcher, protected by his padding and face mask, got up weary but unharmed. Randy separated his right shoulder and tore several muscles on his right side. Season over. The Cardinals cut him a few months later.

"Another hard day," Lanny said. "He believed that perhaps he had come to the end of his career."

Perhaps.

Or perhaps not.

In fact, if you knew Randy back then, you'd know there was no way in hell he was going to let his dream die on a smashup at home plate. No chance. But what he did next was unheard of.

CHAPTER 9

I'm Done with Them

B*ang!*
A baseball slaps against the weathered cement on the backside of a Publix grocery store. It skips off the oil-stained gravel and hops into Randy Poffo's outstretched right-handed glove. He quickly palms the ball with his left hand, sets his feet and launches it back against the wall.

Bang!

The ball rifles off the gray stone and bounces back into his glove. He pivots, palms it again and rockets it back towards the wall.

Bang!

Poffo has been at it for over an hour. Throw. Catch. Throw. Catch. Nonstop. The humid air in Sarasota is thicker than a strip steak. Sweat waterfalls off his body.

Bang! Bang! Bang!

It had been a few weeks since Randy separated his right shoulder — his throwing shoulder. For most ballplayers, a throwing arm injury is a season killer. And for those clinging to the bottom rung of Single-A ball, it might be a career death sentence.

Not for Randy. *No freaking way.* So what if his right arm was useless? He had two arms didn't he? Why not learn to throw with his left?

Delusional? Maybe.

Impossible? We'll see.

One night after the injury, Randy made a commitment to himself (an oath, really) that if he was going to wash out of minor league ball it wasn't going to be because of his bum right arm. That next morning he woke up and brushed his teeth with his left hand. Ate cereal with his left hand. Combed his hair, opened doors and even held drinks with his left hand.

"I did everything left-handed," Randy said of his ambidextrous ambition. "I ate left-handed, drove left-handed, learned to play cards left-handed. It took me eight months."

Most importantly, he willed himself to throw as powerfully with his left arm as he had with his right by following a grueling regimen he concocted himself:

One thousand five hundred baseballs.

Thrown lefty.

Every day.

He'd either throw against the giant wall behind a shopping center near his tiny apartment in Sarasota or at his second-favorite spot, a wall on a tennis court in Payne Park off South School Avenue.

"It was incredibly tough, but I just kept working, throwing the ball against the wall," he said. "I guess persistence was my best attribute."

After getting cut by the Cardinals, he took his battered body and bruised ego to a Cincinnati Reds tryout in Tampa, where he earned an invite to spring training before the 1974 season. With his right arm healing and his left arm throwing a passable ball, he figured if he was going to make it at this point, it would be due to his production at the plate.

Suddenly we have twenty-two-year-old Randy Poffo, a rare switch-hitter and switch-thrower, with everything on the line, spraying balls all over the field in front of his idols Rose and Bench, Joe Morgan, Ken Griffey, George Foster and the rest of the Big Red Machine.

It was dazzling.

During spring training he hit six homers (four lefty and two righty). With two of the bombs on the final day of camp against the Mets, the Reds gave him the last spot on the Tampa Tarpons roster in the Class-A Florida State League.

"I said let him swing the bat here," Russ Nixon, his coach, said at the time. "He is that type of hitter. He wants to play. He has the greatest desire of any kid I ever saw. He is an aggressive hitter."

That desire manifested itself on the field too. Mike Moore, a long-time general manager for the Tarpons, remembers one incident fondly.

"I'll never forget this — one day [manager] Russ Nixon and I got to the stadium at 1:00 in the afternoon, and I peeked out onto the field and saw these baseballs flying across the diamond," Moore said. "It was Randy, all alone, with a bucket of balls, standing in center and throwing them one by one to home plate, all with his left hand. I said, 'Randy, what are you doing?' He looked at me and said, 'Trying to make myself more valuable.' He was that type of guy."

The desire to be valuable came from a slow, crushing realization Randy couldn't escape: no matter how many balls he fired off the shopping center wall, his odds of climbing from Single-A all the way to the majors seemed slim.

"I was getting a good chance with them, and I was going all-out," Randy said. "I had been released once, and if you get a second chance, you're always fearful it may happen again."

Fear led to focus.

Focus led to home runs.

A bunch of them.

Even with the deep dimensions of the Tarpons' home ballpark, Al Lopez Field (340' to left, 400' to center, 340' to right), Randy lit up his new club. Despite concerns about his arm, he pounded nine home runs, had an average over .290 and led the team in RBIs for much of the season until — during a hustle play, of course — he dove in the outfield and broke the index finger on his left hand.

Now unable to throw well with either arm, Randy was moved to DH, but he never felt comfortable holding the bat. In just a few weeks, his average plummeted down near the Mendoza Line. By the end of the year he was still second in the Florida State League in home runs behind future Hall of Famer Eddie Murray, and he led the Tarpons with sixty-six runs batted in. It wasn't enough.

"Randy was a good ballplayer, not a great one," Reds teammate Keith Madison said. "He was an incredibly hard worker. I remember him trying to turn himself into a left-handed throwing first baseman instead of a right-handed catcher."

It was a tall order. First basemen are expected to be durable power hitters with cannons for arms to nail guys stealing second, to turn double plays and toss lasers to third or home. Randy had potential as a hitter, but with his injury, the rest seemed like it was off the table.

He did, however, give everyone a sneak preview of what was eventually to come in the ring.

The story begins during a game between his Tarpons and the West Palm Beach Expos when Expos pitcher Joe Keener eyed Randy warily in the on-deck circle in the first inning. After a few throws home to the hitter, Keener became convinced that Randy was studying his pitches, trying to tip off his teammate in the batter's box as to what was coming. After several glares, he managed to get the batter out, but the pitcher was fuming.

After the Expos had their turn at bat, Keener headed to the mound, still livid. Randy was up first, and instead of waiting to deal with him at the plate, the furious pitcher had had enough. In the middle of his warm-up he adjusted his aim, turned and fired a fastball at Randy's head.

"I was on the on-deck circle," Randy said. "The pitcher thought I was looking at his pitches too closely. So I'm getting ready to hit before the inning started and all of a sudden I turn around and there's a blur coming. And I look and there's a baseball, right against my face. I hit the mound just like that, both benches emptied and we had a brawl."

Like most stories and myths involving the future Macho Man, the details have been embellished, improved upon or mixed up.

In this case, it may be all three.

Tampa Tarpons catcher Don Werner, his teammate at the time, remembers a fight clearly, but the one he recalls was against the Winter Haven Red Sox, not the Expos.

In his version, told to *Sports Illustrated*, the opposing team's coach, Rac Slider, called for a pitching change and as the Red Sox pitcher warmed up, he caught Randy trying to time his pitches.

"So the pitcher just rears back and drills Randy in the helmet," Werner said. "Randy charged the mound and started fighting the guy. We were all wondering what in the world he was doing."

A third version of the story changes a few details about the fight itself. This one was from Jim Selman in the *Tampa Tribune* the day after the incident:

"Right-hander Joe Keener struck Randy Poffo on the batting helmet while he was waiting close by to open Tampa's half of the second inning. Poffo suffered a lump on the back of his head — he turned his face just before the ball hit him. He continued to play, but only after attempting to charge the mound. Plate umpire Parker Lerew restrained him until manager Russ Nixon and trainer Jack Muenchen got Poffo quieted down. The benches emptied, and it seemed for a few minutes there would be real trouble."

Incredibly, West Palm Beach manager Gordon MacKenzie went on the record to say that he didn't think the throw at Poffo was intentional — even though he was still in the batter's box.

"He was looking right at me!" Poffo told reporters, after staying in the game and going 2-3.

Either way, there are two things we know for sure.

One, Randy got beaned with a baseball and two, there was some sort of altercation. Regardless of the excitement from either scenario, or which one is true, the Tarpons still cut him.

"I had a pretty good year at Tampa, but the shoulder still wasn't very good," Randy said. "Then I signed with the White Sox as a left-handed first baseman."

The White Sox signing was a surprise to nearly everyone, including manager Chuck Tanner and farm director C.V. Davis, who came away so impressed with Randy's switch-hitting skills during a 1975 tryout that they invited him to spring training.

"I have to say we were impressed by his ambition and determination," Davis said of the invite at the time. "We'll take a chance on him in spring training, but didn't guarantee him anything. I understand he is a good hitter."

Randy made the first cut, the second cut, the third and the fourth cut, but not the final cut. He was the last spring training invite to not be offered a spot in Chicago's minor league system.

"When they walked up and took my uniform out of my locker, I couldn't believe it," Randy said. "It got me pretty worked up, and finally, I told 'em if I couldn't play baseball, maybe no one else would either. I told them I just might have to burn down the clubhouse and the grandstands."

What happened next wasn't pretty.

Randy went, well, savage. He threw equipment, smashed bags, and although an actual log of the destruction has been lost to history, teammates watched him nearly decimate the entire locker room. But when the storm of rage had passed and he left the ballpark, one fact still remained: he was cut from the team. It rocked him.

Despite learning to throw hard and accurately with his left hand, and despite proving everyone wrong who said, "There's no way in hell you can teach yourself to throw lefty," he'd won the battle but lost the war. After four seasons, three teams and two crushing injuries, Randy Poffo's baseball dreams had come to an end.

For a kid who spent nearly every day of his twenty-four years on earth trying to be the next Johnny Bench, experiencing the inevitable end of his baseball career was like watching a slow-moving tidal wave climb over him while he could do nothing but tread water. It felt like he was about to drown.

"It was probably the most emotional thing that ever happened to me," Randy said.

In a sober final assessment of his former player's career, Tarpons GM Moore stated:

"Honestly, he didn't have the talent to go any further."

Ooooof.

Lost, listless and unsure of what to do after wrecking the locker room, Randy drove aimlessly around St. Petersburg and, looking for the comfort of a familiar face, pulled into the driveway of his old pal Tom Bruno, who was playing in the minors in Sarasota. It was a bang on the door Bruno will never forget.

"He just knocked on my door and said he didn't know where else to go," Bruno said. "He said he'd just got cut. He was kind of lost."

Bruno, who was no stranger to the cruelty of the here-today-cut-tomorrow nature of the minors, invited his buddy in and they talked.

"That time of year it's common," Bruno said. "You're lockering next to someone and then they're gone. You're talking to them and next thing you know they get called into the office and come back and start packing their shit. They're done. It's the nature of the beast."

The two friends talked late into the night and Randy slept on the couch, contemplating the rest of his life. When he woke up, he grabbed his duffel bag and his bat bags, hopped into his beat-up Volkswagen and drove the twelve hundred miles back to Downers Grove.

It was the opposite of how he'd hoped to return.

There were no interviews in the paper. No ticket requests for the hometown kid playing his first game at Wrigley Field. There was nothing. He was just a young guy who got fired from his dream job and needed to figure out what his next move was.

"He was heartbroken," John Guarnaccia said. "He drove up from Florida right to his parents' house. Then he got his bat bag out of the car and walked right up to the big oak tree in front of their house. One by one, he took each of his bats and shattered them. He broke them all. He said, 'My dream as a baseball player is shattered.'"

It was like a scene out of a movie.

We can almost hear the John Williams soundtrack rising as the young man, with tears in his eyes, takes the bats he once loved and slams them into the tree under the moonlight, with his home batting cage lit up in the background.

His mother and father watch helplessly from the window, letting their son vent his frustration and anger and pain. When it's done, the young man stands exhausted. Sweating. Panting.

The bats he once coveted lie splintered and strewn about the yard at his feet.

It's a moving, powerful moment.

It's also the beginning of the rest of his life.

"After that, he said, 'They're finished with me, so I'm finished with them,'" Judy said. "His dad got him started with wrestling right away."

PART II

Randy Savage

CHAPTER 10

The Metamorphosis

Deep down Randy Poffo always knew there was a Plan B.

It was encoded in his genes. Embedded in the marrow of his bones. There was no thought of, "Well, baseball is done, maybe I'll become an accountant."

The Poffos weren't desk jockeys. They were men of action — and entertainment.

"It was always in the back of my mind," Savage said. "I guess it was in my blood."

But now Randy had a new problem.

He had spent years crafting his physique into the ideal baseball player's body. He was lean. Sinewy. He had powerful forearms and a ripped core and legs built for running the basepaths. Randy looked great on a baseball card but he'd get mauled in a wrestling ring.

"He used to do, like, 1,500 sit-ups every morning," Jethro Mills, a pitcher on his team, said.

Jerry Brisco, the WWF's head promoter in Florida in the 1980s, recalled when he first laid eyes on Randy Poffo.

"It was around 1974 in the old Fort Myers armory," Brisco said. "He had good arms, but was small. Because of baseball, he had to keep his weight around 175 pounds and that's pretty little for the ring. But it didn't stop him. The main thing I remember is that he had a cocky attitude once he crawled through the ropes."

Randy knew that his 6'1", 175-pound frame wasn't going to cut it in the squared circle. The best wrestlers in the mid-'70s were thick, beefy men. Jerry Lawler was only six feet tall but weighed 243 pounds. Chief Jay Strongbow was 6'0", 250 pounds. Even Randy's own brother, Lanny, who had already followed his dad into the business, stood 6'2" and weighed 240 pounds. A wrestler giving up seventy-five pounds in the ring would be crushed, like playing chicken with an M1 Abrams tank while riding a ten-speed.

"Randy was a muscle man in baseball, but considered very skinny as a wrestler," Lanny said.

To enter the family business Randy needed to bulk up. Fast. Luckily, the Poffos' weight room lineage ran as deep as their wrestling roots. Their bodies were seemingly built for two things: packing on size and powering through suplexes. Just as Angelo had done at the Navy's gym thirty years earlier, Randy got to work.

"I went home and did weightlifting with a religious fervor," Randy said of the days after his baseball career ended. "It was a compulsion. I wanted to be the best in the world."

With the same commitment and maniacal devotion he displayed throwing fifty thousand baseballs per month against a shopping center wall with his left arm, Randy hit the gym. Body part after body part, day after day, he pushed his muscles to the limit, breaking down the individual fibers so that they'd fuse and grow, willing his frame to expand.

For nearly a year it was all he did: lift, wrestle, eat, repeat.

"I pumped the weights and force-fed myself a high-protein diet," he said.

He hit 180 quickly. Then 190. Within six months he passed 200 pounds and there was no going back.

"Charles Atlas was on the cover of every magazine in our house," Lanny remembered. "My dad bought the Charles Atlas book and that's what started him out. The book was *Charles Atlas: Power Isotonics* and my dad taught us Charles's theory of dynamic tension."

For much of their youth, Angelo insisted on the boys using lightweight dumbbells and he taught them mostly bodyweight routines to hone their muscle. He thought heavy lifting would lead to injuries. After baseball, Randy wasn't interested in honing anything. He wanted to become a hoss — and knee bends and push-ups weren't gonna cut it.

"My brother got into powerlifting and my dad discouraged it," Lanny said. "He used to joke, 'You're not an ant that can lift a hundred times his body weight.' Then when he'd see Randy trying to squat five hundred pounds my dad would call him 'shit for brains.'"

Lanny said that in a rush to get huge, Randy tried different steroids, but it was temporary.

"He took deca durabolin, an injectable, and it worked," Lanny said. "But he stopped when it became illegal. After that it was all exercise until he got much older."

Steaks. Shakes. Chicken. Eggs. He devoured all the staples the 1970s bodybuilding diet had to offer. Those were the days of Arnold Schwarzenegger and Lou Ferrigno. Of Frank Zane and Sergio Oliva. Of consuming hundreds of grams of beef protein daily.

Randy handled the delayed onset muscle soreness, the stomach discomfort of calorie loading and the tendon aches that go along with packing on size fast. The pain never bothered him. He knew his family had endured worse.

His grandfather, who he idolized, often showed up at his childhood home with his eyebrows burned, his skin red or his hair singed.

"He was an immigrant from Italy and fought his way through life like an SOB," Savage said. "He worked in front of the blast furnaces when no one else wanted the jobs. I can remember him coming home with his face all burnt. He made it when others crumbled."

Compared to that, getting jacked was nothing. And like his grandfather, he wasn't going to crumble. He'd forge on — but as he went about building his new body, he needed a body of work to climb the ranks in a sport that was unforgiving to newbies.

It would be cleaner, storywise, if Randy's baseball career ended and *then* his wrestling career began. However, life doesn't often fit into neat chapters — and what very few people know is that Randy actually began wrestling *while* he was still playing ball.

"When Randy signed his baseball contract in 1971, it said specifically that he was not allowed to participate in any other sports like football or wrestling or anything," Lanny said. "But Randy put a mask on and wrestled in Tampa under the name The Spider."

He also took a few spot shows for Gunkel Promotions in Georgia wearing a mask and occasionally performing as The Executioner.

In fact, it was during his stints as The Spider that WWE and WCW Hall of Famer Dusty Rhodes first spotted Randy in the ring at the historic Fort Homer W. Hesterly Armory near MacDill Air Force Base in south Tampa.

"The Armory," as it was known, was built in the 1930s by President Franklin Roosevelt and was the ultimate mixed-use facility. Everyone from the National Guard to the Army Reserves to entertainers and musicians and the University of South Florida's basketball team used the venue. Elvis Presley even performed there in 1955.

Eddie Graham, who ran the Championship Wrestling from Florida brand, used the armory to host a majority of his matches starting in the early 1960s. Randy knew Eddie through his dad and near the tail end of his baseball career, he reached out to get some time in the ring.

"The first time I noticed him was in Tampa," Rhodes said. "It was during Tuesday night wrestling at the Armory. Championship Wrestling from Florida. The only thing on TV was us. There was no Bucs [the NFL team]. There was no football. Wrestling was the only thing in town. I looked down one time and I saw four guys in Cincinnati Reds uniforms about nine or ten rows back."

Those Reds players didn't just happen to be in the crowd. They'd raced down after a Tarpons game to support their teammate, Randy Poffo, aka The Spider.

"They'd drive down as fast as they could to catch wrestling," Rhodes said.

Much later in his career, when Savage was asked about pulling double duty as a wrestler/ballplayer, he played coy.

"That may or may not have happened," Randy said. "I cannot confirm or deny it."

While this isn't a court of law, dozens of eyewitnesses and hundreds of fans saw The Spider perform with their own eyes and, if that's not enough, a picture exists of the character in the ring, which is clearly Randy under the mask.

Fifty years later, we can close this cold case.

Conclusion: he violated his minor league contract.

No matter. With baseball done, Randy was all-in on his wrestling future anyway.

"I love baseball, but I kept hearing about my brother and dad doing so great. I just wanted to get into it," Randy told the *Tampa Tribune* back in 1975. "You never get as much satisfaction out of baseball as you do wrestling. You take all your frustrations out in wrestling. In baseball, some skinny guy on the mound may get you out, or maybe you hit a couple line drives that are caught, and you go home 0-for-4. In wrestling you've got to be mentally prepared every day. People don't like to come see a loser. If you're a loser, you're gone. In baseball you're back the next day. The competition is tougher here. My goal is to hit these weights and get as big and strong as I can."

While the wrestling matches themselves may have been more appealing than baseball games to Randy, in a lot of ways the practice and preparation needed to excel on the diamond were the same as on the mat.

For one, just like he needed reps in the batting cage, he needed reps in the ring. That's why one of his first calls after closing the door on baseball was to Francis Flessner, a wrestling promoter in Detroit who agreed to give Randy a brief shot. Although he won his first match against journeyman wrestler Joe Banic, there were plenty of questions that needed to be answered:

Would guys like working with him?

How would his body hold up wrestling night after night?

And most importantly, would the audiences respond?

"I did real good and they were shocked," Randy said of his time in Detroit. "But I wasn't. I have wrestled all my life because of my dad. My brother and I grew up wrestling. That's all we ever did. It was in the family. But it's hard for a young man to break into wrestling."

Even a young man with connections. That's why Angelo encouraged both of his boys to meet and study under as many veterans in the business as they could.

"My father trained us both," Lanny said. "But he told us not to just learn from him, but to learn from everybody."

For Randy, that meant hooking up with the seven-time NWA World Champion and eventual WWE and WCW Hall of Famer, Harley Race.

Race was a thick-haired, heavy-sideburned, 6'1", 253-pound moose of a man with legendary brute force.

Among his confirmed feats:

He once broke a man's hand just by shaking it.

He shattered a giant block of ice with one punch.

He was the first person to lift Andre the Giant off the mat, hoisting him over his head and giving him a vertical suplex almost ten years before Hulk Hogan did it at WrestleMania for the "first" time.

This was the guy who showed Randy the ropes in a physical and educational sense. "Handsome" Harley Race had been wrestling since he got kicked out of high school for fighting in 1959. He could grapple, grunt and grind with the best of them.

"I knew Randy right from day one when he started wrestling," Race said.

Throughout early 1975 Randy crisscrossed the Midwest, devouring protein, lifting weights, learning from Harley and picking up matches with anyone who would book him.

"Although his dad was a very respected wrestler, Randy went out on his own," Jerry Brisco, the former WWF promoter, said. "He wrestled the little outlaw circuit, the farm and coal mining towns, where nobody was in the audience. He worked his way up until he's become one of our most skilled, polished wrestlers."

In March, Randy headed to Toledo, Ohio, where Angelo and Lanny had been working for the original Sheik.

The Sheik, aka Eddie Farhat, was born in 1926, the youngest of ten children of Lebanese immigrants. After serving in the U.S. Army,

Farhat began wrestling in Chicago for the NWA, honing his gimmick as a raving, rich lunatic from Syria who bloodied himself and opponents with a hidden pencil, threw fire and sputtered pseudo-Arabic nonsense in interviews.

Fans hated everything about him, from his keffiyeh to his painfully slow prayers to Allah before each match to his famous Camel Clutch hold. He even treated his manager/wife poorly to draw heat from the audience — a move Randy would famously steal later in his career. .

In short, the 5'11", 250-pounder was *the perfect heel.*

He was also the promoter of Big Time Wrestling and in the early spring of 1975 he was booking matches with Lanny and Angelo throughout the Buckeye State, along with a bevy of new draws from other promotions. This crew included "Big Money" Hank James, aging former NWA champion Lou Thesz and the young Wild Samoan brothers Sika and Afa Aona'i (now billed as The Islanders).

Another prospect that Sheik was bringing along was the youngest son of his older brother, Lewie Farhat. Lewie had just finished a tour in Vietnam and wrestled under the name Mike Thomas.

"During his time on the Big Time circuit, The Sheik paired up his nephew in the ring with another green newcomer destined to one day become just as big a star as Sheik himself, if not more so: Randy Poffo," wrote Brian R. Solomon in *Blood and Fire*, his excellent biography of The Sheik. "He joined Lanny and their father, Angelo, who had known and worked with The Sheik since the '50s. Randy spent the first fifteen months of his full-time wrestling career working for The Sheik and would feel forever indebted to him for the break."

Lanny remembered the time fondly, and told Solomon, "The Sheik loved my dad, and my dad loved The Sheik. My dad went to The Sheik and told him Randy got released from baseball and wants to become a wrestler. Sheik would always say the same thing: I'll take care of him. That was his code word. Randy owed it all to The Sheik. He thought The Sheik was amazing. He would study him."

With Lanny, Angelo and Randy living in Toledo and performing four, five and even six times a week, the Poffos' new life as a traveling wrestling family began to unfold. Night after night they'd be in a new city in front of new crowds and staying in a new motel. Or they'd drive long hours back to their place near the western edge of Lake Erie, arriving at ungodly hours and exhausted, but ready to do it again the next day.

It was during this time that Randy learned the business from the bottom up. Ring setup. Professionalism. Promotion. Playing to the crowds. Getting paid. All of it. And his quest to pack on size continued at a fevered pace.

"Randy came in as the good guy," Lanny said. "He instantly got over big, even though he was still skinny."

That skinniness bugged the hell out of Randy. He'd look at all these guys over 230 or even 250 and he knew he had to get close to the same muscle mass or he'd always look out of proportion in the ring. A 6'1", 200-pound guy looks like he's half the size of a guy who's a legit 6'2", 250 pounds with their shirt off.

"We tried to work out every day," Lanny said. "I would do push-ups and squats in the locker room before the match. You got idle time in there so you can do something. But I also belonged to gyms all over. If I had time I'd get there early and lift. Nothing heavy. My brother rebelled against that. He thought he needed to get big quick."

If Lanny and Angelo's lifting motto was "nothing heavy," then Randy's motto was "the heavier the better."

Whenever he entered a gym he went straight for the classic Olympic lifts. He'd discovered Mike Mentzer's *Heavy Duty* program, which involved taking muscles to complete failure with heavy weights, perfect form and high intensity. Mentzer eventually won the 1979 Mr. Universe with a perfect score and the 1979 IFBB Mr. Olympia heavyweight division.

Mentzer's routine spoke to Randy. Go heavy. Go hard. Go big. It worked well. After hovering around 200 pounds for a while he finally broke through and began inching to 205 and above on a diet of milk, eggs, meat and carbs.

He also began putting up powerlifter-type numbers on several lifts.

"His biggest accomplishment was that he bench-pressed 435 pounds for 5 reps," Lanny said. "Randy swallowed everything Joe Weider's *Muscle Builder* magazine ever wrote."

As Randy's size slowly grew, so did his reputation. Within months it was apparent to anyone who followed wrestling that the kid had talent.

"The first time I wrestled with him it was different. You could just tell," Lanny said. "I can't explain it. He was so athletic and coordinated. He learned quicker than everyone."

His unique background helped too. As early as May, newspapermen and promoters were using Poffo's baseball career to drum up interest for the shows.

A headline in the *Cincinnati Post* on May 10, 1975, read "Ex-Ballplayer on Mat Show." "Randy Poffo, former minor league baseball player with the Cardinals, Reds and Chicago White Sox, makes his local wrestling debut against Ox Baker," boasted the piece.

Town after town, Randy made his local "debut" at small venues, parks, amphitheaters and auditoriums, places that housed local pick-up hoops games and town council meetings. Or even school plays. In June, Randy and Mike Thomas faced the Islanders in a tag team match at Central Catholic High School in Canton, Ohio, performing where the school held pep rallies.

The Sheik gave the Poffos as much work as they could handle, jam-packing events throughout the Ohio-Michigan wrestling nexus. Akron. Dover. Massillon. Dayton. Ludington. Arcanum. Hamilton. Cincinnati. St. Joseph. Escanaba. Xenia. Greenville. Coshocton. Mansfield.

Angelo and Lanny wrestled together as the "International Tag Team Champions" while Randy pulled tag team duty with The Sheik's nephew or picked up one-on-one matches.

In July, Randy shared a billing for the first time with fellow future WWE icon Andre the Giant.

"Fire throwing Sheik is the return bout with 7 ft. 472 lb. Andre the Giant. The Sheik, a dynamo of excitement, is noted for his gimmickry. This battle sets the tone for the supporting card," a local promotional write-up touted. Randy was on the supporting card, wrestling Kurt Von Brauner in a singles match.

The event was a full twelve years before Randy (wrestling Ricky "The Dragon" Steamboat) would share top billing with Andre (wrestling

Hulk Hogan) in one of the most famous events in wrestling history, WrestleMania III.

In many ways, this random summer Sunday on July 10, 1975, is the perfect inflection point to measure how both Randy and the sport of wrestling entertainment as a whole would rise in the ensuing decade.

The contrast between where Randy started in '75 and where he'd end up in the late '80s and beyond is striking.

Instead of performing at a major arena in a big city (Detroit) for WrestleMania, back in '75 Randy and Andre showcased their talents at the Stark County Fairgrounds twenty miles south of Akron. Instead of wrestling under the giant enclosure at the Pontiac Silverdome, they performed under a grandstand roof. And instead of a live audience of 93,173 and millions more watching on television at home, the fairgrounds venue held a few thousand people with a couple hundred more milling about outside eating corn dogs and funnel cake.

Standing in the fairgrounds ring, covered in sweat on that seventy-seven-degree night after defeating Von Brauner, Randy had no idea what lay ahead. WrestleMania didn't even exist yet. Neither did the Macho Man. Or Randy Savage, for that matter. He was still just Randy Poffo, Angelo's kid, trying to make it in the family business.

After a series of fairgrounds and fairs, the Poffos traveled to Canada for a string of matches around Ontario before heading back to their home territory in Ohio and Michigan for the end-of-summer outdoor season.

On August 28, 1975, he headlined a Labor Day Festival in New London, Connecticut, as part of a tag team match. He partnered up with Lou Klein to take on Kurt Von Brauner and Dr. X. Their wrestling card was just one small-town attraction that night, right alongside a motocross race, horse show, antique car show, demolition derby and tractor pull.

In the fall the crew did a Texas swing, performing in dozens of mid-sized towns throughout the Lone Star State. El Paso. Abilene. Odessa. San Angelo. Each town presented a new opportunity for Randy.

Would the crowd react if I did this?

What if I tried this move?

What if I said this?

When the Poffos returned for several winter shows in Ohio and Michigan, Randy was no longer billed as an ex-baseball player, and by October, he had established himself as the fastest-rising young star in Big Time Wrestling, often being referred to as the "top rookie" in the business. A promotional piece in the *Ludington Daily News* stated that Poffo "has won more matches than any other rookie in recent wrestling memory."

"I'd watch his matches and I could see it," Lanny said of his brother's charisma. "He was a young, good-looking guy. I knew he was going to be a fantastic star."

By the time Randy made a triumphant return as a professional to the Armory in Tampa, it had been roughly ten months since his baseball career had officially ended. Jim Selman, the assistant sports editor for the *Tampa Tribune*, touted Randy's arrival to Tampa as a wrestler, not a ballplayer.

The piece, playing off his ambidexterity, was titled: "Poffo Foes Beware! Either Arm Lethal." In it, Selman took stock of how far the former catcher had come. He hadn't quite fully morphed into the eventual Macho Man look, but he was on his way:

"Poffo is bigger than Tampa baseball fans remember him. He's up from 190 to 208, which still isn't big enough for the massive brethren whom he'll be trying to pin. And, he doesn't look the same. He's more muscular. His hair is longer and dyed blond. With the Tampa Tarpons, he adhered to the Reds' code of short haircuts."

Nearly a year out of baseball and that code was out the window. Forget short haircuts. Forget haircuts at all. In fact, Randy tossed out shaving razors as well and began to grow his signature beard. While we're at it, we can throw out sleeves, button-down shirts, suits, ties, khakis, polos and essentially any article of clothing a boring, regular guy would wear.

Randy was done with all of that.

He was officially on his own path and crafting his own look.

"I helped him put together that image of the Macho Man," Harley Race said. "He had a way about him. He grabbed your attention through his voice. That allowed him to present himself as a type of character. He and Angelo were both great, but his dad couldn't talk like him. That got Randy over with people."

Ahhhh right. We've now come to the two signature pieces of Macho Man lore: the voice and the name.

They're paramount in the legend, interchangeable in terms of importance, and one doesn't exist without the other.

If your name is the "Macho Man" Randy Savage, you can't sound like Mickey Mouse. And if your voice is deep and guttural and grinds like a cement mixer, you can't perform as Randy Sweetheart.

No.

The name and the voice are one.

CHAPTER 11

Goodbye, Randy Poffo

"**I** am fed up to here!" the wrestler with wild hair and a wild beard shouts, staring into the camera.

His interviewer, a much smaller man in a suit and tie, holds a microphone, trying to carry on a discussion. But the wrestler has a prop. It's a steel bar. He's banging it against the ground loudly.

"Do you know what this is?"

"It's a steel bar," the interviewer says.

"It's an inch thick. And over three-quarters of an inch wide," the wild man says.

He holds up the four-foot-long bar to reveal that his opponent's name, Raschke, has been written on one side.

"Do you see that!" he shouts.

"I see that," the man says.

Then, as the camera zooms in, the wild man's eyes get wider and his voice drops a level and he begins to bellow from what seems to be the bottom of his belly.

"I will prove! In front of all my wrestling fans! The power of my teeth and jawwww!! And the strength of my arms!!! And my mind will only concentrate on one name, Von Raschke."

The wild man takes a piece of paper and says he's going to use that on the bar to protect his teeth. The journalist asks, "You're going to bend that with your teeth?"

The wild man yells, "Oooaahhh yeeahhh!"

He then bends the steel bar against his teeth as his eyes pop and muscles strain. When he turns the once straight bar into a U-turn symbol, he lets go and screams into the microphone:

"Oooooooaaaahhhhh yeaaaaahhh!"

The wild man is not Randy Savage.

The wild man is Pampero Firpo.

Longtime die-hard wrestling fans know the 5'8", 230-pound Pampero as the Wild Bull of the Pampas or the Great Pampero. For a short time, he also wrestled as the Missing Link because, well, he kinda looked like the missing link. If you've ever seen an artist's rendering of a caveman then you have a good idea of what Firpo looked like in his prime: untamed bushy hair, a heavy, out-of-control beard and a thick rug of hair covering his chest, shoulders and back.

Born Juan Kachmanian in Buenos Aires, Argentina, he began his wrestling career in 1953 as Ivan the Terrible, before former heavyweight boxing champion Jack Dempsey suggested he try the name Firpo after one of his boxing opponents, Argentinian Luis Angel Firpo, known in the sweet science as the Wild Bull of the Pampas. The gimmick was that the wrestling version of Firpo (Kachmanian) claimed to be the boxing version's son.

Kachmanian liked that story and name much better than Ivan the Terrible, so he ran with it, embarking on a successful and memorable career that included titles from practically every territory that existed in the 1950s, '60s and '70s, most notably NWA wrestling, where he was a three-time champion, Pacific Northwest Wrestling, Mid-Pacific Promotions and as a foe to The Sheik in Big Time Wrestling.

Randy and Lanny watched him together as kids on Sunday mornings in Downers Grove and during their time in Hawaii, when Firpo worked for Pacific Northwest Wrestling.

While Randy followed a similar path as Firpo (decades later) and wrestled for a variety of territories, he had yet to go all-in on a gimmick after his first year in the business. Even as late as the end of 1976, he was still billed under his real name, though he had settled on a "look," which was featured prominently in a giant newspaper spread on the Poffos on December 18 in the *Tampa Tribune*.

Above the headline "Mean, Tough Randy Poffo, A Chip Off The Old Block," a photo showcases Randy and Angelo in the middle of an arm wrestling contest. Randy is on the left side, with the sleeve on his right arm bunched up, showing off his new and growing biceps. He's got a long brown beard and shaggy dyed blond hair. As for accessories, he's wearing brown-shaded sunglasses and a bucket hat.

Angelo, ever shirtless, smiles as he braces his hand against Randy's. In the article, he takes stock of his career and what it's been like transitioning both of his sons into the business full-time after what he estimates to be over 5,400 fights.

"Wrestling pays off well. It's real nice," he said. "I've had my nose broken three times and strained ligaments, but I have no gripes, except that I have been stabbed seven times by fans. I guess that's my gripe."

Translation: Yeah, no big deal — I worked the crowd into such a frenzy as a heel that more than a half-dozen people stabbed me.

Angelo goes on to explain that one of the hardest parts of breaking into the business is that you've got to learn to cultivate anger and hatred from the fans while at the same time ignoring their reactions as nothing personal — even though they're often screaming and shouting obscenities directly at you.

"You can't hit anybody," Randy said. "You'll get sued."

Randy then admits that he's let the crowd get the better of him.

"I'll go into a crowd," he said. "I've done it twice and lost both towns."

Of course he lost both towns.

Imagine you live in a village in the Midwest, maybe it's Loveland or Sugarcreek or Granville, and you show up to a wrestling event at your high school or arts center. Some tanned, jacked guy with crazy hair is taunting you and your town and beating up your favorite "good guy" wrestler.

You boo him and scream at him and tell him you hate him and that he sucks and then . . . *he leaps out of the ring and comes after you in your seat!*

This isn't the decision of a well-adjusted individual, even one who chose pro wrestling as a career. It's the move of a hothead, a wild man ... a savage.

And thus we get to Phase 1 in our Macho Man evolution: dropping the last name Poffo.

Randy had been thinking about it for a while. He loved his dad and brother and was proud of their name and reputation in the business, but something deep down was telling him that he needed his own identity in the ring.

When wrestling fans showed up and saw the name Poffo on the billing, they were expecting a Poffo. Randy wanted to give them something they weren't expecting. He wanted to shock them. He wanted to blaze his own trail independent of the Poffo name while also becoming a star in the business with Lanny.

Hell, once he thought of all the new angles they could explore if fans didn't even know he and Lanny were brothers, the whole family got excited.

Take this write-up in the *Pensacola Journal* that describes the boys: "The Poffo Brothers may be the stars of the future. Blond Randy is talkative and muscular. Brunette Lanny is silent and even more muscular. And there is Angelo Poffo, their macho muscular father ... Randy proudly states that he is the first pro baseball player to turn pro wrestler ... Under the watchful eye of their father, the Poffo Brothers are shooting for the big time."

First, this is one of the few times Lanny, the loquacious, verbally gifted future Genius of the WWE, was ever described as silent. Second, constantly being billed together limited their ability to branch out and forge their own followings and identities, independent of each other and their father's reputation.

With all of this in mind, as Randy went in search of a new ring name through 1976 and early 1977, Ole Anderson, the Georgia Championship Wrestling promoter, happened to describe Randy's wrestling style as fierce, violent, uncontrolled and ... savage-like.

And that was it.

"Poffo sounded a little soft," legendary wrestling broadcaster "Mean" Gene Okerlund remembered. "But he thought Randy fought like a savage."

The name Randy Poffo still appeared on most promotional posters and newspaper billings in early 1977, and the Poffos were mentioned together in a piece in the *Greenville News* on February 13: "In a preliminary match, Lanny and Randy Poffo wrestle Ron Starr and Bill Dromo."

But once Randy heard himself described as savage, he was all-in.

"The 'Savage' part. I gave that name to myself," Randy said. "Because I didn't want to make it on my dad's reputation. I wanted to make it on my own."

And so he did. Two weeks later, on February 27, in tiny print at the bottom of page thirty-three in the *Columbus Ledger* we see this:

> **Wrestling:** The main pro wrestling event Wednesday night at Municipal Auditorium will be a four-man tag team match with Ole Anderson and Abdullah the Butcher taking on Mr. Wrestling No. 1 and Mr. Wrestling No. 2. In other matches, the French Angel will face the Black Atlas, Jack Evans will meet Don Kernodle, Randy Savage will go against Mike Stallings . . .

Is this the first time the name Randy Savage appeared in print?

It might be. It's the earliest reference that turns up across multiple mediums and searches, but with the sheer number of shows the Poffos performed in across so many regions, it's possible that the name popped up in a newspaper somewhere prior to this date. However, it was certainly in the spring of '77 that Randy began to lean into the Savage moniker and use the name publicly and consistently.

A few days later, on March 3, the name Randy Savage shows up for the first time in an ad for a show. Billed as a "Fred Ward, NWA Promotion" at the Macon Coliseum, the Tuesday Night Event (with ringside seats available for $3 and children under 12 admitted for $1) featured a tag team main event (for a $2,000 prize) of Ole Anderson and James J. Dillon vs. Mr. Wrestling Number 1 & 2. Lower on the card we see that Randy Savage will face Bob Backlund.

For the rest of the spring of '77 and the remainder of his life, Randy Poffo would be known as Randy Savage. By the end of 1977 and into

1978, the name grew on Randy until you couldn't imagine him with any other moniker.

"He wrestled like a savage and he looked like a savage with his hair," Lanny said. "But the missing piece of the puzzle was the interview."

Despite ultimately becoming famous for doing the best promos in the business, when Savage first started doing interviews he was a dud. Flat. Off-kilter. Uncomfortable. Not boring, but not memorable.

Lanny, on the other hand, had been born with the gift of gab. He was clever, could think on his feet, had a great delivery and presented like there was no place more relaxing to be than live on camera.

Randy asked him for help.

"It was simple," Lanny said. "I told him, if you wrestle like a savage and you're going to use the name Savage, what wrestler gives the greatest savage interview you've ever seen?"

The moment Lanny asked the question, one man popped into Randy's mind: the Wild Bull of the Pampas, Pampero Firpo.

"Pampero used to do this promo that we listened to when we lived in Honolulu," Lanny explained, dropping into an excellent imitation of the voice. "'You are watching the number one station in Hawaii, ooooaahhhhh yeahhhh!' Then I told Randy to try it."

Randy cleared this throat, clenched his abs, strained his vocal cords and said in a pushed, raspy voice, doing a full impression of Firpo, rolling his eyes and looking crazy, "You are watching the number one station in Hawaii, ooooohhhh yeahhh!"

Lanny stepped back. Paused. Smiled.

"You got it," he said.

This isn't to say that in that moment, Savage instantly nailed one of the most famous voices in 20th-century wrestling.

"He spent the next three months in the bathroom, looking at the mirror, practicing his interviews," Lanny said. "He went from worst to first."

Over time he dialed in the pitch, cadence, tone and timbre to create one of the most unique, imitated talking styles in modern history.

CHAPTER 12

"Ooohhhh Yeahhhh!"

The wholesome, family-friendly version of where Randy Savage's Macho Man nickname came from goes like this: One day in the late 1970s, Judy Poffo was relaxing on her couch, sipping on a smoothie after a swim (she did daily one-mile swims into her eighties) and reading one of her favorite magazines, *Reader's Digest*.

There was a feature in the magazine about the Village People and their hit new song, "Macho Man." The gist of the piece was that the song's title would become extremely popular and cross over into the public lexicon. The magazine predicted it would be the next hot catchphrase to sweep America.

After reading this, and knowing Randy was trying to hone his new "savage" image, she called Randy and suggested that he add it to his wrestling name. He loved the idea and ran with it immediately.

The end.

Sweet, right?

It's maybe, kinda sorta, mostly true. We think.

This is the heartwarming version of the story that was shared in her obituary in the *Tampa Tribune* and it's the story that Randy often repeated later in life. As late as 2004, in an interview with IGN about the video game *Showdown: Legends of Wrestling*, Randy was asked about the origins of the Macho Man nickname:

"The truth behind that is my mom was reading *Reader's Digest* one day, long before the Macho Man song came out, and they said in this article that Macho Man was going to be the next hot term."

Case closed — but not really.

Because in yet another version of "Mom suggested the Macho Man title," Judy said that she came up with the term before the song as well, which negates the reason for the *Reader's Digest* piece referencing the song.

If you're curious about the timeline, the song itself entered the Billboard Hot 100 on June 24, 1978, so it's *possible* that Judy read the article before the song broke through. But suffice to say that at some point in the late 1970s, Judy read the phrase Macho Man and suggested that her son Randy use it in some way.

That settles it, right?

No. Not even close.

Because this narrative isn't the most prominent version of the story or even the one Randy told the most during his career when asked about the nickname.

For that, we have to go all the way back to his days with the Tampa Tarpons and the baseball brawl he caused after getting hit in the face with a fastball in the on-deck circle by Joe Keener.

Yeah, that far back, to 1974.

In this version, after Randy got hit, he bolted for the mound.

"I just ran out there by instinct and attacked him," he said. "I worked him over real good. Next day in the paper, some writer gets on me, says I was acting like some Macho Man. I liked that, and it became part of my name. Some fans put a banner up in the outfield that said, 'Hit it here, Macho Man.' I kind of dug that. It was perfect for me."

Perfect for the Macho Man Randy Savage, yes . . .

Perfect for Randy Poffo, the kid who was trying to make the big leagues and hadn't started a wrestling career yet? Not so much.

Randy repeats a version of this story often, including in several TV interviews throughout his career.

In an article written for the *Cincinnati Enquirer* by Martin Hogan Jr. on August 24, 1986, Randy said, "The pitcher thought I was trying to upset him so he uncorked a throw at me in the on-deck circle. The ball hit my batting helmet, so I went out to the mound after him. I had been in a couple of other fights during the season so the newspaper started calling me Macho Man."

For those keeping score at home, the Macho Man nickname either came from an article Judy Poffo was reading in *Reader's Digest* about the Village People, an article Judy Poffo was reading in *Reader's Digest* that had nothing to do with the Village People, a sign that said "Macho Man hit it here" made by fans at a minor league ballpark or it was given to Randy by a newspaper.

Take your pick.

It's plausible of course that the baseball nickname version happened and *then* Judy made her suggestion years later as well (although we have no record of the phrase "Macho Man Randy Poffo" ever being used).

But if that's true, why did Randy sit on the awesome Macho Man nickname for so long, and only adopt it after he went to Randy Savage and *after* the Village People song became a hit?

No matter the road we took to get here, Randy Poffo wrestled as Randy Savage sans Macho Man for only about a year, from early 1977 to early 1978.

Picture you're a wrestling fan living in Nashville, Tennessee, in 1978. You wake up on a crisp March morning in the middle of the week. It's Wednesday. Hump day. Your job is boring, but you're a wrestling fan and you're fired up to hit the Fairgrounds Arena for the match tonight (you've already bought $2.50 tickets for you and your family).

You don't remember who the headliners are, so you head to your driveway to scoop up the local paper, *The Tennessean*. You flip through to the sports section and on page twenty, in a short feature by sportswriter Al Hrabosky, the Mad Hungarian, you read the following:

MANTELL SEEKS SAVAGE'S BELT; WYNN DEBUTS

Dutch Mantell gets his long awaited chance to lift Randy Savage's Mid-America heavyweight belt . . . Mantell and

Savage, "The Macho Man," have faced one another in tag team competition since arriving on the local scene . . .

If this was you, you were one of the first people in the world outside of Randy Savage's family and a few fellow wrestlers to hear of "The Macho Man" Randy Savage (like Facebook, he'd also drop the "the," it's cleaner).

"He was still developing the Macho Man character," said Dutch Mantell, a longtime friend and opponent. "But every time you saw Randy — I don't care if it was 6:00 in the morning — he was Macho Man. You saw him at midnight — he's still Macho Man. He was always in full-blown Macho Man Mode. I think, really, Randy Poffo morphed into Randy Savage, who then morphed into Macho Man, so he had three distinct personas."

With each persona, he went deeper and deeper into character, almost like a method actor. Just as Daniel Day-Lewis famously stayed completely in character as Abraham Lincoln while filming Steven Spielberg's biopic and Jim Carrey transformed into Andy Kaufman for the entirety of shooting *Man on the Moon*, Randy Poffo disappeared into Randy Savage, who disappeared into Macho Man, almost never to be seen again.

In order to *be* the Macho Man, Poffo/Savage had to *become* the Macho Man 24/7. He also had to make sure promoters were using his name prominently and constantly. For much of mid-1978, that meant inserting his new name into every single thing written about him. It took a while for the local journalists around Nashville, who were charged with covering and promoting Mid-America Wrestling, to get it right.

More often than not, in the early days of the new name, rather than being billed as the "Macho Man" Randy Savage, journalists separated the two, like in this description in a match wrap-up in *The Tennessean* in October:

"Randy Savage, who has dubbed himself the Macho Man, lost to Dutch Mantell in a decision reversed by one of the referees."

A few other ways they'd write it were, "Randy Savage, who now goes by Macho Man" or "Randy Savage, the self-styled Macho Man of wrestling" or "Randy Savage, the self-proclaimed Macho Man."

Occasionally, they'd call him "Mr. Macho."

In the beginning, as long as the new name was in print in the paper and on the billing, Randy was content. He knew that eventually the name would only stick if his gimmick, look and promos made for a memorable performance. And of course, the matches had to be great.

For that, he needed a worthy foe. Someone who could equal his charisma, go toe-to-toe in the ring and who knew how to work a crowd and a storyline. Fortunately, that man was in the same city, in the same locker room and on the same billing as Savage: Dutch Mantell.

Dutch Mantell, aka "Dirty" Dutch Mantell, was born Wayne Maurice Keown in 1949 in Walhalla, South Carolina. After attending Clemson for one year, he was drafted into the U.S. Army and served in the Twenty-fifth Infantry Division during the Vietnam War.

Standing 6' and weighing 225 pounds, Dutch returned home from the Pacific and began wrestling under the name Wayne Cowan throughout the south, until promoter Buddy Fuller decided to give him a new ring name.

"Buddy didn't like the name Wayne Keown, and I didn't either," Dutch said. "So he said, 'I tell ya what I'm going to call you, boy. I'll call you Dutch Mantell.' I said, 'OK. I don't care what you call me — just pay me.'"

Turns out that the new Dutch Mantell was being named after a previous Dutch Mantell, who used to wrestle out of Amarillo, Texas. It wasn't until much later that Dutch: Part II added the "Dirty" and the famous beard, mustache, poncho, bullwhip and cowboy hat to go along with the gimmick that he was from Oil Trough, Texas.

But in Nashville in 1978, Dutch wasn't "dirty" just yet. He'd been in Tennessee for a short time and thought it was a dead end for his career. The talent was limited. The crowds were small. The shows were unoriginal. Night after night it was the same dudes doing the same fights, cracking each other with two-by-fours and smacking each other over the heads with chairs.

Mantell considered himself a performer. He wanted to tell a story. He wanted the audience to *feel*. And there was one guy he saw night in and night out who worked with the same mentality. One guy who was becoming must-watch for the fans — and the other wrestlers.

"When Randy went to the ring, I just had to see what this crazy bastard would do," Mantell said. "Randy was unpredictable and it was fun for me to watch him. We sort of became fans of each other's work. As time went on I noticed I wasn't the only one watching Savage's matches. A lot of the other guys would pile out of the dressing room to watch his match too.

"Pretty soon, Macho Man was selling out the curtain. 'Selling out the curtain' is an old wrestling term meaning that all of the other wrestlers would come out of their dressing rooms to watch your match. It was the compliment of compliments in that other talent thought very highly of your work."

Mantell completely *got* the Macho Man character, noting that it was brilliant on multiple levels. First and foremost, it made the audience think: *Is this guy crazy?* Between all the quick neck twitches and sunglasses touches and arm motions that Randy had added to his interviews, the fans had begun to legitimately question whether "Randy Savage" was sane or insane. Was he acting or not?

Right from the start, the character had a way of wormholing into people's minds. *Does he really talk like that? Is something wrong with him? Is he a lunatic?*

Mantell first met Savage when they were working in Georgia a few years earlier, back when Savage was wrestling as Randy Poffo. But in this third evolution from Poffo to Savage to the Macho Man, Mantell saw a kindred spirit — and an opportunity.

"Business was horrible in Nashville . . . and we were both heels," Mantell said. "I remember I looked at Savage in the dressing room one night and said, 'We're wasting our time, buddy. Heck, we ought to be wrestling each other.' They had nobody else, in my mind, who could do anything. There weren't many fans to begin with and those who were there had no emotion. There was nothing to sink your teeth into.

"So Savage and I got into it, and he's got that wild crazy interview, and I'm kinda low-key as a babyface — it worked perfect."

In Dutch, Randy had someone he could really play off of. Someone he could perfect the Macho Man persona with. And more importantly, someone who not only appreciated what he was trying to do, but was willing to help him elevate the character while raising his game along with it.

It was a revelation for both of them.

Within a matter of months they'd taken a territory that was on life support and injected adrenaline straight into its heart. Towns like Chattanooga and Birmingham and Huntsville, which would be lucky to draw a few hundred people for a standard 8 p.m. show, were suddenly drawing ten times that amount.

The Nashville territory went from starting shows in front of ushers and hot dog vendors to crowds waiting outside to get in a half hour before the match. Venues that sold five hundred tickets were now selling two and three thousand. It was a monumental turnaround in a matter of days.

"When Savage and I were embroiled in this feud, it was in the days before music was played during a wrestler's entrance," Mantell said. "All that would announce a wrestler's entrance was the ringing of the bell. The crowd got amped up just hearing the bell and seeing the combatants as they came through."

For most of the wrestlers, the bell signaled battle. For the Savage/Mantell feud, it bordered on bloodlust.

"When we'd go in the ring for our match, you could literally sense the crowd pulse change, and it would hit me like a brick. It's an addictive feeling," he said. "If medical science could market and merchandise that feeling, it would be the best-selling drug of all time."

Once the opponents locked up in the ring, the energy of the wrestlers rippled out into the stands like a shockwave. Mantell versus Savage wasn't a light, choreographed affair. It was an unleashing of violence. Mainly because Macho Man had one gear: hard and fast as hell.

"One thing you had to have when you wrestled Savage was aggression. If you left aggression in the dressing room, Randy would beat the living crap out of you. So I stocked up on aggression when I wrestled him. I've gone forty-five minutes with Savage and forty-five minutes with Ric Flair. Give me Flair . . . At least with Flair, at some point, he would slow down. Savage had no speedometer. He was wide open, all the time."

The Nashville fans ate it up.

As the rivalry gained momentum and the crowds grew, so did Randy's confidence with this new creation. He knew he had *it*. He had the name, voice, style, vibe and even the baseline look. The final piece of the creation was a costume or outfit or *something* that would make him instantly recognizable outside of the ring.

In early promos in '77 and '78, Randy Savage experimented with a variety of looks. Different leather. Different hats. Different sunglasses. Different jackets. Different colors.

One day he'd look like Sylvester Stallone in *Rocky*, clad in a black leather coat, black jeans, black gloves and even the same hat. Another day he'd rock Harley Davidson–level biker gear with a vest and bandana. In interviews, he'd occasionally wear basic tight maroon or navy shirts with a derby hat that any hipster could buy at a 1970s Macy's, making him look like a jacked-up and insane George Carlin.

In one long-shot attempt at a "look," he even tried out a straw cowboy hat a few times (thankfully, this didn't stick). Towards the end of '78, animal print T-shirts and jackets and sleeveless vests with bright neon colors made their way into the rotation.

In the ring, he tried white trunks, dark plain trunks, dark trunks with the male arrow and circle sex symbol over his crotch, then a few other goofy arrow shapes on his groin, until he ultimately settled on a pair of basic trunks (often purple or hot pink) with three stars on them and the word Macho on his butt.

For a while, he wore nothing but skintight T-shirts over those trunks. In the beginning he wore shirts he picked up from businesses or places he'd worked out at over the years. One of his favorites was an all-white shirt that said Loprinzi's Gym in blue letters across the chest (that he allegedly took from Rip Rogers). He'd pair that with a blue bandana over his shaggy blond hair.

Other matches he'd wear random cheap shirts that looked like you'd buy them for $5 at a rest stop on a state turnpike somewhere. He was photographed behind-the-scenes at several matches wearing a white shirt featuring a blown-up postcard of Georgia that simply said "peaches" on it — just about the complete opposite of the style and flair that he'd ultimately be known for.

These garage store T-shirts soon gave way to homemade shirts he'd create at a small T-shirt printing store in a mini-mall. The shirts often featured a combination of these terms:

Macho

Savage

The Best

Macho Man

Randy Savage

Macho Man Randy Savage

Better than the Best

Macho Man Wants You

Close Enough to Perfect

The T-shirt-and-trunks look was a smart way to keep his name out there. He became a walking billboard for himself around town. If you saw him in the gym, he had a Macho Man shirt on. If you saw him grabbing pizza, he might be wearing a Randy Savage shirt eating a slice. Wherever he went, he stayed in character and, as influencers would say now, on brand.

Occasionally, this "always on 10," "always the Macho Man," "always savage" lifestyle backfired — like the time he fought three policemen and a K9 unit . . . at a Waffle House.

CHAPTER 13

"We Stood in a Mexican Standoff"

A man sits at a booth in his hometown Waffle House on Harding Place in Nashville. He'd worked the late shift and was hungry. On his drive home after midnight he'd pulled off Interstate 24, about nine miles southwest of music row, for an All-Star Special breakfast with a plate of his favorite hash browns smothered, covered and chunked.

The bright fluorescent light from the signature yellow Waffle House wraparound awning reflects through his booth window onto his food. He slides his eggs into some of the maple syrup on his plate and sips his coffee, enjoying a late, quiet dinner as the sounds of cars on the highway rumble in the distance. The headlights rolling by are hypnotizing and he zones out, letting the day wash away. He absentmindedly nods to the waitress who smiles as she fills his cup.

Thwoosh.

The front door swings open, hard and fast, and two thick-shouldered, rough-looking barbarians roll in.

The whole restaurant turns. The entire vibe shifts. The two men take seats at a far counter and the man cocks his head a bit, trying to place one of the guys. He looks familiar. He's seen him before.

Who is he?

The bigger man at the counter turns. He's wearing sunglasses and a bandana, and his bicep muscles ripple through his tight shirt that says "Macho."

That's who he is! the guy thinks.

He's the wrestler who's been all over the paper and posters and local TV. He's the Macho Guy or Mr. Macho or Savage something. The guy looks nuts.

The man watches as the waitress comes over and starts to take the wrestler's order. He hears him say he's starving and then . . .

Thwoosh!

The door bursts open again.

This time, a skinny guy in a cowboy hat walks in. He's got a massive smile on his face. He waves to the staff and they wave back. They clearly know each other.

"Guess what?!" he shouts gleefully. "I just got married!!"

"Awwww!!!" the staff says in unison.

The waitress quickly abandons the two wrestlers to high-five the man in the cowboy hat. Hugs are given. Kisses on the cheek are doled out. It's a nice moment for everyone. Everyone, that is, except for the beefy Macho guy at the counter who seems agitated and pissed off by the delay in getting the much-needed calories into his body.

The man in the cowboy hat is telling his friends about the news, saying things like "I'm thrilled" and "This is the happiest day of my life."

Then the wrestler shouts, "Who! Gives! A! Shit!"

Screeech.

Good mood: gone.

Festivities: over.

Silence.

All eyes are now on the cowboy, who had no idea that he was staring down the "Macho Man" Randy Savage and Rip Rogers (the Disco Kid back then). The two had wrestled in front of a packed house in Nashville hours earlier. They just wanted some damn food.

The cowboy eyes Macho.

Who the hell does this guy think he is?

He swears at Savage.

Savage swears back.

"Well, if you're such a big man, you'll fight me!" the cowboy says.

This suits Macho just fine.

He gets up from his seat . . . blood pumping . . . face red . . . mind raging . . . ready to pound this cowboy's skinny ass into the ground . . . but then . . . he slips and falls.

Whoosh.

The cowboy steps forward to pounce.

Macho leaps up and throws a right hook.

Misses.

The cowboy rears back to fire off a wild roundhouse swing.

Macho ducks, pivots and nails the cowboy with a left jab.

The momentum carries both men to the floor.

A waitress calls the police:

"That crazy wrestler Mr. Macho Man is fighting a cowboy at Waffle House!"

The ground becomes a whirlwind of fists, knees, elbows, grunts and groans. Neither man is landing a clean hit until Macho locks on to the cowboy's head (a front face lock he'd say, later).

Rip, sensing things could get out of hand, wedges himself into the melee and pulls Macho away while Waffle House patrons grab the cowboy and tear him off the wrestler.

"Calm down!"

"Cut the shit!!"

Macho backs off towards his seat, still screaming.

The cowboy inches back, motions like he's getting into a booth . . . bends towards his seat . . . then *grabs a stainless steel table knife . . . and lunges for Macho!*

Macho sees the flash of metal and ducks back behind the counter.

"I have a gun in my car!" witnesses hear him shout.

"You go get it," the cowboy says. "And I'll shoot you with it!"

The cowboy swipes his knife at Macho.

Macho leans back and reaches across the counter to grab his own knife. He jumps out onto the floor and flashes his newly found weapon, then sighs — *he grabbed a butter knife.*

"We stood there in a Mexican standoff," Macho said later.

"Let's go!" the cowboy's new wife says.

Whether the cowboy thinks better of using his knife or decides he might as well start listening to his bride on their wedding night, he puts down the weapon, cusses some more and pushes out the door.

Macho hollers at the cowboy as he pulls out of the parking lot with his dignity and new wife in tow.

Crazy night, right?

We're just getting warmed up.

Moments later, Macho Man sits in his booth, seething. The cowboy pissed him off. The knife pissed him off. The whole night's pissed him off. *And he still hasn't eaten!*

Patrolmen Edward Dies and Raymond Rader enter the Waffle House, responding to the 911 phone call.

"When we got there, he was still hyperactive," Rader said. "He was going strong, you might say. He was cussing everybody in the place, and we told him several times to stop, but he wouldn't, so we placed him under arrest for breach of peace."

But Macho Man would not go gently into that good night.

While Patrolmen Dies and Rader are arguing with Savage, trying to explain that they're not arresting him for the fight but for his behavior in the restaurant *after* the fight, Sgt. S.T. Williams arrives and tries to assist the other two patrolmen with putting on the cuffs.

It goes poorly.

"I realize I was a little hyper," Savage said. "But I wasn't going to let them just place the cuffs on me. When they came at me with the cuffs, I backed off, and that's when they started using the clubs."

Now it's near 2 a.m.

The overnight waitstaff is tired and the patrons are just trying to grab a little grub before returning to their graveyard shift. Instead, they're all standing in the parking lot among a small crowd that has gathered, watching through the Waffle House window as three officers wail on a crazy-ass wrestler who won't listen.

Sirens rip through the night and more cop cars speed into the parking lot, these ones with big logos on the side: K9 UNIT.

Inside the Waffle House, clubs fly and Macho works his way out of his seat, swinging his arms all over the place to avoid the cuffs clasping around his wrists.

"Lie on the floor or we're calling in the K9 unit!" Dies yells, reaching for Macho's wrist.

Macho rips his arm away and decks Rader. The cop slumps to the floor.

"That's it!" Sgt. Williams shouts, yelling for the dog.

The restaurant door opens and a hundred-pound German shepherd tugs at his leash. His bark shreds the air. Saliva drips on the floor.

"Last chance!" Sgt. Williams says. "Lay on the ground! Now!"

Macho Man shoves Dies and the cop releases the giant canine.

Oh shit.

The dog races to Randy, avoids his thrashing legs and sinks all forty-two of its teeth — including the one-inch-long canines — directly into Macho's lower butt.

Dies realizes it's now or never and sprays Macho in the face with Mace. Twice.

Macho frantically rubs his burning eyes while trying to get the dog to unclench its jaw and release his ass.

"Enough! Enough!" he shouts.

The cops pull the dog off and for the first time in nearly an hour, Savage doesn't say a word. He lies down quietly on the ground and puts his hands behind his back. His eyes are stinging with tears. His body is glistening in sweat. His right butt cheek is bleeding profusely.

Four cops. Three billy clubs. Two Mace sprays. One massive German shepherd.

This is the final tally of what it took to subdue a single Macho Man.

"I figured they were going to go for their guns," he said. "They had used their clubs, the Mace and the dog, and that hadn't done any good, so I figured the only thing they had left were their guns."

Dies, Rader and Williams arrested him and each charged him with one count of assault and battery.

"He hit each of us at least one time," Rader said. "But it's not anything we won't get over. None of us were hurt badly."

During the ruckus, Rip Rogers had raced out to call Angelo and they bailed Savage out of jail after posting a $1,000 bond a few hours later.

"I don't have any hostility towards the police," Savage told reporter Robert Sherborne a few days later. "I wanted to explain what had happened, and I think this whole thing resulted from a misinterpretation ... I have to congratulate that dog though. He got in a pretty good shot. He got me on the back of the leg, and it had swollen up and was black and blue, so they gave me a tetanus shot and a shot of penicillin."

The best part of the whole story?

Officer Rader knew Savage and had spoken with him several times earlier when he patrolled his shows.

His final comment:

"I've talked with him before," the officer said. "And he's always a little hyperactive."

A *little*?

In many ways, the Waffle House fight marked the final evolution of Poffo to Savage to Macho. The clean-shaven, soft-spoken minor league prospect for the Cincinnati Reds was gone, forever, vanished deep into this new creation, never to be seen again. There would be no more Clark Kent and Superman. No on/off switch. No more "persona" or "gimmick" or "character." There would only be one man occupying the psyche — one man in control of the brain and body and bluster.

And that would be the Macho Man.

"I saw him a couple days later in Chattanooga as we prepared for the Saturday night show," Dutch Mantell said. "He even pulled his pants down to show me the bite. I had never seen a dog bite before, but it looked nasty. The bite had to be at least 9" long, and I could plainly see the puncture wounds where the dog's teeth sunk in. Then Randy told me, 'Don't pick a fight with a police dog.'"

You think?

CHAPTER 14

The Outlaws

Foam bubbled out of nineteen-year-old Bill Martin's mouth. His eyes slowly glazed and rolled back in his head. His face burned a hard maroon. Wrestler Ronnie Garvin couldn't see any of this. He was behind Martin, leveraging all of his 235 pounds into Martin's body, constricting and contorting his head and limbs.

Garvin had elbowed Martin in the side of the head at the start of the fight to flatten him and was now punishing the kid in the infamous sugar hold, a total body vise grip that is performed in five brutal steps:

Step one: You are put into a full nelson.

Step two: Your face is buried into the mat.

Step three: Your opponent rams both his knees into your back.

Step four: You writhe in pain.

Step five: You pass out.

Bill Martin was transitioning from step four to step five. His arms seared in pain before going numb. His chin ground down into his chest, closing his throat. A black fog enveloped his eyes. All normal signs of the submission hold working its sleepy charm.

Then the foam seeped out of Martin's mouth and shit got real. Quick.

"Stop! Stop! Stop!" Lanny Poffo yelled, running over to Garvin from his corner of the ring.

Garvin couldn't see Martin's face from his position and just figured he was passing out as per normal. Nope. The kid was convulsing and having a seizure.

Garvin saw the concern on Lanny's face just as Martin's muscles began jerking involuntarily. He released the teenager. They immediately propped him up and opened his airway.

"Next thing I know, Angelo is standing over me and Lanny is sitting beside me [putting] a wet towel on my head, asking for me to talk," Bill Martin said. "I asked where I was and what happened. It took several minutes for things to come back to me. My friend Ricky helped me to the bathroom to wash up and told me what happened.

"In essence, Lanny saved my life. Ronnie didn't know how hurt I was so he kept going. He always felt bad about what happened."

Welcome to the International Championship Wrestling tryouts, courtesy of the Poffo family and their new crew of outlaws.

Back in the 1970s, being an "outlaw" outfit in the world of wrestling meant one thing: you were not a member of the National Wrestling Alliance. The NWA, which all the Poffos had wrestled for, included many of the biggest names and territories across the United States, including Eddie Graham's Florida Championship Wrestling, James Barnett's Georgia Championship Wrestling, Farhat Enterprises (The Original Sheik's company), Championship Wrestling in Michigan run by Wilbur Snyder and Dick the Bruiser, Verne Gagne in Minnesota, Southeastern Wrestling owned by Buddy Fuller, and the big dog in the south, the Continental Wrestling Association led by Jerry Jarrett and Jerry Lawler.

It was within this sea of legendary wrestlers and long-established promoters that Angelo Poffo had an epiphany:

I have two thoroughbred wrestlers as sons. I know everything there is to know about this business. Why are the three of us working for someone else? We should start our own company!

It was a bold move, but one Angelo believed he could pull off because of the talent he had in Randy and Lanny. With the growing popularity of the "Macho Man" character leading his stable, Angelo chose to plant his flag in Lexington, Kentucky, directly challenging Southeastern Championship Wrestling and the Mid-American territory while essentially declaring war on their neighbor to the south, Jerry "The King" Lawler out of Memphis, Tennessee.

Within months of starting International Championship Wrestling (ICW), Angelo purchased airtime in nearly two dozen surrounding markets to give his boys the television exposure needed to pump up the new promotion.

"The Poffos built their entire opposition territory on Randy's interviews and Randy himself," Jerry Lawler said. "He was the big star in their company. What they were looking to do was try and cause a conflict with our territory, the established group, and get recognition."

From day one, Macho Man was spoiling for a fight, calling out the Memphis wrestlers every chance he got.

"Randy was very special," said Jimmy Hart, the "Mouth of the South." "When he was running opposition against us, he was on Channel 24 and we were on Channel 5. They would come in and challenge us every week. Randy would come in and go, 'You, Jerry "The King" Lawler! I want you with the utmost intensity!'"

Yet even Angelo and Randy knew that to take on Lawler's entire kingdom they'd need more than a single Macho Man. They'd need bodies. They'd need a roster. They'd need guys like Rip Rogers, guys who say things like, "The only thing I ever wanted to be, even in high school, was a championship wrestler."

When Rogers (born Mark Sciarra) first crossed paths with the Poffos, he was a young dreamer out of Indiana who was taking work wherever he could get it. By happenstance, promoter Nick Gulas made him Lanny Poffo's tag team partner in a Christmas Spectacular show in Nashville. They got along well and when Rogers heard that the Poffos were going to open up a territory, he got ahold of Randy's number and reached out.

"We hit it off so he booked me sight unseen," Rip Rogers said. "I told him I'm built but I ain't worth shit. I just want to learn. Money isn't an issue. Then for the next four years Randy was my roommate, my best friend, my mentor, everything. The first 95 percent of what I learned in the business was from staying with them. Hell, Judy even did my hair."

Randy initially helped get Rogers jobs in several territories as the Disco Kid, but when they officially started the ICW, Rogers was one of the first on board, ready and willing to do whatever it took.

"Was I any good then? No," he joked. "But they needed people who were dependable. I was dependable. I'd get Randy's hand-me-down robes, hand-me-down this, hand-me-down that. They'd teach me the books, the scheduling, editing, how to wrestle, how we'd time heel turns with the TV tapings and anything else that needed to get done."

One of the biggest things that needed to get done was to help train new men to fill out the roster, which brings us back to the first ICW tryouts and Bill Martin having a seizure at the hands of Ronnie Garvin.

Martin was a 5'10", 175-pound power plug from Shelbyville, Kentucky, who attended early ICW shows and, like Rogers, wanted to be a wrestler. Badly.

"Back then there were very few options to get into pro wrestling," Martin said. "It was like a closed society. Like a band of gypsies. Unless you were a big college football or wrestling star, or you came from a wrestling family or had a close friend in the business, you couldn't crack it."

Still, he and his buddy Ricky Cook were dead set on breaking into the business, but the first year of their efforts turned up nothing but dead ends — until one day they heard the news they'd been waiting for.

ICW needed wrestlers and was holding an open tryout.

"Just tell me where and when," Martin recalled thinking.

After signing, they ran into George Weingeroff, a well-known wrestler and referee working with the Poffos. They were talking after an ICW event and the young, green prospects could hardly contain their excitement about the tryout. They couldn't wait. When George heard this, he smirked.

"You guys better show up in shape," he said. "I mean real good shape. That camp is going to be tough."

Heeding Weingeroff's warning, the two athletes trained as if they were prepping for Hell Week to become Navy SEALs.

"Ricky and I took his advice," Martin said. "We were already working out with weights and running some, but we stepped it up a lot. We were lifting until failure, running three or four miles a day and up to seven or eight on the weekends. Then we'd wrestle each other or anyone else we could find around our jobs."

When the boys walked into the tryout, they saw eighteen other wannabe wrestlers who were all over the map in terms of size. Six-foot jacked guys. Short fat guys. Tall chubby guys. Beefy strong guys. Beefy not-strong guys. Guys who wouldn't weigh 150 pounds if they were carrying a bag of bricks and other guys who had passed 300 pounds years ago.

Bill and Ricky sized up the competition. They were confident. They were in tremendous shape and had the muscle to prove it. Then they glanced at the pros waiting for them in the ring, a veritable gauntlet of badasses eyeing them up, staring at the fresh meat like salivating sharks with chum in the water.

The Poffos and Weingeroff were there, along with Rip Rogers, the sugar hold expert Ronnie Garvin, and 5'10", 245-pound Pez Whatley, a former University of Tennessee at Chattanooga wrestler and powerlifter.

Shit. This is gonna be rough.

Lanny took the lead in running the tryout, which was designed with one goal in mind: weed out the losers. For getting on the same card as the Macho Man, wimps need not apply.

The day began with calisthenics, an Angelo Poffo special. Air squats. Sit-ups. Crunches. Push-ups. Jumping jacks. Dozens of them. Then hundreds of them.

First the men sweat. Then they hurt. Then some quit.

Once satisfied that the newbies were officially warmed up, Lanny set up a series of head-to-head competitions designed to test each man's grit, guts and heart.

"We had a push-up competition, which I won, then a squat competition, which I won," Martin said. "Then a sit-up competition which Ricky won. I got third. Some guys were starting to puke. I was in good shape, but I was a little tired. Then Lanny said, 'We're ready to start the class.' Two guys walked right out. They were done."

Good.

With men in attendance who had done over 6,000 sit-ups straight (Angelo) and thrown 1,500 baseballs against a wall lefty every day for weeks on end (Macho), there was no sympathy for weaklings who couldn't hack bodyweight exercises and one-on-one lifting contests for a few hours.

"First thing they did was randomly pick two guys to wrestle each other to go for a pin," Martin said. "I got paired with a 300-pound guy who was so tired. I beat him easily. They went all the way around the room until everyone wrestled. Then they matched up the winners against each other until there was only one man left. I won. Ricky came in second. I thought we were done."

They weren't. Next up was a "King of the Ring" competition, meaning one man goes in the ring and wrestles until he loses or beats everyone in the class.

"I willed myself to go through the whole class until I started over again and then Ricky beat me," Martin said. "I was so exhausted. My body was shaking. Then Ronnie Garvin walks in the ring and asks, 'Who is the best?' Lanny pointed to me. Ronnie looked me dead in the eye and said, 'I am going to put you in a submission hold and you are going to try to stop me.'"

As you now know, Bill Martin didn't stop him, but the upshot of surviving a near-death experience in the sugar hold was that Martin made the ICW squad and was eventually named Rookie of the Year.

It was through these tryouts, event outreach and recruiting that Randy rounded out the ICW team, which eventually included 6'1", 242-pound "Cowboy" Bob Orton Jr. and the human tank, 6'2", 275-pound Bob Roop, a former high school state wrestling champion, football player at Michigan State and Special Forces medic in the Army.

Was it enough to take on the king?

They'd soon find out.

CHAPTER 15

Terminal Adolescence

"Me and Randy had the world's dirtiest apartment," Rip Rogers said. "We had a couple bean bags. Old chairs. A bunch of mattresses we threw on the floor. There were York weights and dumbbells in the living room. We each had a bedroom but a lot of guys would stay there. The kitchen was empty. We had a blender. Protein powder. Skim milk. Egg whites. But we usually ate out. We did nothing but wrestle every night, train like a bastard and chase girls. Every night was an adventure."

Ahhhhh, the glamorous life of running an outlaw wrestling promotion on a budget in Lexington, Kentucky, in 1979.

The glorious living quarters Rip "The Hustler" Rogers describes above were in the Zandale Terrace Apartment community about 1.5 miles due south of Lexington and the University of Kentucky campus.

They destroyed the place.

"If you walked into that apartment you'd see nothing but holes in the wall," Rip said. "Sometimes Randy was mad at the world for no reason and he'd punch the wall."

Not that Rip and Randy were trying to impress anyone outside of fans at wrestling events. They'd often be on the road three, four or five nights in a row, running shows everywhere from Johnson City, Tennessee, to Carbondale, Illinois, to Cape Girardeau, Missouri. Whatever place they rented was just a spot to sleep in and store their weights. Neither one of them had any real belongings beyond the gear they needed to wrestle. No furniture. No wardrobe to speak of. No keepsakes.

"I had one suitcase," Rogers laughed. "I'd wear the same shit for a week."

After the spot in Zandale Terrace the roommates moved to a different dumpy apartment before ending up in an old house next to a Baptist church on the same street where Angelo and Judy lived.

The exact address has been lost to history, but for our purposes, we'll say it was #1 Meathead Central. At any given time there could be a half-dozen cars on the front lawn and a dozen wrestlers in the back, blasting music and having a curling contest with dumbbells.

"We'd grab forty-pounders and say, 'Get 'em up as many times as you can,'" Rogers remembered. "I'd get fifty reps in a row. Then Pez would get fifty-one. Then Randy would get fifty-two and say he was champion. But I was built, man. I'd go double Randy's number and he'd get so fucking mad. He'd tackle me."

One time Randy challenged Rogers to a knee pulls competition. Neither would give up. They each did over five thousand (Rip won) and it took them over two and a half hours. The next day Rogers threw down the gauntlet for an air squat battle. He outlasted Randy again, clearing several thousand before his wobbling legs gave out. Once again Randy screamed at Rogers, pissed off that he lost.

There were weights all over the property. It looked like a Gold's Gym had exploded and nobody picked anything up. You'd have ten-pound and twenty-five-pound plates on the front lawn. Dumbbells were in every room. The backyard had barbells and plates and a bench press. It was an outdoor flex factory.

Randy loved the Olympic lifts and believed he was the strongest in the ICW crew, but everyone knew that was bullshit. They had Pez Whatley in their midst, a true blue behemoth and competitive powerlifter.

"Randy was very powerful," Bill Martin said. "But Pez Whatley was the most powerful guy at ICW."

The thing was, Randy ran the company and nobody wanted to make the boss look bad.

"Pez could crank out sets of incline bench at 405. Then Randy would get out there and put up 405 on the flat bench a few times and dare anyone to beat him. Nobody would try," Rogers laughed. "Then when Randy would leave, Pez would put it up five times like it was nothing. He wasn't stupid. Don't upstage the boss."

When they got bored slinging iron, the squad might head a few blocks over to the park for some pick-up hoops. To any of the kids on Randy's high school freshman basketball team, he'd be unrecognizable. The once fleet-footed guard of his youth was long gone. In its place was a stocky, 225-pound wrecking ball who loved to foul.

"We'd beat each other to death," Rogers said. "He was so coordinated and he had great eye-hand skills. And he had a long trunk and short legs. He had legs like a guy who was 5'8" and a wingspan like a guy who was 6'3". Basketball was his weakest sport, though. He'd play hard defense. Everything was so intense. We'd smash each other."

Hoops. Weights. Women. These were the staples of extracurricular activities the ICW crew enjoyed in what little down time they had — and there was very little down time.

While Randy's Macho Man was the main attraction for the promotion, wrestling was only one of about a dozen hats he wore within the company. Truth be told, everyone who wrestled with ICW also had to handle about seven other responsibilities to keep the operation running with what amounted to sweat, Scotch tape and second-hand equipment.

Angelo, Judy, Randy and Lanny sat at the top of the "corporate" structure, although there were no official titles. Judy handled all the commissions and payouts, but chipped in on everything from wardrobe and hair to food and travel. Angelo was the voice of reason and the big-picture strategist. He mapped out the territories they'd work in, the television hits and the venues, and work on the storylines. Randy and Lanny covered nearly everything else from the taping to the rings to the ring trucks to the event logistics and promotions. Lanny even did post-production voiceover work as an announcer for many fights.

Aside from the wrestlers themselves, ICW's assets included two travel vans that were purchased for $16,000 and one ring truck to transport the mat, ropes and posts that cost $30,000. Then there were several thousand dollars of television and sound equipment, studio time, costumes and a variety of other odds and ends needed to produce three to five live wrestling shows a week.

Nothing was fancy. Everything was used. The company ran on Angelo's ethos: squeeze every last drop out of every last penny and then try to squeeze it again. The stories about his cheapness (frugality, if we're being polite) are legendary. He was known to order hot water at restaurants and add ketchup packets to make tomato soup. On road trips he'd stuff four, five or six guys into a single hotel room, while he himself slept on the bathroom floor — as a sixty-year-old.

His distaste for wasting even a single dime carried over into the ring, where one of his gimmicks was to wrestle as the Masked Miser. In fact, it carried over into *everything*, especially lodging.

"Lanny and Randy would try to get free rooms from guys who were already leaving, or sleep in their car or trunk," Bob Roop said. "They were making money. It wasn't like they were broke. The boys had to see how normal people lived, and maybe [would have] gotten the impression their dad was — there's one thing about being frugal, and there's another about being so fucking tight you won't spend a nickel."

When it came to transportation, Angelo was a next-level budget traveler. If he wasn't jamming nearly a dozen guys into a van and driving them himself, he was loading hundreds of thousands of miles onto a single car — efficiently and slowly.

"I made the mistake of telling Randy that I could drive anything with a stick," Martin said. "And I could. I grew up on a dairy farm. My dad worked me like a full-grown man when I was twelve years old. But once I told Randy and Angelo I could drive, I drove us to 80 percent of the shows. It would be me, Angelo, Lanny and Randy in Angelo's old Mercedes with a diesel engine. That thing had 500,000 miles on it when I drove it and later Angelo told me it crossed 600,000.

"Well, I'd be behind the wheel on these two-hour drives and four-hour drives and six-hour drives and I'd want to get there. The old speed limit was fifty-five miles per hour but we'd be in the middle of nowhere with hundreds of miles of flat road in front of us and I'd push it to sixty-five, but Angelo wasn't having it. He'd say, 'Keep it on fifty-five. That's where I get the best gas mileage.' Not a penny wasted."

Sometimes they'd stop to eat. Sometimes they wouldn't. Martin never knew ahead of time so he'd bring a banana or candy bar to hold him over in case Randy decided a pit stop wasn't in the cards — or Angelo chose to save a few bucks on food that week.

If they did stop, fast food was a luxury. Occasionally they'd hit a truck stop with an all-you-can-eat buffet. More often than not, they'd pull into a Kroger (only if it was near a gas station — remember, no superfluous miles) and send Martin in with a few bucks to buy a loaf of bread, Kraft cheese and a pound of bologna to make sandwiches in the car because it was the cheapest lunch meat.

"Lanny was always into eating healthy and he hated bologna," Martin laughed. "He'd say, 'You're gonna eat that shit? Do you know what it's made of?'"

Randy didn't care what he ate as long as it had protein. He'd supplement whatever calories he consumed with endless shakes and amino acids anyway.

And nobody made big money. A rookie wrestler like Bill Martin earned $25 per day, with free travel and lodging if he drove and stayed with one of the Poffos. The real compensation wasn't the dollars. It was the knowledge and the discipline:

How to wrestle.

How to do media.

How to set up a ring.

How to run a promotion.

Bill Martin was down for all of it, but in the beginning he had to get over one major hurdle — he thought Randy Savage might be, in a clinical sense, insane. And it spooked him. Really everyone.

"Hell, I thought he was crazy," Dutch Mantell laughed.

"Back then he didn't listen to anybody," Rogers said. "Too much emotion."

Martin echoed the thought.

"I was a tough guy," Martin said. "I never lost a fight. I was very physically strong from life on the farm. All the guys at ICW were surprised by my strength and to that point, I'd never been scared of anyone my whole life. But Randy lived that Macho Man character. I thought he was nuts. All the twitches and moves. And he would fight anybody. If there was going to be a fight, he'd be involved. I was a little scared of him."

Like Rogers, Martin often witnessed Randy's intensity as it manifested in various destructive ways.

"I've seen him rip dressing room doors off the frame if he saw something didn't go right for one of the wrestlers in the ring," Martin said. "He'd scream and cuss and lose it if an event didn't go as planned. Once he pulled the hinges clean off a door. He tried to open it and it was stuck and he yanked it off."

While his actual sanity was up for debate, two things about Randy Savage were never in question at the ICW: his intensity and his dedication.

Everyone who spent time with him in those days believed he was destined for greatness one way or the other. They were there night after night. They saw the crowd's reaction to him. They noticed that it was just . . . *different*.

The way the audience gawked at his flowing robes. The violence in their booing (he was a heel). The way they responded to his early entrance music (from the movie *Fame*). The heightened buzz during his matches.

"He had 'it,'" Lanny said.

To all involved, his trajectory to the top was palpable. It was also inevitable.

When asked in 1981 about his goals to win a championship belt on live television, this was his response:

"Back when I threw my baseball uniform away, I looked at myself in the mirror . . . yeah . . . I stared at myself . . . And I said, 'Randy! You're gonna be a world champion in professional wrestling. That's your new goal! You'll be the World Heavyweight Champion before you're thirty. Get busy. Get workin' hard. Get intense training. Get workin' out.'"

He was twenty-nine years old at the time of the interview — right on track.

"Randy was so dedicated to wrestling and becoming a star," Martin said. "I knew in my heart that one day he was going to be a big star somewhere because of his attention to details and his drive. Randy would not miss a workout. He never stopped."

Martin recalled a period where Randy found a training partner who really pushed him at his favorite gym in Lexington, the Sinthe Sports Center. Randy got it in his head that this was *the* place he needed to train at to be the best and he wasn't going to let the ICW's heavy travel schedule get in the way.

One day he approached Martin and asked him if he could pay him to do some extra driving. On its face, this didn't bother the rookie. He didn't mind driving with Randy. In fact, he often enjoyed it — it was the calmest the hyperactive Savage would ever be. They'd have long talks about their favorite baseball players and teams and what was happening in the majors. Randy would share stories about the minor leagues. They'd talk hoops or football — both far better than Angelo's preferred driving entertainment, listening to opera. Ugh.

But Randy was asking Martin to drive *just him*.

"I already drive you everywhere," Martin laughed.

Randy explained that he didn't want to stay out on the road loops anymore. He wanted to come home to Lexington every night so he could train in his gym.

"Um, what?" Martin asked.

This was an absurd idea.

A typical road loop for the ICW would be a four- or five-day swing around the region with shows on consecutive nights. They might be in St. Louis one night, Decatur the next, then Bloomington or Dayton the next night and then Charleston and back to Lexington.

Usually, the sane members of the ICW would stay in motels near their events along the loop because, you know, that made complete sense. Not Randy. He was asking Martin to drive him back to Lexington *each night* after shows so he could train in the morning at his gym before they drove to the next show.

St. Louis to Lexington: five hours.

Terre Haute to Lexington: four hours.

Indianapolis to Lexington: three hours.

Columbus to Lexington: three hours.

These were round trips of six to ten hours, with the first leg happening overnight after a show that might end at 11 p.m.

"Randy was paying me to drive him while he slept in the back so that he could work out in the morning," Martin said. "Then we'd get back in the car and meet up with the rest of the ICW."

One particular trip illustrates the true level of Randy's obsession.

"We were leaving one event about four hours from Lexington late at night after a show and we hit a wreck on the road," Martin explained. "There was no way around it. We were up all night, inching along. When we finally got back to Lexington it was 7 a.m. Neither of us had slept in two days.

"Randy wanted to go right to the gym. I couldn't believe it. I pull in and Randy grabs his gear and tells me to follow him. I was weak as a kitten. Exhausted. And he gets going with full intensity. He's screaming and yelling and the veins are popping in his muscles. I don't know how he did it."

Part of what motivated Randy was the desire to be the best wrestler ever. The other part was a side hustle that few people know about the "Macho Man" Randy Savage.

During his early ICW days, in addition to keeping the promotion afloat and headlining shows, he took a crack at competitive bodybuilding with Rip Rogers.

The Incredible Hulk stood glistening onstage. The green paint was gone. In its place was a golden tan designed to highlight every muscle, fiber and flex under the hot lights for those in the audience.

Lou Ferrigno, all 6'5" and 285 pounds of him, was putting on a show. And the former Mr. Universe titleholder and Mr. Olympia runner-up knew what the crowd came to see: His gigantic 59" chest. His 19" neck. His 23" arms. All of it.

As he strutted along the platform, he paused and unfurled a sun-blocking front double biceps pose, stealing attention from all the other competitors.

He was the star of *The Incredible Hulk* television show. He starred in the *Pumping Iron* documentary. He'd signed on to play the title character in the movie *Hercules*.

If you were in attendance, you'd be forgiven for thinking he was the only big name on the stage. But you'd be wrong. A few bodies over, in dark brown trunks, sporting about 8 percent body fat, stood the future worldwide wrestling superstar, Randy Savage, shredded and posing his ass off. A little further down the line from him was Rip Rogers, with his blond hair and dark brown beard and white trunks. Both men were much smaller than Lou physically (who wasn't). But one of them would one day become a bigger star.

This was the 1982 Mr. Kentucky bodybuilding contest.

In the 1960s, '70s and '80s, the University of Kentucky's Rupp Arena was home to Wildcats basketball stars like Dan Issel, Pat Riley, Kenny "Sky" Walker, Rex Chapman, Sam Bowie and dozens more. But on this night, it was home to Rip, the Hulk and Macho Man.

Ferrigno was guest posing and giving a seminar on bodybuilding, which Savage and Rogers attended. When the scoring came in, Savage took seventh overall and Rogers took fourth. They were competing in contests as often as they could, usually the next day and one town over from a wrestling show.

They competed in the Volunteer Classic in Tennessee. Mr. Indiana. Mr. Central Kentucky. The Indianapolis Classic. In these shows there often weren't even weight classes, just an overall physique competition.

"Randy would beat me in Nashville and then I'd beat him in Indy," Rogers said. "He won a few trophies. I won a few trophies. We'd be posing in front of 2,400 people in Rupp for the Kentucky championship. Then we'd go to these seminars. We went to Arnold's seminar. He was coming right off the Conan movie. We took it seriously."

One of the sponsors of the Mr. Kentucky show owned the Sinthe Sports Center, and after he met Randy and Rip, he told them if they'd promote his gym with ICW, he'd give them lifetime free memberships. This is another reason Randy was so maniacal about getting back to Lexington to lift every day — the gym was free.

"It was the best weight room in the state," Rogers said. "Anyone who had anything to do with sports trained there. There were no 24-Hour Fitness places back then. But Sinthe was open 6 a.m. to midnight, so we could lift after shows or first thing in the morning. I think I competed in twelve contests over eighteen months at one point."

Randy didn't compete in that many because he realized that the aesthetic physique needed for bodybuilding shows ran counter to one of his larger, long-term goals in wrestling, which was to pack on mass to look bigger and stronger in the ring.

He eventually dropped the side hobby. There was no way his 6' frame could get to 230 or 240 with under 10 percent body fat and stay there while also wrestling night after night. Even with the steroids he tried, it wasn't possible.

The other issue was focus.

By 1982, the Macho Man had established himself as a major draw in local wrestling around Kentucky, Tennessee, Indiana, Illinois and Ohio. He'd become a strong, legitimate counterweight to the region's other huge star, Jerry "the King" Lawler. If the ICW and Randy were ever going to up their game to take on one of the best in the business, the time was now.

CHAPTER 16

You Come at the King,
You Best Not Miss

Hallmark greeting cards.
Or Batman.
Maybe Superman.
Any DC comic, really.

If you'd asked Jerry Lawler in third or fourth grade what he was going to do with his life he'd have said for sure, 100 percent, no doubt about it, he was going to be an artist and make a living sketching Justice League battles or clever illustrations for Happy Mother's Day wishes.

He drew through grade school and middle school and high school. And he had talent. Even his art teacher, Helen Stahl at Treadwell High School in Memphis, thought so.

"She saved a portfolio of my work that I'd done through three years that I'd been her student," said Lawler. "And actually she submitted the work to the University of Memphis."

On the strength of his drawings he was awarded a full-tuition Commercial Arts Scholarship to the school, where he dabbled in cartoons and worked on his craft. Not one to be shy, he would often send his work to local media personalities who he admired. Two of them were Dave Brown and Lance Russell, commentators for a Saturday morning wrestling show in Memphis that he used to watch regularly with his father, who got him into wrestling in the first place.

This means right about the time a young Randy Poffo was belting home runs in high school for Downers Grove, his future archrival was getting his first break in wrestling — as a cartoonist.

"He's a great artist and cartoonist and he would go to the matches on Monday night down at old Ellis Auditorium and he would draw cartoons of the matches that he saw," Dave Brown said.

In an alternate universe somewhere, the Macho Man and The King never draw blood in the ring. Jerry Lawler simply draws Randy Savage in his sketchbook. Weird to even think about.

"Lance and I would put these cartoons on the air," Brown said. "One thing led to another and finally we got Jerry down to the studio, introduced him, showed some of his artwork and from there it progressed until he got into the business."

Even Lawler's childhood wrestling idol, Jackie Fargo, reached out to him about his drawings.

"Jackie Fargo was like Elvis at the time," Lawler said. "Especially for a wrestling fan."

Incredibly, unlike so many of his contemporaries with college football or NCAA wrestling backgrounds or a powerlifting pedigree or a gym rat mentality like Randy Savage, Lawler wasn't even into exercise.

"I never worked out a day in my life," he said.

To further separate him from the usual wrestling rabble, he also never touched alcohol, drugs, cigarettes or coffee. He was addicted to one thing and one thing only: wrestling. From his first match on August 17, 1970, against Mark York (which he won), he never wanted to do anything else. Even more, he was willing to start at the bottom and grind his way up.

Like Bill Martin, he began his career working for nothing — $15 a match — which would hopefully be enough money to fill his gas tank to drive to the next show. And the next and the next. The schedule early on was relentless.

During an interview on his 50th birthday, he shared a typical day with his hometown television station.

"We'd do Saturday morning TV in Memphis and then drive to Jackson TV. They had a TV match in the afternoon there. Then from there, drive to Nashville where they had matches at like three o'clock in the afternoon, a live show. Get out and wrestle there. Get back in the car, drive down to Chattanooga, do a show in Chattanooga at 6:30. Jump back in your car again. Drive down to Birmingham and have a show in Birmingham at 10:30 that night."

Hectic. Harried. Worth it.

By keeping up this schedule for several years, Lawler quickly became wrestling royalty throughout Tennessee, and he won his first title in 1974 by taking down his one-time idol, Jackie Fargo. From that point on, he was known simply as The King. He sold out hundreds of shows. Was the biggest wrestling draw in the state. Became part owner of the Memphis Wrestling Company. And, from Randy Savage's perspective, he was public enemy number one.

If the Macho Man was going to take himself and ICW to the top of wrestling, all roads led through Memphis and Jerry Lawler.

Randy's ongoing archrival in the ICW was his brother, Leapin' Lanny Poffo (though nobody outside of the company knew they were brothers). They were the two big fish battling it out in their tiny little puddle on the sidewalk of wrestling.

"In our own promotion, I was the main babyface and he was the main heel," Lanny said. "Also in the Maritime provinces, when we had bought in to the territory with Emile Dupre. We did very good business.

"What I loved about working with Randy is he knew everything that I could do well, then he called the match. He made sure that I looked so good in that match, no matter what the finish was. He was totally unselfish, and then he would do something terrible to me, then, *boom*, I'd be down. He upstaged me every night, but we got over. He loved being the villain. It gave him tremendous creative power."

The bit worked. Fans rooted for Lanny and rioted against Randy. The Macho Man character played so well that occasionally people got so invested they couldn't distinguish the performance from reality.

One night, after a show at a high school in Eastern Kentucky, Randy was walking out the back door of the gym when an elderly lady approached him as he moved towards his car. He slowed, figuring she wanted an autograph. Instead, right when she got in front of him, *she cracked him over the head with a tire iron!*

Fortunately, Randy was able to duck and block the swing a little with his arm so his skull didn't crack open, but it was a harsh reminder of how good a heel he'd become.

"Randy had beat her guy and she was upset," longtime friend Keith Madison said. "He spent the night in the local hospital. He showed me the scar."

Show after show, Lanny, as the promotion's lead creative and writer, would craft new storylines and angles to keep up the in-ring heat between the brothers. Meanwhile Randy honed his skills on the microphone, dropping gem after gem in interviews, like this one:

"The best thing you can do is just stand back and let the Macho Man talk! Because there's nothing you could say that I couldn't say better myself! Yeah!"

With each media hit he got louder, cockier and crazier.

"Freak out! Freak out! I'm 100 percent mentally insane! 100 percent pure athlete! Yeah! The greatest wrestler aliiiiive!!!"

"This was a period in the wrestling business where if you were crazy on-screen, you were crazy off-screen," Bruce Prichard said in the Vice TV documentary, *Dark Side of the Ring*. "You had to live your gimmick, and Randy played crazy really well. He lived it 24/7."

As Randy's local star power grew, he rightly believed that if he and the ICW wanted to grow and compete with the big-boy territories, they had to bring the heat to outside promotions and champions — namely, Jerry Lawler.

They pulled no punches.

Savage issued endless challenges to Lawler's crew, going so far as to offer $50,000 to any fighter with the guts to show up to an ICW event to fight. When nobody appeared, he publicly offered Lawler $100,000 to bring his top three fighters into the ring against him at the same time. Again, crickets.

After those attempts failed, he began laying down the gauntlet on TV and at the end of every show. "Fight me, Lawler! You can run but you can't hiiiiiiide. I know where you live! I'm comin' to you! Yeah." Angelo would even take out ads in local papers daring The King to take on Macho Man.

"He'd go on TV every week and knock Lawler and Bill Dundee and our matches," Jerry Jarrett, co-owner of the Continental Wrestling Association and Lawler's partner, said. "I remember sitting in our locker room in Memphis. We had this private dressing room where everyone would sit and joke around or watch television. One of the boys asked, 'Jerry, why does Randy Savage spend his whole hour talking about us?' I said, 'You'll have to ask somebody else because I don't know how crazy people think.'"

Crazy or not, both Lawler and Jarrett knew what Savage was up to.

"When you're on the bottom rung of the ladder, you usually think the way to get attention is to try to get the rub off the established guys," Lawler said.

Rub off or piss off. Didn't matter.

In his quest for attention, everything was fair game.

On nights when ICW wasn't wrestling, Randy and his crew would occasionally drive hours across the state and buy tickets to a Lawler show just to get kicked out on purpose. They'd purchase front row seats, show up yelling and cussing out Lawler just long enough for security to be called in, and then they'd holler at Lawler and Jarrett the whole time they were escorted out, saying the CWA was ducking them.

"They'd be in the back and when the guys parked and walked in the back door, they'd be there yelling at 'em and challenging 'em in front of the fans," said Jim Cornette, a former CWA manager. "Or they'd sit ringside a time or two in Rupp Arena when they were allowed to buy tickets."

When Savage couldn't make it to a Lawler event, he'd offer an open invitation for Lawler to meet him in the ring at an ICW fight night and then act shocked that Lawler didn't show up (even though Lawler never knew about it and didn't care).

"Randy Savage would go out and say, 'I'm going to wrestle Jerry Lawler this Saturday night in Lexington!'" Lawler said. "Of course, I was never going to be there. I didn't even know this was being done. Then Randy would go out to the ring and say, 'Would you look at this? Jerry

Lawler's a coward!' That was their philosophy on how to make a name for themselves."

You had to admire Macho's gumption. The man didn't even care if he broke the law. In fact, he'd even confess on video after he did.

In his second most famous incident of trying to goad Lawler, he showed up to his home, unannounced, fixin' to get it on.

"They came to my house one day when they knew that I was down in Memphis on TV," Lawler remembered. "They brought a film crew, and Randy came to my house in Hendersonville, Tennessee, when I was two hundred miles away in Memphis. And he broke a window out of my house. He threw a rock through a window."

In Lawler's retelling, Savage screamed about him and played up the event for a few camera guys he'd brought along.

"They filmed him doing it," Lawler said. "He came up and beat on the door and everything, knowing nobody was home . . . and they went back and showed that on their TV program."

George Weingeroff remembers the incident differently and says it was a brick, not a rock, that Savage tossed through the window. And he says Savage didn't bring a video crew but instead went on the ICW television show afterwards, looked dead into the camera and shouted, "Lawler! I'm the guy who threw the brick into your house!"

Either way, Lawler already knew that because, Randy being Randy, he went through the trouble of writing his name on the damned brick.

Using TV to start trouble was a favorite Macho Man tactic. Sometimes he'd confess to his antics. Other times he'd air video of them. And in other cases, he'd interrupt Lawler's TV appearances, a gambit he used to his advantage throughout their rivalry.

The King would be mid-interview, having a calm, reasonable conversation with a TV host, and then — *whoosh* — Macho would barge in, already lathered in sweat and full of rage to light up The King:

> You know something, Jerry Lawler?! You make me laugh.
> But you make me sick at the same time! Yeah! You disgust
> me in how you talk! You don't know how many times I've
> laid awake in bed at night and thought of that silly little

grin you put on your face . . . Give me that silly little grin when you're in the ring with me and I'm gonna have a real good time with ya! I am the greatest wrestler who ever lived! And I'm talkin' past, present and future! Talking one hundred thousand light years in the future! Yeah!

For the vast majority of the feud, Lawler had decided that it was best to not even acknowledge Savage or the ICW. Don't punch down. Don't give them the satisfaction. Unfortunately, for a few wrestlers on the CWA roster, turning the other cheek wasn't so easy. You can only call out a man so many times before he decides he's gotta make a stand — even if it nearly kills him.

This brings us to the most infamous clash between Savage's ICW and Lawler's CWA, the moment where tensions completely boiled over, where the consequences could have been deadly.

Welcome to the Savage–Dundee gunfight.

Here are the details . . .

Location: The American Fitness Gym parking lot near Nashville.

ICW Players: Randy Savage, Angelo Poffo, Rip Rogers, Pez Whatley, George Weingeroff.

CWA Players: Bill Dundee.

What you need to know about this story is that there are multiple versions and multiple motivations behind each one, but all versions end with Dundee having broken bones in his face and needing six weeks off from wrestling.

The Macho Man variation of the story goes like this:

Randy Savage was cutting a promo outside American Fitness, tearing into CWA, as per usual. Eat. Work out. Wrestle. Rip on Jerry Lawler's crew. This had been his routine for months on end. Only this time, while he was filming, Bill Dundee, the 5'7", 200-pound spark plug and Lawler's #2 man, appeared in the parking lot of the gym while Savage was talking.

Dundee already had two strikes against him. One, he was tight with The King. Two, several years earlier he had worn wrestling trunks that said "Macho Man" on the rear end and he brought them out recently to anger Randy. The third strike, on this particular day, was breathing the same air as Savage.

The instant Dundee got a look at Savage's crazy eyes and the ICW crew in the parking lot, his stomach turned cold. Outnumbered and caught off-guard, he made for his car, opened the trunk and pulled out a Smith & Wesson revolver. According to Jim Cornette, a former photographer, promoter and manager with the CWA, Dundee revealed the gun, but Savage went ballistic and wrestled the firearm away from him.

"He brought it [the gun] out, but Savage blocked it, grabbed the gun and whacked him with it. Savage drilled Dundee on the side of the head and broke his jaw," Cornette said.

This is the story the Macho Man ran with, obviously. It makes him look the most . . . macho. Allows him to say, *Lawler's crew pulled a gun on me and look what happened!*

If you were a Randy Savage fan in Tennessee or Kentucky in the very early 1980s, you *loved* this version. Told you everything you needed to know about the wimps at CWA and the hard-asses at ICW.

Only . . . it may not be completely accurate.

Bill Dundee's version is a little different.

In his telling, he was innocently talking to ICW wrestlers Pez Whatley and George Weingeroff, leaning against his car, when Savage came out of nowhere and clocked him.

"Randy ran by and sucker punched me in the eye," he said.

Then *after* the punch, he says, he managed to get to his car and go for his gun.

This is how Dundee explains the encounter in his autobiography, *If You Don't Want the Answer, Don't Ask the Question*:

> I got sucker punched. There was a bunch of them, one of me, I grabbed my gun and that ended the fight. I have read that I had a broken jaw, that I was pistol-whipped, I read a bunch of stuff. What I told you is the truth, as sure as my name is Bill Dundee.
>
> They drove off and went to the police station to file charges of assault with a deadly weapon against me. Jarrett

got a lawyer for me and I filed charges against them. We had to go to court and instead of exposing the business, both sides decided to go broadway and drop all charges. However, I told Savage on the way out of court that I had taken his best shot and he hadn't yet had mine. They went on their TV saying that Savage had fought me in a parking lot and broke my jaw. Normally, we ignored them. However, I did go on TV and show my eye off. I said I had been attacked by four monsters.

In the actual Memphis TV footage, Dundee said he had been attacked by nine-foot tall gorillas, not monsters. And in one retelling he stated that he and Randy wrestled and "rolled around the ground like women," in another he said they "never left their feet," and in yet another he pointed the gun at Angelo and Macho Man ran away.

The way the details change with each telling over the years, we'd be forgiven for labeling Dundee an unreliable narrator. Also, there's one major hole in his story: George Weingeroff wasn't even there, so there's no way he was talking to him in the parking lot.

"I went to Knoxville to go to the World's Fair that day," Weingeroff said. But . . .

Rip Rogers, who says he was in the car when the punch happened, lends credence to the sucker punch version:

> We had an off day in Hendersonville and Randy wanted to go to the local gym. So I think we're going to work out and then as we pull in I see Dundee walking out of the gym. He was just an employee of Jerry's. Just a wrestler. He walks by the car and says, "Hey, Randy," and Randy sucker punched him in the goddamned jaw! I said, "Randy, what the fuck was that?!" He said it was about some old Macho Man trunks Dundee used to wear.

Lanny was also at the World's Fair in Knoxville that day, but suffice to say he didn't side with Dundee's version.

While there's no disputing Dundee's injury or that there was an actual confrontation, there is a wide gulf between being sucker punched without a gun and being pistol-whipped with your own gun.

"The way I heard it from the guys that afternoon was that Randy confronted Dundee about wearing the 'Macho Man' shorts and sucker punched him," Weingeroff said. "Dundee was not gonna fight Randy. He was scared shitless and said he had to get Jerry Jarrett's number from his car. When he walked to the car, he took out his gun and Randy tried to wrestle it away. Angelo was able to talk him down and promised Dundee nobody would use the gun if they both let go. Then they did. Nobody got beat up with a gun."

The end result, however, was the same.

These two crews hated each other.

"It really was a war," Weingeroff said.

"The animosity between Randy Savage and myself went beyond the ring," Lawler admitted. "It became really personal."

It even went to court.

The legal action began in late summer 1979, when the Poffos filed a $2.4 million lawsuit in U.S. District Court claiming that nine wrestling businesses had violated U.S. antitrust laws. In the *Lexington Herald-Leader*, staff writer Jack Brammer wrote, "The Poffos claim that nine other wrestling promoters have agreed among themselves to use only professional wrestlers who are affiliated with their organizations. The Poffos say this has hurt them financially by preventing them from obtaining several wrestlers — those working for the nine wrestling businesses — for their events. They also claim that other promoters have blacklisted them as professional wrestlers and have fixed admission prices to wrestling events at a non-competitive level."

The lawsuit, which sought both damages and a temporary restraining order, listed a who's who of the family's old friends in the business. Nobody was spared.

Headlining the list, of course, was Jerry Jarrett and Jerry Lawler's Continental Wrestling Association, but an all-star cast of colleagues found their name in the brief: Nick Gulas, Eddie Graham, James E. Barnett,

Ed Farhat, Wilbur Snyder and Dick the Bruiser, Buddy Fuller, and even Angelo's old pal Verne Gagne in Minnesota.

The case, predictably, went nowhere. But it served its purpose, which was to give Angelo and Randy the official pretense to talk about "their lawsuit" and how they'd been wronged.

"It's like a Mafia," Savage said of the promoters in the lawsuit. "Wrestling is a monopoly. They get together in a room and divide up the country. They'll say, 'This guy owns New York,' and nobody is allowed to go there. It's like saying you can't open a pizza place on a street because there's already one there."

Part of their gripe was also with how other promoters treated their wrestlers. In this aspect, the Poffos viewed themselves as the good guys — saviors of the industry.

"It's a prostitute-pimp relationship," Savage said. "The promoters use you up and throw you away. You can go into a town, buy a house and become their slave."

The other aspect to their grievance was much more crucial because it involved the lifeblood of their business — big venues and revenue.

By the early 1980s, the ICW had been effectively banished from the largest venue in the state, the University of Kentucky's Rupp Arena, which was a major problem for a wrestling promotion based in Lexington.

They'd been allowed to perform there one time and it was a strong gate.

"We sold 2,500 tickets and the gate was $10,000," Angelo said at the time.

After that, they'd been locked out for a couple reasons, both of their own doing. Tom Minter, the executive director of the Lexington Civic Center, told them that Rupp Arena already had a contract with another wrestling promoter to do a once-a-month show, and he didn't believe that the area could support two shows.

This reason was likely bullshit.

The "other wrestling promoter" in this case was Lawler, who commanded sold-out shows on the first or second Thursday of every month. It wouldn't be a leap to suggest that Minter knew where his bread was buttered and chose to punish the Poffos to keep Lawler happy.

The second reason was likely 100 percent true and would ultimately prove to be fatal for the ICW in a myriad of ways.

"ICW is not the type of organization we want to do business with," Minter said.

This was because in addition to lambasting Lawler in the media, Randy and his boys took to the airwaves and launched a second war against the arena officials running Rupp Arena for barring them. They hurled insults, made threats and accused the officials of "taking money under the table" from Lawler to keep them out.

It was only after the Rupp Arena officials complained to the TV station for airing the "unfounded remarks" that the Poffos issued a non-apology. The truth was that the Rupp ban not only hurt their bottom line, it hurt their brand. They were trying to be *the* wrestling outfit in the state and that's not possible if you can't step foot in Rupp.

"It's like you were the New York Yankees and you couldn't play in Yankee Stadium," Rip Rogers said at the time.

No Rupp, no cash, no cachet.

Angelo estimated that with the proper amount of promotion and a regular presence in the arena, they could consistently sell four thousand tickets, which could mean a $40,000 payday per night, once or twice per month. That's a potential half-million dollars or more per year if done right.

"A couple of shots at Rupp Arena would be all it would take," said "Cowboy" Bob Orton Jr.

Missing out on that pay dirt was slowly killing the company, and it forced them to scratch and claw their way throughout the state, making up for the smaller venues with a volume of shows at a pace that was unsustainable for the long term.

"As long as we can't get into Rupp Arena," Savage said, "we're going to look small time."

After several years of banging away against their rivals, they'd wrestled in over thirty Kentucky towns, largely in high school gyms or National Guard armories. The hour-long show on Channel 36 in Lexington, where they lobbed their weekly vitriol and threatened violence upon Lawler, reached about a dozen cities.

"Angelo was so cheap it killed us," Weingeroff said. "We'd film Thursday mornings and start at 8 a.m. Kids are at school. People are working. Nobody is in the audience. But it would save money. Angelo didn't understand how empty it looked. We'd do these other 6 a.m. tapings on Tuesday mornings. And Angelo would bring a stopwatch to time the crew on their breaks to make sure they weren't wasting time. These were guys he should have brought whiskey to for working so early for us. Instead, he pissed off all the guys who were helping us."

Weingeroff, Rogers and others tried to intervene and offer opinions, but Angelo wouldn't hear it. He was as stubborn as he was thrifty. He'd rather produce a shitty show and save money than spend money on a quality show.

"We didn't get results from the studio shows, but instead of figuring out why they weren't working and making them better, Angelo says 'screw it' and buys all his own equipment," Weingeroff said. "The product was even worse. Lights would be shaking. Quality was bad. It was horrible. But if you complained you weren't a team player."

Angelo even went so far as to buy a $15,000 editing machine, which didn't matter, because the quality of the tapes they had to edit was garbage. Then the machine broke.

"It should have been a goldmine," Weingeroff said. "We could have owned Lexington and Louisville and Cincinnati and a few others. Instead we pissed everybody off and nobody wanted to work with us."

None of this mattered to Randy. He and Angelo believed that everyone was out to get them and that was it. Their failures were singularly the result of a vast conspiracy by Lawler and his cronies to keep them down.

In an effort to drum up business, Savage leaned on every single connection he had — including old baseball buddies who were dumbfounded how the once quiet, stoic Randy Poffo had turned into this loud, bombastic . . . creation.

One ex-teammate he called on was Doug Flynn, a former Tampa Tarpon with Randy who also happened to be a Lexington native. Unlike Randy, Flynn's talent carried him to the Major League, where he had a respectable eleven-year career as a utility infielder. He collected nearly 1,000 hits with the Reds, Mets, Rangers, Expos and Tigers, winning two

World Series titles with the Reds in 1975 and '76 as a backup infielder. He also won a Gold Glove with the Mets in 1980.

In 1981, Major League Baseball players went on strike and Flynn used the time to pursue his other passion: music. He sang with the Greg Austin Band, performing all over Kentucky.

One night he looked up from the stage and saw a thick, massive dude walking towards him with a strut. The guy was wearing a bandana and a leather jacket and a pair of custom jeans with the words "MACHO MAN" written on the side.

"He looked like a biker," Flynn said. "I was thinking, 'What have I done to him?' I thought I was dead."

It was just his old pal Randy strolling up to say hi.

Flynn was floored that the man in front of him was his pal Poffo. After reconnecting, Flynn used the opportunity to pull a prank on their mutual friend, Keith Madison, also a former Tampa Tarpon.

Madison didn't make it to the Major League, but instead of turning to pro wrestling as a second career he chose a more familiar path, taking the job as the head baseball coach at the University of Kentucky in 1979.

A few nights after running into Randy, Flynn invited Madison out to dinner with their wives. He picked Madison up and they carried on with their normal chitchat on the way to eat. When they got to the restaurant, Flynn said to Madison, "Hey, would you mind if someone else joined us?"

"Sure," he said.

Madison had no idea who Flynn invited but when he looked out the window, he noticed a tough-looking guy approaching the car.

"We're in the back seat with the windows down," Madison said. "We stop, and here comes this huge guy with long hair, wearing kind of wild clothes, and I'm like, *What in the world is this?*"

The long-haired guy walked right up to the back seat, poked his head in and said, "Madison, Poffo here."

The three ex-Tarpons had a great reunion and over the next few months Randy enlisted their help.

In one instance, several angry people dialed into the ICW's Lexington TV show to call Randy a liar. He had mentioned a few times that he'd been a minor leaguer for the Reds and Cardinals and the callers weren't having it. No way did they think for one second that the beefy, colorful Macho Man was once in the minors.

"Randy said nobody believed he had really played minor league baseball," Flynn said. "So I did an interview in which I talked about playing with him in Tampa and that he was a good player."

In a more up-close-and-personal favor, Savage asked Flynn if he'd be willing to be the guest referee in a steel cage match at the local Henry Clay High School. Savage figured he'd cash in on Flynn's local drawing power and put some butts in the seats. After all, the guy had two World Series rings. The audience would love him.

Nope.

"I walk in and the fans are calling me names I'd never heard before," he said. "It was like, BOOOOOOOOO! They're screaming, 'It's not fair, you are his buddy. How can you be a fair referee?'"

Playing into it, Flynn took the microphone and ripped into Randy, saying that just because they were teammates doesn't mean they were friends.

"In baseball you need to be a team player, and Randy is here because he's not a team player," he shouted. "He's just in it for himself!"

Savage played along, grabbing the microphone and blasting Flynn for being a traitor and for only showing up to shut him down. The crowd loved it.

"That was great," Savage told him afterwards. "Wanna come on the road with us?"

Unfortunately, neither local celebrities, lawsuits, laying the verbal smackdown on Lawler nor any other trick or stunt Randy could muster was able to overcome this one insuperable fact: the ICW was losing money and losing talent. Angelo and Randy and Lanny had no choice but to shut it down.

"If we'd buttered up the TV executives and cozied up to the people who ran the big venues and arenas in the area, things could have been different," Weingeroff said. "I put $10,000 of my own money into the ICW and I wanted it to succeed. It should have. But we pissed off everyone. We put out low-quality TV. And it failed."

CHAPTER 17

Loser Leaves Town

Randy Savage stands in front of a brick wall. His skin is crimson with rage. His face is wet with sweat. He's wearing a pink bandana on his head, a string tank top that hangs off his shoulders and a thin chain on his flexed neck.

He grips a microphone as the light from the 1980s camcorder sprays his face. He rocks back and forth on his feet, twitching with anger. His head snaps left, then right, flicking back and forth like a lizard's tongue. Then he opens his mouth and unfurls an iconic diatribe. You've got to imagine his voice in your brain. Hear the tone and guttural cadence. Ready? Go:

> Freak out, freak out, YEAH! Message from the Macho Man to Jerry Lawler and his dad. Yeaahhhh . . . Wait a minute . . . I wanna tell you somethin' from the Macho Man Randy Savage . . . wait a minute wait a minute wait a minute, man! Freakin' out in my MIND! Jerry Lawler's dad is dead! Yeah. Jerry Lawler's daaaad is dead! He ain't healthy, man! He's in his grave somewhere turnin' over and over and over! You know why, Jerry Lawler, your dad is turnin' over in his grave? Because you come to the well TWICE! And you left empty-handed, yeah! Last time in

the steel cage you went against the Macho Man Randy Savage, yeah! And that name means somethin' allllll over the world . . . Yeah it does, yeah . . . And Jerry Lawler, your dad, man, he is really embarrassed about it, yeah! Because what you've done is you've gone past your due retirement, yeah! You should've retired before you faced the number one world's greatest athlete in the world today! Yeah. Me. Yeahhhh ME, Jerry Lawler! Well you're cryin' and you're cryin' and you're cryin! Man! Don't you have no PRIDE!! Think of your dad, Jerry Lawler. Think of your DAD being DEAD! And you're comin' after the Macho Man!

Cut to Jerry Lawler standing in a bland television studio. A red curtain hangs behind him. He's wearing a shimmery blue jacket over his bare chest. He's calm. Serious. An interviewer gives him the opportunity to respond to Savage's comments. His voice is measured:

I said last week that he had the luxury of having his father run down to the ringside when he got in trouble. And, ahh . . . My father's been dead since 1969. Before I ever started wrestling. But he used to take me down to the wrestling matches . . . He really admired wrestlers and I think he would have been really proud that I became a wrestler. And for me to stand here and listen to a piece of trash like Randy Savage even say my father's name or my dad on his mouth makes me sick to my stomach. So let me tell you something, Randy Savage. When I get in that ring, I promise you one thing, brother. I want you to have your dad sittin' in the back . . . and I'm gonna give you a beating like you've never had in your life! I'm gonna pull every stinkin' hair out of your stinkin' head. That's a promise from The King to the stinkin' Macho Man!

Wait a minute, you're thinking.
What the hell?

Didn't the ICW go broke?

Weren't they forced to shut down?

Did The King finally accept Macho Man's challenge?

Addressing the final question first, yes, Lawler ultimately agreed to take on Savage. The reason: money. *Lots* of it.

Following the implosion of ICW the Poffos were stuck between a rock and a bunch of boulders. They couldn't book matches through their own promotion. Other promotions despised them. Venue operators loathed them. The wrestlers they employed were now unemployed. They owed people money. It was bleak. In an effort to blaze their own trail they'd burned nearly every bridge they had and now found themselves stuck on an island of irrelevancy.

Shortly after letting the roster disband and selling whatever assets they had, Randy Savage took stock of his options, which didn't take long because he had none.

He'd spent the last five years meticulously building the Macho Man character from the ground up. He'd immersed himself in the fiber of his creation — disappeared inside of it. Perhaps a few specks of Randy Poffo remained in his body, maybe deep down inside his cells, in the mitochondria, yeah, but that was it.

For all intents and purposes, he *was* the Macho Man, a creature who carefully evolved over time for one specific purpose: to wrestle in front of packed houses.

Now that purpose had been taken away. *Snap.* Just like that. Suddenly, he was purposeless — a boat without water, a soldier without a war.

With time to reflect, it occurred to him that maybe he'd pushed Lawler a bit too far. Maybe he'd been out of line. Despite all the psychotic ranting and delirious behavior, Savage always considered himself a man of honor. Especially when it came to business and the business of wrestling.

Perhaps he'd behaved dishonorably.

It was this last thought that spurred him to pick up the phone to call Jerry Jarrett, the founder of the Continental Wrestling Association and partners with Lawler.

"Jerry, I just want to tell you that I appreciate the way you acted throughout this because I've been a real fool," Savage told him. "I admire you and I wanted to tell you we're going to get out of your hair."

Jarrett paused a moment, then asked Savage what he was going to do next.

"I'll try to find someone who will hire me," Savage said.

Jarrett again paused. Then he had an idea. A big one.

"Well, you know, you have been plugging this match against Lawler and Dundee for over a year now," Jarrett said. "Why don't we get some mileage out of this?"

"You think you might be able to work with me?" Savage asked.

"If you give me your word that this is business and not some stupid stunt, then we can make a lot of money," Jarrett said.

Savage gave Jarrett his word that he was serious and that he'd be a team player from that point on. To show just how sincere he was, he also penned a personal letter to The King, apologizing for his behavior.

The "Mouth of the South" Jimmy Hart, who'd attended Treadwell High School in Memphis with Lawler and was his wrestling manager, remembers sitting in Lawler's kitchen reading the apology together.

"Savage wrote, 'In all due respect, you have a great product. We tried to come in and do something that was unethical at the time and it didn't work. If you could ever use us, we're available,'" Hart said.

Despite the years of bad blood, Hart, Jarrett and Lawler all came to the same conclusion: they were about to make a boatload of money.

The program between Lawler and Savage couldn't have been planned better if they'd done it intentionally. Without an actual endgame, they'd been building up their rivalry for years throughout both their territories across several TV stations and nearly every newspaper in several states. It was perfect. Most importantly, Savage and Lawler spent much of that time genuinely disliking each other. Their hatred wasn't faked.

If you'd polled wrestling fans throughout Tennessee and Kentucky in the early 1980s and asked if the rivalry between Savage and Lawler was real or manufactured, nearly 100 percent would have voted "real." And they'd have been correct.

Now Lawler and Savage had a chance to cash in on all that pent-up emotion.

Hell. Yes.

And to continue the reality-based storyline, instead of rolling Macho Man into the CWA fold, they decided to bill the match as "promotion against promotion."

"Lawler had originally planned a main event for the next week between the Road Warriors and the Fabulous Ones," Hart said. "But we just had to change that. I said, 'King, with you and Savage main-eventing, this card will be a sellout.' Jerry agreed and we reached out to Randy."

Done deal.

"We brought them into the fold," Lawler said. "We worked out an agreement to have this big company battle. Like a loser leave town, but not just the wrestler but the entire company."

With the wheels in motion, they turned Savage loose. Antagonizing Lawler. Angering Lawler. It was an all-out blitz. The Macho Man was everywhere. TV. Radio. Print. Even in person at Lawler events.

"We had Randy show up to a Lawler match," Jarrett said. "And we acted like it was an invasion."

Savage would show up, alright. Shades. Bandana. Chains. Wild hair. Wilder voice. Screaming at Lawler to fight him. And then, when the audience couldn't take it anymore, when something *had to give* . . . Lawler said, "Let's get it on."

Within hours, the Lawler vs. Savage fight became the talk of the South. They billed it as the Grudge Match of the Century.

And it was set for Thursday, March 8, 1984, at Rupp Arena.

The *Lexington Herald-Leader* gave the fight the full media treatment. Staff writer Jim Warren was assigned to write the Lifestyle section's front page feature on the Macho Man and came away with a unique impression of Savage, who he described as a man whose trademark is "maniacal intensity."

"Sit down to talk with Randy Savage and you'll get a surprise," Warren wrote. "He is an unexpectedly articulate and soft-spoken fellow who sprinkles his conversation with references to the writings of Henry David Thoreau, Maxwell Maltz (*Psycho-Cybernetics*) and Norman Vincent Peale."

If you're under seventy years old then you likely don't know that *Psycho-Cybernetics* was a very popular self-help, self-improvement and personal development book from the 1960s. Its main thrust was to explain "how thinking of the human mind as a machine can help improve your self-image, which will dramatically increase your success and happiness."

Whether Savage used the book to improve his self-image or to help create the Macho Man image from scratch we don't know, but one thing is certain: it worked.

The Macho Man that Warren spent time with in the spring of 1984 was intense, focused, driven and hell-bent on using his match with Lawler as a springboard to reaching the top of his profession.

"It's going to be total war," he said. "There's no doubt that he [Lawler] has a great record. And I consider myself to be at the top of the profession. It's going to be like finding who is better, Mickey Mantle or Willie Mays. Here's a chance to knock him back ten yards and for me to take a giant step toward superstardom. It's the biggest match of my career. I'm gonna beat him and beat him bad."

Not only was Macho Man counting on this match to help him break through to the next level, the once anti-Poffo executives at Rupp Arena had done a complete one-eighty. They were no longer in the Never-Poffo business. Now they were all-in, counting on Randy to help them break records.

"The largest wrestling crowd we've ever had for professional wrestling in Rupp Arena is 9,400 people," said Bill Humphrey, the Lexington Center operations director. "A big-hype event like this has the potential to draw 11,000 to 12,000, so a new record is possible."

The Poffos' old nemesis Tom Minter, the executive director of the Lexington Center, added, "The advance ticket sales would indicate it could be our biggest wrestling crowd ever."

Savage was thrilled. This was everything he ever wanted for himself and the ICW, and man, was he ready.

"I prepare for a match by getting crazy, getting wild, getting psyched up," he said. "A guy with an attitude of just going in and tearing up the gym, you better watch out for that guy. I'm very intense when I do any-thing, weight lifting or anything. I let my intensity fly on TV or in the ring. I do wild things. I don't know why, but I do. It's colorful, but at the same time I'm expressing myself."

In his mind, nothing short of the entire world would be watching him "express himself" against Lawler.

"Whoever wins this match is going to be known in Japan and every-where," he said. "Everyone knows this is going on and [they're] going to be watching."

Savage was right.

For the first time in its history, a wrestling event sold out the famous Rupp Arena. Crowds lined up outside hours before the event. It was standing room only inside. Vendors sold T-shirts and banners and hats and all manner of swag. You were either a Savage guy or a Lawler guy. The arena was a house divided — though not 50/50. The cheers for the popular "King" outweighed the smattering of people rooting for the Macho Man. In fact, any show of positivity for the heel, Savage, only intensified the vitriol against him. For many, it was truly good versus evil.

"The first time we worked together, when it was 'promotion against promotion,' we sold out the arena with 23,000 people," Lawler said. "That was unheard of in wrestling."

It was also just the beginning.

After the referee ruled the debut match a "no contest" because it turned into a free-for-all street fight outside the ring, the two stars began one of the most lucrative and exciting runs in Memphis wrestling history.

"Savage vs. Lawler I" was the tip of the iceberg. For the next twelve months they'd wrestle weekly, crisscrossing the territory, battling it out every way imaginable. They did cage matches. They traded the championship belt. They fought for new belts and old belts. They joined new tag teams to face off against other talent, often with Lanny joining Randy (nobody knew they were brothers) to take on their new tag team archrivals, the Rock 'N Roll Express with Ricky Morton and Robert Gibson.

Then the first Thursday of every month, Savage and Lawler made their way back to Rupp Arena to headline an event. When they'd exhausted all of the storylines involving their own rivalry, and milked every last drop of hatred for each other that they could, they flipped the script and created a new angle where the two feuding stars became a tag team.

It was a delightful turn, giving Lawler and Savage a chance to play off each other against new stars in the promotion like King Kong Bundy and Rick Rude. To sell the turn more effectively, they had Jimmy Hart switch loyalties to Bundy and Rude. This brought out a harsher, more fired-up version of Lawler and gave Macho Man a chance to turn his insanity up to 11.

In one of their first promos as tag teammates, we get a glimpse of how their chemistry balances out:

"We don't have to wait until Monday night, Rick Rude, Jimmy Hart and King Kong Bundy!" Lawler bellows to a live studio audience. "Let me tell you something. I want you to listen and listen real good! I don't like this man [*pointing to Savage*]! And he don't like me! But brother, we both hate your guts! And when we get in that ring we're gonna show you how much we hate your guts. We don't have to be great friends to beat your stinkin' brains out and that's exactly what we're gonna do!"

Meanwhile, as Lawler is talking, Macho Man is having what could easily be interpreted as a psychotic episode next to him. He's flicking his tongue. He's pacing. He smashes his head repeatedly against a steel chair. He looks like he should be committed to an asylum ASAP. And then he opens his mouth and screams at the audience and spins from the crowd, often talking with his back to the camera.

"In the Twilight Zone now! In the Twilight Zone! That's where we're at right now. Yeah! Monday night! Mondaayyy! Yeahh! And Rick Rude, bring 'em on two by two! Yeah! Lawler and Savage doing their thing! Doing their thing! Bring 'em out right now! You wanna see some action? Come our wayyy, man! Oh yeah! I don't like you either, Lawler. But we're in the Twilight Zone now! Jimmy Hart! Yeah! Jimmy Hart! Come near me now because I'm QUICK! And Bundy's slow. And Rick Rude is DUMB! Oh yeahhh!!"

The new platform with the CWA gave Savage the chance to experiment with the Macho Man character with a wider audience. No longer was he cutting promos in front of empty studios and bleary-eyed cameramen at 7:30 on a Tuesday morning.

With Lawler, he'd found a megaphone — a way to amplify his persona in front of larger TV audiences and exponentially larger crowds. As he upped his verbal game, he continued to push the boundaries of what his body could handle in the ring as well.

"Robert and I wrestled Randy and Lanny everywhere," said Ricky Morton, one-half of the famed Rock 'N Roll Express. "Randy liked to give people their money's worth. He was a great storyteller. He was so creative in the matches too. We were the first wrestlers to ever go through a table."

The pride in Morton's voice is palpable because these days you can hardly watch an episode of *Monday Night Raw* or *Friday Night Smackdown* for fifteen minutes without one giant dude tossing another giant dude through a three-foot-by-six-foot standard table. But in the early 1980s, it hadn't been done yet.

"Back in those days we'd call matches by the fly," Morton said. "Meaning, we'd figure out what we were going to do in the ring. Randy was really athletic and agile. He tried a lot of crazy, crazy stuff. One night we were working and he leans into me during the match and says, 'I'm gonna pile drive you on this table.' People weren't used to that stuff then but I trusted Randy . . . And he pile drived me and we went through the table and it broke! What a trend we started."

After they crashed to the floor, Morton clutched his neck and writhed in pain. Savage dove on top of him, concerned, and through a covered mouth asked, "Are you okay?"

"I'm fine, I'm selling!" Morton said.

It played beautifully. The fans in attendance thought Morton had a broken neck, which made every blow from Savage afterwards seem all the more sinister and vicious. Morton, thinking quickly, told Savage he was going to sell the table injury into the following week. It became a major angle: did the Macho Man break Ricky Morton's neck? Nobody knew.

"Randy was magical telling that story," Morton said. "And I kept selling. We'd do a tag team match against Randy and Lanny and then when I'd wind up in their corner, Angelo would wrap his towel around my neck and choke me . . . The people would lose their damned minds."

Randy also used the opportunity to soar higher and higher on his famous flying elbow drop. You know the one. It's quintessential Macho Man. He'd get his opponent down in the middle of the ring, climb up to the top rope . . . point to the sky with two hands . . . swing his arms down . . . coil . . . and . . . *whooosh!* . . . sail into the air and crash down onto his opponent.

If you've ever wondered what it's like to be on the receiving end of a patented Macho Man elbow drop, here's an explanation from Morton, who handled hundreds of them:

> First thing you need to know is that he'd come off that top rope at what felt like one hundred miles an hour. When you first see it, you're going, "Holy shit." You just don't know what to expect because when you see it on other people it looks so damned vicious. You're lying there and he's dropping with an elbow or sometimes a double axe handle or even a knee and then, nothing. You didn't feel a damn thing. That's how good he was. He'd practiced that move night after night after night. He'd land on his hip and knees and side and shoulder with perfect timing. When he dropped that elbow, he was the one taking the bump because you didn't feel it. Didn't knock the breath out of you or nothing. Everyone trusted him.

Elbow drops. Pile drivers through tables. Sellout crowds. Championship matches. By early 1985 Randy Savage had accomplished nearly everything in wrestling that he wasn't able to in baseball. He'd moved from Single-A territories all the way up to high Triple-A with the Continental Wrestling Association. He'd nearly maxed out what could be done locally.

The only thing left to do now was "go to New York," which was the wrestler's inside term for getting the call from Vince McMahon to join the major league in the then-WWF. On this, he'd get a monster assist from his pal Jimmy Hart.

————

"Can you tell me about the Nutrilite Vitamin B dual action formula?" a polite elderly lady asks on the phone. She's looking to buy some Amway supplements and she's been given the number of a salesman named Randall.

"Sure," a deep, gravelly voice responds. "Uh, each bi-layer tablet releases eight *essentialllll* B vitamins . . . Yeah . . . Two instantly! And six more slooooowly . . . Dig it . . . For eight *hooouuursss* of energy support to fight fatigue. Fight it! Crush fatigue. Kill it! With vitamin B! Ohhhh yeahh!"

The woman hangs up, scared.

Did she call the right number?

Yes, she did. The number was Randy Savage's. And sure, he probably didn't handle his calls with the Macho Man persona turned up to a 10, but it likely wasn't at a zero either. The bigger question is, why was he taking vitamin sales calls in 1985 in the first place?

The answer, as always, is money. Because even though Savage had been packing arenas with Lawler and was a local celebrity, wrestlers simply didn't make enough money to live off of — at least if you were a heel.

A babyface, like Lawler, could slap his name on anything and make a buck. People had been trained to root for him and wanted to do business with him. Merchandise. Grocery stores. T-shirt and poster signings.

A big-name babyface could make big-time money to supplement his income.

Heels, on the other hand, were a victim of their success. Wrestlers took kayfabe seriously in that era — they wanted to keep up their staged performances completely in real life, never breaking character in public. Heels and babyfaces used to have different locker rooms. They'd train at separate gyms. They wouldn't even travel together.

The upshot was that audiences truly believed the "good guys" and "bad guys" hated each other. They also truly believed that the good guys were "good" and the bad guys were "bad." This meant that an exceptional heel like Macho Man couldn't capitalize on his name locally. People weren't lining up to pay money for him to sign T-shirts or to take pictures. He wasn't getting appearance fees to emcee events or parties. And since wrestling didn't provide enough to pay the bills, he had to look for other anonymous sources of income — like selling vitamins for Amway.

Little did Macho know that his side gig hustling CoQ10 was going to give Jimmy Hart the exact cover he needed to poach Savage and take him to New York.

The way Jimmy Hart tells it (and has a thousand times) is that one day he was sitting at a Denny's in Nashville, Tennessee, pondering a "Moons Over My Hammy" or possibly a "Grand Slamwich" when he decided to call in to see if he had any messages. There were no cell phones back then. No texting. No DMs. If you wanted to find out if someone was trying to get ahold of you, you had to call an answering service, a home office or your house to see if someone left a message.

On this particular check-in, he was told that Vince McMahon tried getting in touch with him. Hart, naturally, assumed it was a prank — one of the boys trying to screw with him, as always.

Although . . .

McMahon *had* spent the early 1980s in an all-out assault on the local territories. One by one he poached talent, took over TV rights, lured fans and tried to put the entire NWA conglomerate out of business.

Sure, he'd bought out stars from other regions, but did he really want Jimmy Hart?

For weeks, Hart didn't believe it. Put it out of his mind, really. Until he got another call, from his friend Hillbilly Jim, who basically said, "What the hell is wrong with you, man? Vince is trying to bring you to New York!"

Convinced that it was real, Hart flew to meet McMahon, accepted the offer (and the fury of Lawler for leaving) and joined the WWF in time for WrestleMania I.

"I remember it like it was yesterday," Hart said. "In one corner there was Liberace and on the other side there was Muhammad Ali. Cyndi Lauper. It was like a dream come true."

A few months later, Hart got another call, this time from Vince McMahon's right-hand man, George Scott. There was no ambiguity this time. His marching orders were crystal clear. Vince and George had seen tapes of Randy and they wanted him in the WWF. Now. Go get him, Jimmy.

Hart got queasy in the pit of his stomach. He knew how pissed Lawler had been when he'd left, and he wasn't nearly the draw that Savage was. The thought of going back to Memphis to poach Savage put him in a cold sweat.

As he formulated a game plan, he zeroed in on one theme: Lawler couldn't find out that Hart was talking to Savage on behalf of Vince. If, ultimately, Savage decided to leave Memphis with him, then it was up to Savage to handle that on his own. But no way did he want Lawler to get wind that he was actively trying to meet and recruit the Macho Man.

Then a light bulb came on.

Amway!

"I got ahold of Randy and told him I had someone to buy $500 worth of Amway products from him," Hart said.

Savage was thrilled. This was a lot of money and Hart knew it would get his attention.

"I'm at a TV [shoot] right now but meet me at the gym afterwards over on Summer Avenue," Savage said into the phone.

Hart raced over and when Savage showed up, he instantly dropped the façade.

"Look, Randy, I lied," Hart said. "I was just kidding you. Let me tell you what: WWF would like to see if you want a chance to come here."

Savage was so paranoid he didn't believe it. He thought it was some kind of a sting operation to catch him not being loyal to Lawler and Jarrett. He wasn't taking any chances.

"He got me out of the car. He patted me down, like he thought I had a wire on me and was going to tape this information and give it to Lawler and them," Hart said.

After soaking up the info, and realizing Hart was 100 percent serious and not bluffing, Savage knew there was no decision to be made. He was going to meet Vince. But first, he had to tell Lawler and Jarrett the right way. He wasn't going to just take off. This time, he handled things with the CWA professionally.

Following his talk with Hart, he set up a meeting with Jarrett to share the news and offer him whatever runway they needed at CWA to make his departure work for them.

"I've got a chance to go to the WWF," Macho told Jarrett. "How much notice do you need?"

Jarrett said later, "He was the only wrestler who got the call from Vince to go to the WWF, who told Vince, 'Only after I give Jerry whatever notice he asks for.'

"I told him we'd need just two weeks to get the belt off him. When Vince called me and asked about bringing Randy up, I said, 'I love that man. You know what I think? Randy is the most honorable wrestler I've ever known.'"

And with that, after toiling for over a decade in the minor leagues of baseball and wrestling, the time had come for Randy Poffo, aka Randy Savage, aka the Macho Man.

He was off to The Show.

PART III

The Macho Man Cometh

CHAPTER 18

Liz

It's a meathead love story as old as time.

A dude rolls into his regular gym at 6 a.m. to throw some iron around. He's jacked up on caffeine and ready to rip. He's hammering chest and back today. Bench. Flyes. Rows. All of it. He's fired up.

As the smell of sweat and chalk and plates hits his nose and the clanging and banging of other lifters catch his ears, he strolls by the front desk to flash his membership card.

Nine days out of ten he barely registers who's behind the counter. Man. Woman. Monkey. They say, "Have a great workout," and he nods without looking up.

But on this day...

As the dude is about to show his card, his brain registers something different. A new front desk girl. Brunette. Almond brown eyes. Pretty face. Bright skin. Charming smile.

Whoahhhh.

Their eyes connect.

The front desk girl's heart skips a beat.

She's beautiful. She's used to guys checking her out. High school. College. They're all the same. And lord knows she's seen her share of gym rats strutting past her, flexing to snag her attention. It never works.

But this guy...

There's something about him. His muscles are massive. His hair is all over the place. His clothes are bright neon. His beard is thick. And his eyes — they're *intense*. And they're laser-focused on her and she feels seen. Vulnerable.

"Hi, I'm Randy," the meathead says.

"I'm Liz," the girl replies.

This encounter took place at the Sinthe Gym in Lexington, Kentucky, smack dab in the middle of Randy's run with the ICW.

"It was instant attraction," Lanny said. "We worked out there regularly and then one fine day a new girl came in and that was Elizabeth Hulette."

One story that's been shared throughout the years is that Elizabeth made a comment about how red Randy's eyes were (plausible) and that he was quick to make a remark asking her to come to the other side of the desk to get a closer look.

The version Randy preferred is that it was "love at first sight" because, well, from his perspective, what's not to love?

A perfectly romantic meathead mindset.

"I was impressed by her beauty and intelligence," Savage also said.

Liz was warm, sweet, quiet and charming, the true yin to Savage's yang. The two hit it off quickly. And once Randy learned that Liz had been a communications major at the University of Kentucky, he rolled her into the ICW fold with a job. They taught her how to edit, work the sound, time the promos and prepare tapes for air.

"At the end of the day the ICW was a mom-and-pop shop," Lanny said. "We all had to learn how to do everything and once we learned something, we taught it to the next person. Liz had a communications degree and was eager. She adapted to everything."

Also, she was gorgeous. You didn't have to be Roone Arledge to know that she belonged in front of the camera, not behind the scenes in some dark editing bay. They put her to work as an announcer, providing color, segues and wraparounds to pre-taped action from the live events.

One of her early telecasts, where Macho Man faced off against Adrian Street, features Liz wearing a classic '80s blue blazer (with shoulder pads), her hair styled and her charm on full display.

"Hello everybody and welcome to another sensational hour of international all-star wrestling, I'm your hostess, Liz Hulette," says the fresh-faced twenty-five-year-old in her perfect Kentucky twang. "We've got a fantastic program for you, bringing you some of the finest professional wrestling stars from all over the world. We want to get started with our first match, so let's get to ringside."

She's polished. Professional. Already seems too big for the small-time studio. Her timing was also perfect — both personally and professionally.

The day before New Year's Eve, on December 30, 1984, Randall Poffo and Elizabeth Hulette got married.

Randy's original plan was to secretly sweep his Kentucky bride away, marry her in private, then show up with her back in Lexington as a happy couple with rings on their fingers. His whole life for the last five years had been about attracting attention and he wanted this special day solely for the two of them, alone, to remember forever. No crowds. No cameras. No performances.

It was a sweet idea . . . that Elizabeth's mom wanted no part of.

You're not marrying my daughter without me present.

"Randy wanted to elope," Judy said. "But Elizabeth's mother said no. She wanted to have the wedding in her house. Randy agreed to that, but he didn't want anyone there, so he only invited the two of us, his mother and father."

That's how, on a warm day that almost reached seventy degrees in the middle of winter in Frankfort, Kentucky, the future "First Lady of Wrestling" became the new Mrs. Poffo. It was a humble, sparse affair. Even Lanny wasn't there.

"I was wrestling that night," Lanny said. "He'd have been upset if I canceled the show."

Lanny didn't miss much. After the short ceremony at the house, there was no steak dinner or a big night on the town. No band or first dance or speeches. Nothing.

"They had some refreshments," Judy said. "That was it. It was very quiet. But that was Randy. He didn't want anyone around. He didn't want anybody to know that it was so special to him, so he was quiet about the whole thing."

Quiet about the ceremony, yes.

Quiet about his wife's talent, no.

Fast-forward about six months to Savage meeting with Vince McMahon to plan his arrival in the WWF universe.

His first question was, "You got room for my brother?" McMahon agreed to bring Leapin' Lanny Poffo along.

The second question had to do with Vince's idea to give the Macho Man a valet. In wrestling, a valet is an attractive woman who accompanies a wrestler to the ring. She's there for three reasons: to add sex appeal, pique curiosity (why is *she* with *him*?) and to distract. She can disarm her wrestler's opponent with a look, misdirect the referee as needed and incite the crowd at key moments in the match.

With Savage's patented (savage) behavior, the WWF brass thought pairing him with a pretty valet would enhance his character and get a pop from the crowd. Not so much beauty and the beast, more like beauty and the brute.

Randy was warm to the idea, as he'd seen The Sheik use his wife, Joyce (as Princess Saleema), successfully in the same role for years back in his early NWA days in Chicago. McMahon's first choice was Melissa Hyatt, aka Missy Hyatt.

Missy was tall (5'8"), with platinum blond wavy hair and a "look" reminiscent of Farrah Fawcett (a good thing). McMahon had been trying to find a role for her within the WWF and this seemed like a good opportunity.

Savage had other ideas.

"They were discussing what type of manager or valet the Macho Man should have," Lanny said. "Missy's name came up. So did some other tall blondes that fit that type. They were beautiful women. But Randy was thinking, 'If I'm going to have a beautiful woman with me, I want Liz.'

So he said to Vince, 'My wife isn't really tall or blond, but she's really pretty. How 'bout you give her a screen test and see how she does?'"

McMahon agreed and flew Liz to the WWF headquarters in Stamford, Connecticut. Her time in front of the camera for the ICW paid off. She was phenomenal. Everyone loved her. Blew Missy and everyone else out of the water.

The new couple was ecstatic. Not only was Randy getting his dream shot with the WWF, he got jobs for his brother and his wife to go along with him. The only thing left now was to plan the angle for his WWF debut and to figure out a dramatic, showstopping strategy to introduce Elizabeth as his manager.

CHAPTER 19

The Number One Draft Pick

Bo Jackson rushed for 1,786 yards and scored 17 touchdowns for Auburn University in 1985 on his way to what Jeff Pearlman dubbed "the most inevitable Heisman triumph in history" in *The Last Folk Hero*. Not only that, Jackson had positioned himself as the no-doubt-about-it, number one overall pick in the next NFL draft. He was *the guy* every NFL front office wanted. Not just a running back — a *franchise* back. The type of talent that only came around once every decade or so.

They envisioned him on billboards, on the cover of their game programs, on local media, filling highlights on ESPN, on the front page of newspapers and magazines . . . all of it. He'd be instant must-see TV.

It was during this same year, 1985, that Vince McMahon believed he'd discovered his own Bo Jackson: the "Macho Man" Randy Savage.

Like Bo, Randy was a rare two-sport athlete (though his baseball days were well behind him). Like Bo, Randy was going to be must-see TV. And like Bo, Randy was going to be the number one, most sought-after talent for the current roster of WWF managers.

Instead of being evaluated by the Tampa Bay Bucs, Atlanta Falcons or Houston Oilers, Randy's skills were being measured by the watchful eyes of Mr. Fuji and Bobby "The Brain" Heenan and "Classy" Freddie Blassie.

This was how the WWF would introduce the Macho Man to the masses. Not as some new guy or potential winner, but as *the new star*, the Bo Jackson of the WWF.

On June 17, 1985, at the Mid-Hudson Civic Center in Poughkeepsie, New York, in front of 2,596 people, Randy Savage made his WWF debut. Built snug into the upper corner of the East–West Arterial in the city, the cozy arena was just over an hour from the WWF headquarters in Stamford, making it the perfect place to reveal new talent.

"That's where it all started," WWE Hall of Famer Tony Atlas said. "We would go back and forth from there to Allentown, Pennsylvania."

Lanny remembers the details of wrestling in the arena well: the early arrival time, the local media tour and most of all the rabid fans and length of the shows. The WWF did so many tapings and matches in the arena, from promos to matches to Piper's Pit, that main events sometimes didn't end until midnight.

"When you went to Poughkeepsie back then you knew you were in for a long night," Lanny said. "We would get to the dark match and people still wouldn't leave."

A "dark match" is a non-televised match that often features the biggest WWF stars putting on a show for the fans in attendance. If a prominent name isn't featured heavily in the TV shoot, this is a way for the live audience to see them perform.

Randy Savage's debut was decidedly *not* a dark match.

It was a showcase. A launch party, if you will, announcing their new franchise talent to the world. Savage's first contest was against 5'10", 235-pound Aldo Marino, previously Ricky Santana, actually named Ricardo Ortiz.

Marino wasn't a big name. He was a jobber, a guy who specialized in making the stars look good while he lost. Before that night in Poughkeepsie, he'd trained at the renowned Great Malenko wrestling school in Tampa, Florida, and then kicked around Texas for a while before getting some spot work for the WWF. Little did he know that on this steamy Wednesday night in the Hudson River Valley, he'd become a part of wrestling history.

Legendary announcer Howard Finkel introduced the two men. Marino stood in his corner, wearing black trunks and what can only be described as a bright yellow server's vest from a restaurant.

The Macho Man, on the other hand, went all-out for his premiere.

He wrapped a glittering gold-and-red-striped headband around his hair, leaving enough fabric to flick and whip with every twitch of his head. Beneath that he slid on some classic dark sunglasses and to cover his body he chose a robe that belongs in the Louvre. It was the size of a bedspread, hanging off his body over his full wingspan, from wrist to wrist. It was jet black, with a shimmering two-inch gold collar wrapping around the neck and going down his chest.

On the front, under each arm, were dueling giant snakes facing off against each other. One was gold. The other was silver.

Finkel introduced him:

"From Sarasota, Florida, weighing 239 pounds, Randy . . . Macho Man . . . Savaaage!"

Randy spread his arms wide, pointed his fingers and spun around, revealing the glorious back of his robe, which featured two enormous, intricate, dazzling bright red dragons with horns and gnashing teeth, ready to fight each other. The only thing standing between them was the name Savage written in massive gold script. It was a work of art.

When the time came to remove the robe, Savage unveiled a vintage pair of his classic pink trunks, with three stars across the front and "Macho Man" written on the back in white. He had on wristbands, hand wraps, knee-high neon yellow boots and yellow kneepads.

After the bell rang, commentators Vince McMahon and Bruno Sammartino set the stage:

"The Macho Man, Randy Savage, who is quite the competitor, making his WWF debut," Vince McMahon said. "That's a colorful robe there. A well-built young man, Bruno."

"Yes, he is," Sammartino said. "I'll tell ya, he's made quite a reputation for himself. I've heard a lot of great things about him. Not too pleasant as far as his style. He's a very good wrestler but a very mean individual. But he has certainly been a winner and he is well known all over the world."

After a few quick takedowns in the first thirty seconds of the match, a who's who of legendary wrestling managers appeared ringside. We've got Bobby "The Brain" Heenan in a suit and casual blue dress shirt, Mr. Fuji with his customary tuxedo, top hat and cane, Classy Freddie Blassie in some version of a hot pink jumpsuit and Jimmy Hart wearing a bright red shirt and a sports jacket covered in multicolored pastel hearts.

While Macho Man pummeled Marino with all the tools in his wrestling bag (standing elbow off the top rope, double axe handle off the top rope, two flying elbow drops) the managers evaluated Randy like he was running the forty-yard dash at the NFL combine.

"This fella's got quite a reputation," Sammartino said. "I'm sure that's what these managers are out here for. They're looking him over. They'd all like to manage him."

With every Savage move in the ring, McMahon and Sammartino hammered home just how special this new Macho Man character was.

"I don't believe I've ever seen any one individual attract so many managers at ringside to take a closer look," McMahon said.

After two massive, signature flying elbow drops, Savage pinned Marino in what was ultimately a three-minute match. More importantly, the managers got a good look at their prospect, and even more important than that, the fans got a good look at the managers taking a look at Savage.

Before Savage was even officially announced the winner, Heenan, Fuji, Hart, Blassie and Johnny Valiant were all in the ring shaking the Macho Man's hand.

"My goodness! I can't believe what I'm seeing!" McMahon shouted.

All of it added up to one message:

Pay attention, folks, because the Macho Man is the *next big thing*.

Part two of the WWF Macho Man Welcome Tour involved a guest spot on "Rowdy" Roddy Piper's famous talk show, Piper's Pit. Appearing on "The Pit" was wrestling's version of a comedian getting the coveted invite to be on Johnny Carson back in the day. It was a nod to the wrestling world that you mattered.

Piper, born Roderick Toombs, was a kilt-wearing, bagpipe-playing, pot-stirring, shit-talking superstar with unmatched charisma and an unmistakable voice and sense of humor. Once kicked out of junior high school in Winnipeg, Manitoba, for carrying a switchblade, Piper found himself living on his own as a teenager. He stayed in youth hostels and eventually fell in with pro wrestlers who gave him work, trained him and taught him the business.

He spent his twenties climbing the ranks of the west coast territories, from San Francisco and Portland to Los Angeles, where he perfected the "Rowdy" gimmick before heading to the WWF.

By March of 1985, Piper had become such a huge draw that he was a crucial player in WrestleMania I, headlining the event at Madison Square Garden with his tag team partner, "Mr. Wonderful" Paul Orndorff, against Hulk Hogan and Mr. T.

"Once I got inside Madison Square Garden, it was like being at the Academy Awards," Piper said. "There were stars everywhere, from all walks of life. I was rubbing elbows with Liberace, the Rockettes, Andy Warhol and countless others. Frank Sinatra, Gloria Steinem, Rod Stewart, Little Richard, Dick Clark. The A-list just went on and on. And once we got through the ropes, Muhammad Ali, who was a special referee that night, was waiting there to greet us."

Not bad for someone who was nearly homeless as a teen and was kicking around gyms and going on lunch runs for older wrestlers barely a decade earlier.

This is why Roddy played the role of kingmaker and chief shit-talker with the WWF. He could hold his own with everyone from Ali to Mr. T to the supposed future of the company, the "Macho Man" Randy Savage.

Within thirty seconds of Piper shouting "Hello, peasants!" into the microphone from the Pit, with plaid wallpaper and a photo of himself in a Superman shirt over his right shoulder, Randy Savage made his first appearance on the show, crashing the set like an eighteen-wheeler with no brakes.

"Macho Man Randy Savage is here! On Piper's Pit! And what a historic event, baby! Look at me! In living color, yeahhh!"

For the special occasion, Savage wore a white tiger-print headband with a matching skintight sleeveless shirt. His robe was big and red and magnificent, with hundreds of shiny fake diamonds spelling out "Macho Man" in blue and "Savage" in red and gold on the back.

"You're gonna love this! Hulkamania is dead! Starting now! Macho Madness! Ohhh yeah! All around the world, yeah!"

"This man here! Is the number one draft choice in professional wrestling today!" Piper said to his audience. "Every manager in wrestling that has any sense is after this fella right here! And I'd like to know, what is it like to be the number one wrestling draft choice in the entire wrestling world?"

By this time in the interview, Savage had jumped up on a chair, spread his arms, and with his back to the camera, completely obscured Piper. The only thing fans at home could see was his giant robe reading "Macho Man."

"It's unbelieeeevable, man! All 235 pounds! Going down the aisle with my million dollar robes! Roddy Piper, I want you to feel Macho Madness right now! I want you to wear one of my million dollar robes, baby!"

"Wait a minute, I can be Macho Madness?" Piper asks, smirking, enjoying the spectacle.

"There's gonna be some changes! Yeahhhh! No more Hulk Hogan!"

Then Piper, wearing the Macho Man robe, jumps on a chair and yells, "This is Macho!!!"

Chaos.

Charisma.

Crazy.

The three Cs of vintage Macho Man interviews.

And in one fell swoop, in under four minutes, Randy Savage was christened a WWF star by Piper and put a bull's-eye squarely on Hulk Hogan's back.

"It was magnificent," Lanny said. "Randy really got over on Piper's Pit. It was huge."

In no time, the Macho Man was omnipresent in the WWF universe, and every appearance plugged the angle that he was the number one unsigned talent in the company. Even basic media round-ups in the newspaper introduced him as "the number one free agent in wrestling, Macho Man Randy Savage." It was like Vince McMahon threatened the entire wrestling world with a fine if they didn't mention "number one free agent" and "Macho Man" in the same sentence.

Of course, everything was building up to a major reveal that they all hoped would shine the light on Savage even brighter: the announcement of Elizabeth as his manager. But before that, they had to squeeze every last ounce out of Savage's "free agency" angle for suspense and content.

"The other managers were vying for his talents. It was enticing," Lanny said. "Never been done."

It was also smart. For new wrestling fans who hadn't yet heard of Savage, what better way to legitimize him fast than to have headlining managers bidding against each other for his services?

On an episode of *Tuesday Night Titans* (Vince McMahon's signature wrestling talk show) shortly after defeating Aldo Marino, Macho Man stood in front of a panel of managers and took individual pitches like he was a young Michael Jordan listening to sneaker executives . . .

BOBBY "THE BRAIN" HEENAN:

You're the most sought-after free agent in professional wrestling today. And I'm the number one manager today. You like the way you dress? You like your style of living? I can improve all that. I can take you shopping every day in Beverly Hills. I can introduce you to stars and agents. I can take you places you've never been. Give me a shot, you'll be a rich man soon.

JIMMY HART:

Randy, the only thing I can say is this. Be home! When opportunity knocks you answer. This is the opportunity of a lifetime for you. I am your basic cut-rate, discount manager . . . My clothes aren't made in California, they're made in Memphis . . . Save your money. I'll make you money.

And one day you will be the heavyweight champion of the world. That is a promise from me to you!

CLASSY FREDDIE BLASSIE:

You don't want to start at the bottom. You want to start right at the top. I'm the only one here that managed a world heavyweight champion. I'm the only one loaded with diamonds. Wouldn't you like to have diamonds like this? Wouldn't you like to have walking-around money like this *[flashes a wad of cash]*? This is just walking-around money with Freddie Blassie. Thousands here! And I guarantee ya, there's more where this came from!

Despite these enticing offers, Macho Man remained unsigned throughout June and July, and every match he performed in featured all of the managers in tow, following him ringside, drooling over the chance to oversee his career.

Then, finally, on July 30, back in Poughkeepsie, New York, it happened. As Savage walked to the ring to face jobber Jim Young with Heenan, Hart and Blassie in attendance, Howard Finkel introduced him like this one final time:

"Out of Sarasota, Florida, weighing 235 pounds, the man who is in demand by wrestling managers galore, the number one free agent, Randy 'Macho Man' Savaaage!"

In the ring, Savage removed his green and silver robe while the managers looked on from the floor.

"It is reported that he is going to announce who his manager is and it's not, allegedly, one of these gentlemen. Maybe he's double-crossing everyone," Vince McMahon said.

Unfortunately for Jim Young, the wrestling match was standing in the way of the big announcement, so Macho Man dispatched him in about 60 seconds. He was tossed out of the ring, tossed into the ring, hit with a devastating suplex and then a flying elbow, and lights out. One. Two. Three. Done. Time to move on to the major news of the night:

Who will be Macho Man Randy Savage's manager?

Savage didn't waste any time, grabbing the microphone right after he was announced the winner.

"We got to know who the manager's gonna be of the future WWF World Champion," he said. "Right behind that door there is the Macho Man's new manager. Everybody get ready . . . This is a big, big moment . . . And heeeere . . . she comes!"

An orange door swung open and out walked Liz, now Miss Elizabeth. She looked like a supermodel. The men in the booth could hardly contain themselves.

"Oh oh oh, ohhh my," Bruno Sammartino said.

"Oh my goodness," McMahon said.

"What is this, some movie star? Who is this?" Gorilla Monsoon asked.

"Myyyy goodness. Take a look," McMahon added. "What a beautiful woman. My goodness! She is absolutely gorgeous!"

A buzz swept over the audience. Catcalls rained down. Whistles seemed to come from every direction. When Savage took Elizabeth's hand to show her off around the ring, the vision he'd discussed with McMahon at the WWF offices several months earlier came to fruition.

You couldn't take your eyes off them: Macho Man, the quintessential jacked athlete, and Miss Elizabeth, looking like she belonged on a Hollywood red carpet.

The crowd was completely captivated.

Mission accomplished.

"When Elizabeth appeared that night she walked down the aisle of wrestling history," Lanny said.

Keep in mind, however, that as beloved as the Macho Man is today, the WWF's goal in 1985 was to make you hate him. He was being groomed as the ultimate heel to eventually square off against the company's ultimate babyface, Hulk Hogan. A big part of that was to have the audience root *for* Miss Elizabeth and *against* Savage.

"Liz was a demure, quiet soul," Bruce Prichard said. "They were polar opposites. They wanted you to hate Macho Man and love Liz."

For that to happen, Savage had to give the audience a reason to loathe him. This was a lay-up for Savage. All he had to do was turn the Macho persona on full tilt and sprinkle in a little chauvinism.

He began by belittling her in their very first appearance together on *Tuesday Night Titans*. When asked why he chose Elizabeth to manage him over Hart, Heenan and the others, he compared her to a flowerpot:

> First of all, just realize one thing, when you got a piece of talent like myself, wrestling anybody in the world, I mean past, present and future. I mean, you really don't need much in the corner. Like I could grab a vase or a flowerpot and stick it in the corner right there and go out and whip Hulk Hogan and drop a big elbow on him and beat him one, two, three. But! The pizzazz factor would be lacking with a flowerpot! Yeah! That would be lacking, yeah! But with Elizabeth in the corner! Yeah, with Elizabeth in the corner, she's a small part of Macho Madness. A small part. But that's okay. The pizzazz factor.

With that shot across Miss Elizabeth's bow, his behavior towards her took care of the rest. He told her where to stand, what to say, when to say it, when to talk, when to shut up, and when to get off camera so he could have the spotlight. It was uncomfortable and uncouth and it worked to perfection. Quickly, as Scott Hall said, the fans "were hatin' on Randy for browbeatin' the girl."

All Savage needed to do now was put himself in position to challenge Hogan.

CHAPTER 20

Arriba!

Paul Roma was laughing his ass off. He was prepping for a match in the locker room of the Mid-Hudson Civic Center, checking his socks, his boots and his tight TNT network T-shirt over his 235-pound frame, when in walked the goofiest-looking guy he'd ever seen.

"You have to understand, I came from a non-wrestling world," Roma said. "I didn't follow pro wrestling. I played football. I was coming off the bodybuilding circuit. I had no clue. Nobody prepared me for the characters."

Especially a character like this one.

"I'm in the locker room and I see a guy walking towards me with the bright colors and 'Macho Man' written on his pants and I started chuckling," Roma said. "I turned to Mario Mancini and I asked, '*What the hell is that?*'"

"That's Randy Savage," Mancini said. "Keep it down. These guys take this stuff very seriously."

"He was walking around, chest out like he had two watermelons under his arms," Roma said. "It was brand new to me. To walk around like you're King Kong, arms out, like your back is a landing strip. That was funny."

Roma made his WWF debut about six months before Savage, in December of 1984. Born Paul Centopani, he'd been working mostly preliminary matches at the start of 1985 when he first encountered the Macho Man in Poughkeepsie. Roma was built like an NFL linebacker and would eventually become part of the popular tag team the Young Stallions with Jim Powers, but in that moment, he was young and amused.

"When I came up I was told that when you're out of the ring you become Paul Centopani, but when you're in the ring or around the ring, you're Paul Roma," Roma said. "I was able to do that. Some people couldn't.

"Randy dove into his character like nobody else. He'd walk through the airport with tassels and a cowboy hat, drawing attention to himself. He'd get to a gate with Elizabeth and sit far away from everyone. He'd be wearing his gimmick, but trying to avoid people. That was a far cry from the way I was taught by Mr. Fuji. But Randy lived it."

From August 1985 to the following February, Savage shot up through the ranks of the WWF like a rocket ship. By the end of the summer he was considered a World Top 10 wrestler by *Wrestling Observer* magazine and the number two contender in the WWF for Hulk Hogan's title behind the Dynamite Kid and ahead of "Mr. Wonderful" Paul Orndorff.

In a mix of house shows and live shows, he faced off against everyone from pikers to main-eventers. Rick McGraw, Jose Luis Rivera, George Wells, Ivan Putski, Dynamite Kid, Ricky Steamboat, Tito Santana, the Junkyard Dog and even Hulk Hogan in a house match.

"After a few months we found out what Randy Savage was all about," "Mean" Gene Okerlund said. "High flying moves off the top rope. The elbow. All the good stuff."

Roma faced Savage for the first time during this run at a WWF show in Madison Square Garden in front of 18,000 people.

"He was just getting going and it was no big deal at the time," Roma said. "I recall that during that match he came off the top rope with the elbow and he hit me with his hip in the top of the head and my face. He goes, 'Sorry man ... but can you take another one?' I said yes and he came off the second one and I was afraid to look in the mirror. He asked if I was okay, but I heard he overshot a lot."

The hardest part for Roma, whether he was wrestling Savage, Bad News Brown or "The Million Dollar Man" Ted DiBiase, was that the outcome of the matches was decided beforehand.

"I wanted to win at everything," he said. "It was hard to comprehend you had no say in the matter."

In 1985 and '86, there was no way Savage, the company's juggernaut, was going to lose to a new guy like Roma. The Macho Man was being fast-tracked to the top. There was no time for speed bumps. Only wins — wins against preliminary guys, wins against performers and wins against prime-time players — every moment of which was leading up to a match for the WWF Intercontinental Championship belt against Tito Santana in early 1986.

Although Macho Man liked to call himself the world's greatest athlete in wrestling because of his minor league baseball days, the WWF was littered with legit athletic talent in the 1980s. Paul Orndorff was a fullback and tight end for the University of Tampa who racked up 2,000 all-purpose yards and scored twenty-one touchdowns in his career. He was even selected in the 12th round of the 1973 NFL draft by the New Orleans Saints.

The Junkyard Dog, born Sylvester Ritter, was a dominant 6'4", 300-pound lineman for Fayetteville State University. He was an all-conference, two-time honorable mention All-American who got drafted by the Green Bay Packers before being injured at camp.

Ted DiBiase attended West Texas University on a football scholarship as well.

In a coincidence, Tito Santana also suited up for West Texas University on the gridiron. The 6'2", 230-pound former high school star played tight end, making twenty receptions and scoring five touchdowns his senior year. He was drafted by the Kansas City Chiefs but only played one year of pro ball, with the BC Lions of the Canadian Football League.

All of this is to say that while Savage was a superior athlete, he was not in rarefied air in the WWF. In fact, size-wise, he was still on the small side — no matter how much he lifted. Where he separated himself in those early days was with his character (obviously), his ring speed and his aerial acrobatics. The former football players listed above were much bigger than Savage in real life. Tight ends. Linemen. Fullbacks. You could see it in their thighs and quads and cores. These weren't low body fat, high muscle definition guys. They were tanks. They could all move weight.

Savage, despite being billed at 235, had skinny legs. He was top-heavy and against guys like Hogan, JYD and DiBiase, he still gave up between two and six inches in height and as much as fifty pounds. And it bugged him.

Psychologically, this was one of the main reasons that Randy adopted his elaborate costumes. Yes, they were loud and drew attention and helped him style and profile like his contemporary Ric Flair, but they also created the optical illusion that the Macho Man took up more space than he really did.

"Even though he's 20 or 30 percent bigger than me, relative to that game and that height and the look of [other wrestlers] he's not big," Michael Braun, Savage's longtime fashion designer, said.

Occasionally, when they'd be working together, Savage would mention that he was small. Braun understood what he meant.

"Here's a guy whose biceps are bigger than both my thighs put together," Braun said. "What he's trying to say is, 'The clothes help me and help the character visually for me to be believable.' The voice. The visual. The clothes."

Wrestler Diamond Dallas Page had the unique perspective of being a fan of Savage and then getting to wrestle him.

"I don't think he was six foot," Page said. "The way he moved and walked with his arms. He always looked like he was 6'3" to me. He was just one of those guys. Walked on his toes. He exemplified the way you should do this business, especially if you're not a giant."

For Savage, not being a giant was not going to be an excuse.

This was why he put such pressure on himself to nail every other part of his gimmick. He had no say in his height or genetics, but everything else involving the Macho Man presentation was under his domain. From the costumes to the microphone work to the events themselves, Savage was obsessed and meticulous; and while extreme attention to detail gave him an edge, during his first year in the WWF he didn't see eye-to-eye with some veterans like Tito Santana over his obsessive-compulsive nature when planning matches.

Santana happened to be the Intercontinental Championship belt holder when Savage entered the WWF. He'd won the belt in the summer of '85, just as Macho Man joined the company. Now, he found himself directly in the path of Macho's ascendance. The WWF viewed the Intercontinental Heavyweight Championship as a critical stepping stone for Savage on his way to a collision with Hulk Hogan, cutting Santana's reign short.

Santana didn't care. He was a pro's pro. Since joining the WWF for a second time in 1983, he'd become one of the more popular wrestlers on the roster and he'd recently finished a years-long angle for the belt with Greg "The Hammer" Valentine that included lumberjack matches, no-disqualification matches and steel cage matches.

He was not one to quibble about winning or losing a belt, but the way Savage prepared was different from what he was used to.

"When Macho Man first got into the WWE, he'd come out with about three pages of notes [on] how he wanted the match to go," Santana said. "And us legends, we didn't use notes. We just went out there and called the match."

This "call-it-on-the-fly" strategy worked for most of the established stars. Didn't matter if it was a house show, pay-per-view or title match, they'd have a general idea of what they wanted to do and who was going to win and go from there. Unfortunately for Savage, until he established himself as a superstar who could dictate matches and plan how he wanted them to go, he had to learn how to get along the hard way.

"It wasn't easy for him at the beginning," Santana said. "Because he'd come up with a whole list of what he wanted to do . . . He'd have it all written out . . . And sometimes he'd get totally lost. But once he learned, he became one of the best."

Savage's title shot with Santana happened on February 8, 1986, in the legendary Boston Garden, home of the Celtics. When the WWF arrived in Beantown on a freezing winter night, the Celtics were on a 13-game winning streak on the way to 67 wins and an NBA championship against the Houston Rockets. It was a fitting destination for Randy Savage to win his first WWF belt. The only difference was that instead of being serenaded with cheers like Larry Bird, Robert Parish and Kevin McHale, the angle was for the Macho Man to be victorious and vilified.

What was the best way to do this?

Cheating, of course.

The night in the Garden kicked off with Lanny Poffo beating Paul Christy in the opening match, followed by Sivi Afi vs. Barry O, George "The Animal" Steele vs. Tiger Chung Lee and then Big John Studd vs. Hillbilly Jim.

Then, in the middle of the card, we got Savage vs. Santana.

For the special occasion, Savage wore a billowing, hot air balloon–sized, blue sequined robe with "Macho Man" written in silver and gigantic stars spread across the back. Miss Elizabeth wore a matching blue dress. After Savage was announced as the challenger, proof of his drawing power was immediately evident. Heel or not, a majority of the Garden clapped and cheered for him, and then turned it up louder when Miss Elizabeth was announced.

Santana, wearing a simple "Arriba Santana" black shirt, received an uncharacteristic amount of boos mixed in with the cheers. After an eight-month buildup for Savage, the angle had paid off. His road from Memphis to the land of Mike's Pastry outlets left fans ready for him to become a champion.

Compared to the plodding pace of the previous matches, these two appeared to be on hyper speed. Sprints. Clotheslines. Double axe handles. Santana going for his signature Flying Jalapeno move. Eye pokes. More flying axe handles. False finishes. After nine minutes of fury, Santana was able to secure Macho Man with his devastating figure four leglock.

He sold the agony, fought through it, and was able to turn the move over into the ropes. Once free, Savage went for a foreign object (a small metal pipe) in his trunks several times (in perfect view of the cameras), fended off suplexes and another figure four leglock, before finally clocking Santana with the object and knocking him out. Macho Man dove on top for the cover and . . .

One . . .

Two . . .

Three . . .

"We got a new champion! We got a new Intercontinental Champion, Monsoon!" Jesse Ventura shouted on the call.

"Do you believe in miracles?" It's not, but it's as good as it got for Macho Man up to that point. Before referee Danny Davis raised his hand to signal the victory, Savage tossed the small steel pipe out of the ring, grabbed the belt and hugged it like it was a lost puppy who just returned home.

"You gotta call it brilliant," Ventura said, referring to the pipe.

"I call it cheating," Monsoon replied.

While Santana lay "unconscious" on the mat, Macho Man, selling an injured knee from the leglock, writhed around the mat, limping and clutching his coveted new belt.

"The rest is history," Santana said. "He became a real good worker and good talker. I enjoyed all my matches with him. I never had any problems with him."

Later, in an interview with "Mean" Gene Okerlund, with Macho hugging the belt to his chest over a purple leopard print shirt, he gave an interview that blurred the lines between the real man and the Macho Man:

> Talkin' about history, talkin' about history, yeah. One date, aww yeah, just in my mind. February 8 in Boston, Massachusetts, at the Boston Garden, yeah. Where Larry Bird plays basketball! Yeah. And the Boston Celtics are a real tough team. But uh . . . I think if I played basketball, maaan . . . the way I am . . . and the super athlete that I am . . . I would overshadow Larry Bird! Because on that particular night in Boston I was the greatest professional in the world! Oh proud! Yeah, I'm proud! . . . And a lot people out there . . . You know . . . They're gettin' into Macho Madness really super strong. And Macho Madness, yeah! Growin', growin', growin' . . . and more seductive than sex!

"You can't say that," Okerlund says perfectly as the straight man.

"I *can* say that," Macho says, snapping his fingers.

CHAPTER 21

Intercontinental Champion

Gym. Travel. Wrestle. Repeat.

This was the glamorous life for Randy and Liz, the newly married, newly famous couple. They'd gone from kicking around small towns like Chattanooga, Clarksville and Kingsport with a home base in Lexington to jetting in and out of Philadelphia, Washington DC and Chicago with a new home base in New York City.

They'd gone national. It was nice. It was exhausting.

Savage found himself flying through the tri-state area with enough frequency that he bought a condo on Staten Island out of sheer convenience.

"I'm in and out of Newark so much that I need a crash-type place," he said.

Did he care about resale value? Good restaurants nearby? Easy parking? Nope.

He only cared about one thing: proximity to a weight room.

"When I look for a place, I try to find a place where I get along with the gym," Savage said. "And when I met Ralph, we hit it off."

Ralph is Ralph Venice, the former owner of the old Bath Beach Body Building gym in New Springville, dead center in the middle of the island.

"Whenever I'm in Staten Island," Savage told the local paper after buying the condo, "I do all my working out at Bath Beach."

The gym was Savage's anchor. His sanctuary. It was that way in the minors, in Lexington and now as a main eventer in the WWF.

On the road, he relied on his bodybuilder pal Paul Roma to point out the best places to get a pump because neither man was willing to let their physique suffer from their insane travel schedules. This commitment to the iron was something that separated Roma from the pack in Savage's eyes. There was a mutual respect there that he didn't have with other wrestlers. He let Roma behind the character a little bit.

"Lifting was a priority and everything depended on the flight," Roma said. "If I was able to have breakfast before getting on the flight and I knew the town and I knew the gym, then we'd land, check into the hotel and go right to lift."

As soon as they'd hit the ground Savage would pepper Roma with questions.

"Hey, Roma," he'd ask. "What's the gym we're going to here?"

"I'd tell him I knew of a Gold's Gym in this town or a World's Gym near downtown in another city. I trained with Hercules mostly. He was the only guy who could train with me because of my methodology. But Randy knew what he was doing. By that time he was doing a regular bodybuilding rotation. Bench, curls, shoulders, shrugs, leg days. He'd get a full sweat going and have the belt on. When I see someone training hard as hell like that I respect him. I don't put anyone over like that. I'd see him on the way out of these gyms and say, 'You busted your ass today.'"

"Thanks, Roma," Savage would say. "I appreciate that."

The training sessions gave Roma a glimpse into Savage's psyche — showed him what Savage valued.

"Guys like Jake 'the Snake' smoked, drank, took drugs," Roma said. "That was how they were. I didn't see that out of Randy. He cared about his character too much. So what if he couldn't have a natural body like theirs? He was willing to work.

"He also liked to see who he could trust. He liked to know that if you talked to him, your conversation wasn't going to be shared with everyone. Like he'd ask me about the best foods to eat post-workout . . . But he only did that once he knew I wasn't the type of guy to run around to the other wrestlers and say, 'Randy asked me what I should eat today.' That

Randy Poffo ditching his clean-cut minor league baseball look

A young, skinny Randy Poffo in an early wrestling interview

Angelo and Lanny flexing at the start of Lanny's career

BELOW LEFT: No longer Randy Poffo. Randy Savage is born.

BELOW RIGHT: Randy shows off his new 210-pound physique.

The Macho Man plays to the crowd.

Full beard. Full cape. Headband. We've reached early Macho Man status.

Macho Man holds up a coveted ICW championship belt.

Macho Man and Miss Elizabeth get
ready for a match.

Leaping through the air for a signature
elbow drop

Macho and the First
Lady of Wrestling

Fired up. Energy on 10.
Macho incites a crowd.

Full height angle of
Macho's famous leap
off the top ropes

Center of the ring and
attention. Macho and
Elizabeth with a title.

Macho enjoying his
run as King

Macho whips Hogan into the ropes.

One of many battles between the Hulkster and Macho

No more robes. Macho Man has gone full neon.

Lanny Poffo reading one of his famous poems

The Macho King in all his glory

Promo photo with Hulk
Hogan at the peak of his fame

Randy Savage loved showing
off his famous scepter as king.

Macho Man in an early photo
of his orange and yellow Slim
Jim colors

Randy Savage gives the crowd a
fist pump and "oooh yeahhh!"

Randy Savage decked
out for the Match Made
in Heaven

The Macho Man and
Elizabeth say "I do" at
SummerSlam.

Classic Randy pose
before going off the
top ropes

Randy joins the nWo in the WCW.

Randy Savage
pummels fellow icon
Ric Flair.

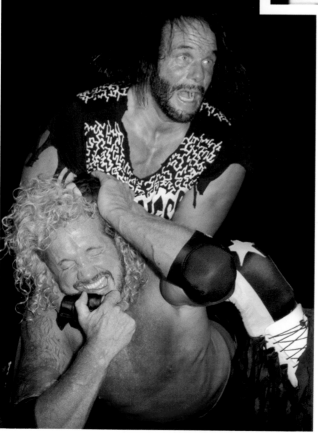

Macho Man in
one of his classic
matches with
Diamond Dallas Page

Reconciling with
Miss Elizabeth for
their WCW run

Lanny Poffo inducts
the Macho Man
into the WWE Hall
of Fame.

didn't matter to me. But some guys would do that. He didn't trust many people for that reason."

In the world of wrestling and meatheads, there aren't many more important things two dudes can bond over than training — sharing what works and trashing what doesn't. Roma was an avid fan of certain supplement companies and he'd share them with Savage. He'd talk about the dangers of fast food and fried foods, and Macho Man listened.

"I know some people looked at Randy and thought he was an asshole or that he was a dick," Roma said. "But you have to take the time to get to know who he is and what he was about. He didn't let everyone in, but he wasn't a phony at all. He didn't care if you liked him or not, but he was the same with everybody."

Even as Savage got his first taste of true stardom as the Intercontinental Champion, he was gaining a reputation for being a bit of a loner within the WWF. He'd spent the early part of his career crammed in a sedan with Angelo and Lanny. People who *knew* him — people who knew what he'd been through. As he made a name for himself, he kept his inner circle as small as possible.

Wrestlers who got a peek behind the curtain all say they could tell when Randy didn't trust someone. They would watch in amusement as he forced his way through a conversation. He was polite but quick; curt and concise. Or he might just blow someone off. Depended entirely on his mood.

While he was one of the boys in the minor leagues, playing poker and screwing around in the locker room, those days were long gone. Legendary card games would take place on airplanes or in the WWF locker room with all the big names, and Savage almost always passed.

Andre the Giant asked him to play all the time. Roma and others did too.

"If he had wanted to, he'd have cleaned them out," Lanny said.

"I think he was a deep thinker and I got that about him," Roma said. "He wasn't into a lot of that stuff. Some guys might say, 'Look at that asshole.' But he wasn't that . . .

"I'd see him get really mad at people. Irate even . . . But you know what? He was great with kids. One time later in my career I was with my little boy and we were talking to Miss Elizabeth and he came over and was really nice. He joked around with him . . . Then he said, 'Roma, you're killing me, man. Elizabeth wants a kid like this.' It was a joking thing. Not many people saw that side of him. I have all the respect in the world for how he was."

The "Randy was great with kids" theme is something that comes up over and over again in conversations with people who knew him and spent time with him, even at the height of his fame. At some point they'll stop and say, "Not many people know this, but Randy was incredible with kids" or "Did you know Mach would do anything for kids?"

This included the kids of his rival wrestlers.

One grade schooler who got to see the playful side of the Macho Man up close was Travis Orndorff, the son of "Mr. Wonderful" Paul Orndorff.

"Or, as Randy called my dad, Mr. So-So," Travis laughed.

This jab came from a terrific bit of trash talk by the Macho Man before an Intercontinental Title defense against Mr. Wonderful in Philadelphia at the Spectrum:

> I'm really looking forward to defending this, yeah . . .
> The Intercontinental Heavyweight Championship belt
> against Mr. Articulate! Yeah. Paul Orndorff, yeah. Mr.
> Wonderful . . . He calls himself Mr. Wonderful yeah . . .
> BUT IN COMPARISON! To the Macho Man Randy
> Savage you're Mr. So-So. Yeah . . . And I am pointing my
> finger at you and saying Paul Orndorff, you haven't got a
> chance! NO YOU HAVEN'T! . . . Paul Mr. Wonderful
> Orndorff! You're so-so! IN COMPARISON!

"Back then my dad was wrestling seven days a week, hitting three or four towns within a decent distance," Travis said. "They'd get a huge tour bus and the guys would drive. If the cities were close my dad would take me."

The WWF tour bus in the mid-1980s wasn't some sad Greyhound used to shuttle Little League travel teams to tournaments. This thing was a beast. It was fifty feet long and had tables, two-seater rows, a few beds and enough room to haul twelve to fifteen of the largest guys you can imagine over state lines. It was a Guns N' Roses concert tour bus, but for giants.

Travis was in third and fourth grade in '85 and '86 when his dad started to let him travel with "the boys." It was every eight-year-old's dream: free time behind the scenes with the giants (Andre), dogs (Junkyard), animals (George), dragons (Ricky) and all kinds of "men" (Million Dollar, Honky Tonk and of course Macho).

"The Junkyard Dog taught me how to play poker," Travis laughed.

Wrestlers would pass the time on the bus as you'd expect: movies, cards, shooting the shit, busting each other's balls, napping, eating. Randy Savage usually sat in the back, keeping to himself. The guys knew he wasn't one for idle chitchat and they mostly left him alone.

On one ride, Mr. Wonderful decided to have a little fun with the Macho Man. He sent his young son over to pull one of the oldest pranks in the book.

"The first time I met Randy I was sitting on the bus with my dad and he nudged me on the shoulder with an idea to mess with the Macho Man," Travis said. "So I got up and walked down the aisle towards him and when I got to him I said, 'Hey Randy, you have something on your shirt.' And I pointed to a spot on his shirt. When he looked down I flicked his nose. Everyone was watching. He gave me a stare for a minute like he was going to be pissed, but then he started laughing."

Every time Savage saw him after that when Travis was little, he'd put his finger on Travis's shirt, get him to look down and flick his nose. In the moment, Travis thought it was just a cool thing to do with one of his wrestling heroes, but as he got older, he realized how special those moments with Randy were because not everybody got them.

"Randy was not the big, boisterous person without the camera on," Travis said. "He was very chill. He was introverted. But he was always gentle with me. He was always funny with me. Over the course of my life I was around hundreds of wrestlers who never even noticed me. But Randy always made me feel noticed. Even in those minor moments. I was a kid but he always treated me with respect. It was a huge compliment."

As Travis got to know Randy a little bit, he noticed that the Macho Man rarely let his guard down with other people. He stayed in "Macho mode" most of the time and few people saw the humorous side to him.

Travis also got to witness firsthand how Savage's obsession with matches would differ from other wrestlers. While most guys would prepare for a match with a two- or three-minute chat, Randy would insist on hours-long conversations.

"When my dad and Terry [Hulk Hogan] would talk before a match, they'd talk for four minutes and the finish was already planned," Travis said. "Randy would pull my dad or someone in the hallway for an hour. I remember bouncing around the locker room and I'd see Randy talking to someone for a long time and I'd ask what they were doing and my dad would say, 'Oh, you know, he's just planning his match. Randy is very meticulous.'"

Randy and Paul didn't develop a close friendship over the years, but they had a high level of mutual respect. They recognized in each other the full package: the skill set, the body, the wrestling savvy. Mr. Wonderful was known to be one of the strongest guys in the WWF and Savage acknowledged that. He always held powerful guys like Orndorff and Pez Whatley in high regard.

"Randy was strong," Travis said. "But he wasn't 'my dad' strong. My dad had ungodly strength. He was over 6'2" and over 250 pounds."

The respect Savage had for Paul and Travis Orndorff lasted throughout his life. Travis remembers a series of little moments where they'd run into each other throughout his childhood: once at Disneyland, where Macho bought him a Coke; another time when Macho congratulated Travis after he won a karate tournament.

In one instance, Paul and Travis ran into Savage when it had been almost a decade since they'd seen each other. As soon as Randy saw Travis, he pointed to Travis's shirt and did the nose prank.

"Every time I saw Randy he was happy and respectful to see me," Travis said.

Savage's affinity for kids even extended to a random teenager who unbeknownst to the wrestler or the teen would one day portray the Macho Man on a hit television show.

Kevin Makely grew up in Poughkeepsie, New York, and went to as many of Macho's early shows in the Civic Center as possible. He worshipped Savage, even dressing up as the wrestling icon for Halloween on several occasions. Macho was *his guy*.

One night, as Makely headed towards the bathroom in the Dutchess Diner after a WWF show, the door opened and out strolled the Macho Man in full gear. Jeans. Sunglasses. Leather jacket. Bandana on his head.

Makely froze, until Macho saw that the kid was starstruck and stuck out his hand.

"He didn't blow me off at all," Makely said. "He shook my hand and took the time to talk to me for a bit. I was just a kid in a diner. He did the voice and the movements and all of it. It was stellar."

Who knew that three decades after the meeting, Makely, an actor, would portray his idol on *Young Rock*?

When Luis Rojas was eleven years old he won a *WWF Magazine* "Lunch with Your Favorite Manager" contest. Out of 400,000 entries, Rojas was selected for a dream meal with Miss Elizabeth and her better half. It included a limousine ride to the hotel with his dad and sister and tickets to that night's wrestling match.

"I freaked out when I found out I won," Rojas said. "Randy Savage is my favorite wrestler."

When the Rojas family arrived at the Marriott in Miami where the famous wrestling couple were staying, they weren't sure what to expect. Sometimes winners of such contests find out that "lunch" ends up being a smile, a handshake, an autograph, a quick photo session and that's it.

Not so with Randy and Liz.

Rojas's eyes widened when he saw the couple actually walking towards him in the restaurant. Miss Elizabeth was wearing a white summer outfit and Savage was full Macho Man, with jeans, an animal-print sleeveless shirt, leather wristbands and a bright headband.

Then they sat down and told Rojas to "fire away." Through bites of food, Luis asked why Randy chose Miss Elizabeth, what Miss Elizabeth thought when he first asked her, and what it's like to be his manager.

"I just make sure everything goes smoothly when we get into town," she answered. "I try to keep the little things from bothering him. It's hard work but it's a lot of fun."

Luis's sister, Vanessa, had her own questions for Elizabeth as the four sat on a bench and talked after the meal. Jerry Brisco, a former WWF promoter, wasn't surprised that Elizabeth was drawing the same focus as Randy.

"There's never been anybody as a manager that's caused the attention and created disturbances like Elizabeth," he said. "There's never been a lady manager known nationally like that. There are other female managers in wrestling right now but they're all imitations. Her beauty surpasses any of them."

The Macho Man and Miss Elizabeth stayed right up until it was time for all of them to leave — Rojas in a limousine to the arena to watch and Savage and Elizabeth behind them to perform. But before they left, Luis made sure to let his favorite wrestler know one thing.

"I think you'll beat Hulk Hogan whenever you wrestle," Rojas said.

"Ohhhh yeahhh," Macho replied.

Luis Rojas, like millions of other fans, had fallen hook, line and sinker for the long-game storyline that the WWF was laying out: Hulk Hogan and the Hulkamaniacs versus the Macho Man and Macho Madness.

But they were in no hurry.

After Savage took possession of the Intercontinental Heavyweight Belt, the WWF spent the next year creating angles with different wrestlers to increase the importance of that belt and let the audience simmer with other rivalries.

They also wanted time for Macho's "#1 Heel" status to be cemented, though he was so unique and charismatic that his popularity rose just as much as his bad-guy image. This led to somewhat contradictory responses from fans. He'd get massive ovations *and* complaints about his staged behavior towards Elizabeth at the exact same time.

While Savage was successfully defending his title against a slew of challengers like Ricky "The Dragon" Steamboat and Jake "The Snake" Roberts, the WWF fans were dividing themselves into pro–bad guy and anti–bad guy camps. Some viewers became so upset with Macho Man's antics, they wrote into their local newspaper.

One reader in Illinois sent the following to the editorial board of *The Dispatch* in 1986:

CIVILIZE THE SAVAGE

I'm a big fan of WWF Wrestling. I watch it every Sunday, and I watch "Wrestling Mania" on Saturday nights. What I'd like to SPEAK OUT about is the Macho Man, Randy Savage, the way he treats Elizabeth. He treats her really bad, even on television, in front of hundreds of thousands of people. I don't know whether this is an act or if this is the way he treats her, but if it is an act, I think the acting stinks. I think he should change, and I think he should treat her a lot differently. I think there is something really wrong with Randy Savage.

This kind of reaction was *exactly* what Savage was going for. He'd have been delighted reading it. *We're getting over. Oh yeah!* Then his next thought would be, *How can we turn up the heat?*

The answer to that question was a multi-level storyline beginning with veteran wrestler George "The Animal" Steele falling in love with Elizabeth and wanting to protect her from the brutish Randy Savage. The storyline worked because Steele's gimmick was that he was part caveman, part child. He was a wrestling version of Forrest Gump, but instead of being smitten with Jenny, The Animal was head-over-heels in love with Elizabeth, though he barely spoke and had the IQ of a bowling ball.

This was all the more amusing because the man behind the green-tongued, turnbuckle-chomping Animal was Jim Myers, who was the character's total opposite. Far from being a simpleton, Myers was a former Michigan State football player and educator. He had earned his master's from Central Michigan and was a high school teacher and football coach at Madison Heights in Michigan while he wrestled.

"Truth be told, Vince had no real long-term plans for Randy and me. None of us knew how our feud would go over," Myers said in his autobiography, *Animal*. "Randy was the heel and I had become a loveable cartoon character. It soon became apparent the possibilities were endless, and most of them revolved around Miss Elizabeth."

As their rivalry unfolded, a pattern developed during their matches that audiences began anticipating. The Macho Man and the Animal would wrestle. At some point the Animal would catch Elizabeth's eye and he'd become transfixed.

Every fan watching would have the same reaction: *Uh-oh . . . Don't do it, George! Stop staring! Stop looking at her, George! No . . . Don't touch her, George!*

George couldn't help himself and as he'd reach to stroke Elizabeth's hair or to touch her hand, he'd unleash the wrath of the Macho Man. The formula was so powerful that viewers found themselves rooting for Miss Elizabeth to end up with a toddler-brained Neanderthal over Savage.

The in-ring collision between Savage and Steele was only the visible part of their struggle. Behind the scenes there was a clash of styles and preparation. Savage, just as he'd done with Tito Santana, approached Steele with a step-by-step plan for their first big match. Steele was nearly fifty years old at this point. He'd begun wrestling when Randy was in Little League in Downers Grove. In fact, he knew Randy when he was a little kid because he'd worked with Angelo in Detroit.

Needless to say, the outline was received poorly.

"Randy showed up in the locker room with a script that was probably four or five pages long," Steele wrote. "I felt like he wanted me to audition for something by Scorsese. What was this, pro wrestling or Broadway? Now, I was an old-school guy. I learned the business in the backseats of cars going to and coming back from shows in places like Kalamazoo and Muskegon . . . I went to school between bites of bologna sandwiches and swigs of beer . . . Everything was impromptu. There were no scripted scenarios, there were only instincts."

The way Steele and Santana and the earlier generation of wrestlers were taught was to communicate in the ring and pay attention to the crowd. If something was firing them up, keep doing it — drive the crowd into a frenzy, pull back, then do it again. To a guy like Steele, the concept of mapping out every moment of action in the ring wasn't just crazy — it was insulting.

"To be honest, I took offense to what Randy was proposing," he said. "So I pretended to read the first page, slowly crumpled the paper, tossed it in the trash can. I did the same thing with the rest of the pages, very slowly and very deliberately. All the while, Randy was going ballistic. I just told him to calm down, listen to me in the ring, and we'd have a great match."

Though the matches weren't "great" in a classical sense. By this time, Steele was far past his prime and Savage was in the peak of his.

"Randy respected what George had done in the business. He knew he used to be a great athlete. But he didn't like the matches very much," Lanny said. "There was only so much he could do."

Translation: they weren't sprinting around the ring, countering each other with exciting, high-flying acrobatic moves. From a wrestling standpoint, the Macho Man was in a much different class than the Animal. Instead, the matches served one purpose: to enrage the crowd further against Savage and to continue to manufacture "concern" for Elizabeth.

These fights also highlighted a growing problem that more and more wrestlers were noticing off-camera: Randy's jealousy over Elizabeth.

At times, it seemed he was buying into his own fictional storylines. Instead of seeing Jim Myers, the happily married 50-year-old coworker with a daughter older than Elizabeth, he saw George Steele, the bald, hairy old wrestler trying to take his woman in front of his own eyes.

During one particular match, when Steele carried Elizabeth out of the ring, Savage was heard shouting backstage, "What are they going to think that George is doing with my wife?"

The question, if asked sincerely, was laughable.

The audience was going to think exactly what you'd staged for them to think!

That he's protecting her from you!

Over time the schtick became a sticking point. Vince would tell Steele to do something that would incite Macho Man the wrestler and it would piss off Randy Savage the person. The Junkyard Dog would make a joke about Miss Elizabeth the WWF manager and Randy would take it as a joke about Elizabeth, his wife.

Understandably, things could get confusing with so many storylines to juggle. But there was no real-world scenario where Randy Savage the man had to worry about Elizabeth, his wife, leaving him for a 275-pound, hirsute 50-year-old from the Paleolithic Era — on national television no less.

Thankfully for all involved, this particular angle played itself out over the course of 1986 and 1987 before it became shoehorned into the next major storyline for the Macho Man: a feud with one of the most beloved wrestlers of all time, Ricky "The Dragon" Steamboat.

"My brother believed with all his heart that Steamboat was the greatest babyface in the business," Lanny said. "He was a pure good guy and Randy felt the two of them would be sensational in the ring. He asked to work with Steamboat directly."

What happened next was magical.

CHAPTER 22

Dragon, We Got 'Em

You're not as cool as seventy-year-old Ricky "The Dragon" Steamboat. Period. Full stop.

You have a home office; he has the "Dragon's Den." You wear old sweatpants and a T-shirt; he rocks a pristine red karate gi with dragons etched on the front and his initials, RS, monogrammed on the chest. You have photos and trinkets and a few framed accomplishments hanging up; he has half the damn history of wrestling on his wall.

And that's just the beginning.

He's got plaques commemorating his induction into three (yes, three) wrestling halls of fame: the NWA, the DCW and the WWE, the last of which includes a photo of his hall of fame class.

"There's me, Howard Finkel, Dory and Terry Funk, Koko B. Ware, Cowboy Bill Watts, Stone Cold Steve Austin and Kevin Von Erich from the famous wrestling family," Steamboat says proudly.

Next to that is a section of the wall he calls "Mid-Atlantic Memories." This is a collection of photos from his time wrestling in the territories in the late 1970s. One image stands out. It's Steamboat, mid-air, ready to drop the hammer on a large man standing in the ring.

"I'm coming off the top rope with a chop against Harley Race," Steamboat says. "That was the first time I wrestled with a world champion. It was a one-hour timed match."

As he moves around the Dragon's Den, familiar faces pop up in every framed photo. Steamboat and Jay Youngblood. Steamboat and Jimmy "Superfly" Snuka. Steamboat and Steve Austin. Steamboat and Ric Flair.

"The Nature Boy [Flair] was heavily responsible for getting me to the main events," Steamboat says. "Flair got me up and our feud went on for seventeen years."

A slew of trophies sit on a long shelf adjacent to the hall of fame plaques, with framed photos of Steamboat posing in bodybuilding trunks onstage. He dabbled in physique competitions during the early part of his wrestling career, taking top honors in several. His favorite is a first place finish in the WBBG Southern States competition, edging out his buddy Snuka in a pose down.

Next to the trophies, surrounded by a photo of Steamboat with Muhammad Ali backstage at Madison Square Garden (from WrestleMania I) and an original cover of the Steamboat *Tales of Wrestling* comic, hangs the centerpiece of the wall — the seatback of a blue stadium chair.

A chair?

Yes, but not just any old chair.

"This is a seatback from the Pontiac Silverdome," Steamboat says. "They tore it down, but I requested to get seat #3 to represent WrestleMania III and my match there with Randy Savage."

The chair displays the following inscription:

"Seatback from the Silverdome, March 19, 1987, World Record Attendance, 93,173."

Above the seat is an original yellow billing for WrestleMania III with Hulk Hogan and Andre the Giant as the main event and Randy Savage and Ricky Steamboat listed below. On top of that is a photo of Steamboat holding Savage over his head in a chokehold from their match.

"Always have to pay homage to the Macho Man and the classic match that we had at WrestleMania III," Steamboat says. "We never used the catchphrase that we wanted to 'steal the show,' we just wanted to go out and have the match of the night."

While that last statement may be the truth, make no mistake: Savage and Steamboat 100 percent *did* steal the show. To many, they created the most memorable match in wrestling history.

The rivalry between Savage and Steamboat began as these things often do, with one man dropping another man onto a metal barricade throat-first, then leaning that man up on the barricade by his voice box and hitting him with a double axe handle from fifteen feet in the air, *then*, while the man with the injured voice box writhes on the wrestling mat after being dragged by his hair, the first man grabs the bell that signals the beginning and end of each match, carries it with him to the top rope and leaps off with it, slamming it into the other man's neck and smashing his larynx.

The above sequence took place on a *WWF Superstars of Wrestling* episode that aired on November 22, 1986, four full months before the next year's WrestleMania. The man with the crushed larynx was Steamboat. The man doing the crushing was Savage.

To keep this storyline in context, it's important to note that Savage was the Intercontinental Champion and that Steamboat had just pinned Savage for nearly twenty seconds in front of a pro-Steamboat audience, but the referee had been knocked out and couldn't make the count. When the referee finally came to and started counting, a second referee ran into the ring and stopped him, again saving Savage from a loss and giving him time to recover while Steamboat argued his case.

This was the scenario they concocted to ignite the feud between the Macho Man and the Dragon, and it worked on multiple levels. First, Savage's attack on Steamboat's windpipe was cruel and vicious and visceral. It made you hate Randy. *Why is he doing this?? Somebody stop him!!!*

Ricky sold it like a champion, and as he clutched his throat and struggled to breathe, the injury *felt real*. This leads to the second reason it worked. The "injury" wasn't an absurd physical injury that wouldn't make sense if he came back too soon. Who the hell knows how long a larynx takes to heal? Nobody. This leads to the third and fourth reasons as to why it worked so well. The injury allowed the WWF to film live "check-ins" on Steamboat's condition with doctors and from hospital rooms without any real frame of reference people might have like with a broken arm or collarbone. It also took Steamboat out of shows until WrestleMania, giving the feud time to boil over.

"From the time he dropped the bell on my throat until WrestleMania, we had a three-month buildup," Steamboat said. "In other words, we had the time to elaborate on the storyline. If you drill into their heads week after week and it goes for three months, people will have a better, fond memory of why these two guys are having this blow-off match."

During those three months, Steamboat wasn't wrestling at all, keeping up the impression that he was "recuperating" from his injury.

"About a month out from WrestleMania I asked the home office if Savage and I were going to have any tune-up matches," Steamboat said. "Vince said, 'No, you're going to make your debut on the day of the show.'"

This gave the two performers the time they needed to prepare for what they both hoped would be the greatest match of their lives.

"My brother loved Steamboat as a performer. He believed that Ricky was the most talented guy out there," Lanny said. "They were the same size. They were both athletic. They could match each other with speed and agility. This gave them tremendous chemistry. Randy knew what Ricky was capable of doing in the ring and he thought they could bring the best out of each other."

While Tito Santana and George "The Animal" Steele were from an earlier generation of wrestlers who bristled at Savage's desire to orchestrate a match move-by-move ahead of time, in Ricky Steamboat he not only had a contemporary, he had a kindred spirit.

"That's what I worked on my whole career," Savage said in an interview later in his life. "Putting matches together and scouting my opponents to see who would blend with my style of work."

Steamboat blended with him effortlessly, like chocolate syrup and milk. Even better, he cared about every bit of the performance as much Savage did. He was a perfectionist, after the Macho Man's own heart. This was a guy who studied the best actors in Hollywood and used what he learned about acting in the ring. Whenever he watched a movie, he'd pull himself out of the film and focus on the individual performances.

How did this actor show pain? How did they play off another actor's emotion? How are they showing fury with their eyes? Steamboat said he watched *Raging Bull* a dozen times to study Robert DeNiro's boxing work in the ring.

So this time, when Savage put together pages of notes in preparation for his match, he wasn't presenting them to someone who'd pretend to read them and toss them in the trash like George Steele. He was dealing with someone who had their own pages of notes as well.

It was a match made in heaven.

"The Macho Man was anal about every step of the match and so was I," Steamboat said. "We knew from the numbers that were talked about ahead of WrestleMania III that it was going to be a big event. The pay-per-view numbers, the seats that were being pre-sold. All big. Andre and Hulk Hogan were headlining the show, but Savage and I were the match right before them. And we wanted to go out and have the match of the evening."

For most matches at the time, the two wrestlers would know the finish of the match but then call everything else in the ring. They might talk *some* strategy and come up with false finishes (pins where a wrestler kicks out before the count of three), but maybe not. In a big-time match, you might get a half-dozen false finishes. Maybe more.

Savage and Steamboat wanted to have a championship-caliber match, and with Steamboat sidelined from on-camera wrestling until WrestleMania, Savage spent every free minute with him running through the match step-by-step.

"It was like paint-by-numbers," Lanny said. "Randy's expectation was perfection."

Steamboat remembers the process well, right down to the yellow legal pads they used to map out their ideas.

"We wrote down the entire match going on our gut feeling," he said. "Every step. When we got to the end it was 150 steps. Then we spent the rest of our time quizzing each other. I'd say . . . 'step number thirty-four is this' and then I'd say, 'Randy, what's next?' And then in his voice he'd say 'number thirty-five is this and number thirty-six is this . . .' We'd go back and forth over and over again leading up to the match."

Legendary WWF interviewer Mean Gene Okerlund, who'd conducted many of the interviews with Macho Man and Dragon in the buildup to the fight, knew about the amount of creative energy being expended on it by the two stars. Typically, the WWF home office would have an equal hand in deciding how the match would go, but not this time.

"I know that Vince and Pat Patterson had a lot of input early on," Okerlund said. "But somewhere along the line, I believe Randy Savage and Ricky Steamboat made the final decisions as to what they were going to do on their own. It didn't come from Vince McMahon. It didn't come from Pat Patterson. And look at the product you got."

Savage even went so far as to request which referee he wanted for the match — in this case, Dave Hebner.

"Working with Randy, everything had to be on a dime," Hebner said. "We went to the office where they have all the rings set up. We worked our butts off a month before to go over everything and get it right. Nobody had ever done this. I had to know everything that was going on, which is an awful lot of finishes for me to remember. I couldn't sleep the night before knowing that tomorrow I was going to have the biggest match in the world."

In the days leading up to WrestleMania III, Hulk Hogan's image was everywhere. Billboards. Magazine covers. Newspaper spreads. He was the face of the WWF and their biggest event. The two photos that got the most ink were a tough-guy headshot of him pointing straight at the camera and another where he was wearing the heavyweight championship belt and giving a full double biceps pose.

A third ubiquitous image was a "tale of the tape" graphic the WWF created comparing their headliners, Andre the Giant and Hulk Hogan, side by side. They list Hogan as 6'8", 294 pounds with a 58" chest (and his famous 24" pythons). Andre is billed as 7'4", 525 pounds with a 71" chest.

However, the biggest story in the mainstream media heading into WrestleMania III didn't involve a match at all. Instead it revolved around the stunning popularity of wrestling itself. The fact that millions of people now cared about "fake wrestling" caught many old-guard journalists off guard. They didn't understand the appeal and looked down on the people who enjoyed it.

As a result, it seemed every North American newspaper's pop culture or sports editor assigned their oldest, crustiest columnist to write a snarky article about pro wrestling. This piece from the *Windsor Star* is a terrific example:

WRESTLEMANIA: A POPULAR DISEASE

For decades, professional wrestling has been derided for its fakery, farcical nature and stature as the absolute lowest of lowbrow activities.

Wrestling and its dedicated followers, of course, couldn't care less — just ask the 92,926 fans expected to jam the Pontiac Silverdome Sunday for WrestleMania III. The Barnum-and-Bailey-like World Wrestling Federation says WrestleMania III will be the largest indoor sports/ entertainment event in history, and no one seems to be disagreeing.

Just what does it take to draw that many people? Well, Super Bowl XVI could muster only 81,684 faithful football fans to the Silverdome in 1982. This fall, Pope John Paul II might match WWF Champion Hulk Hogan's drawing power at the Pontiac arena. Like it or not . . . the WWF has nurtured wrestling into the cultural event of the year.

One thing this sneering screed got right is that fans didn't care what anyone else thought. They'd turned the Hogan, Andre and Macho Man–led organization into a juggernaut.

"According to the World Wrestling Federation, 70 million Americans watch its televised matches each month," a *New York Times* news service piece reported. "With just 850,000 seats available at 163 closed-circuit sites across the country, and with a pay-per-view hookup limited to 6.5 million households, the vast majority of fans will have to wait until the WrestleMania III video cassette hits the market . . . So many people have been buying the WWF's videos and other merchandise that the federation will introduce Super Stars of Wrestling ice-cream bars next week."

Aside from the big announcement of the upcoming wrestling bars (which were delicious), it was in this landscape, with non–wrestling fans curious what the fuss was all about and wrestling fans by the millions trying to see Hogan take on Andre, that Savage and Steamboat had dedicated themselves to perfection.

"Randy put effort into all of his matches," Lanny said. "Didn't matter where. But this was the most effort ever put in by two men."

Hercules. Hillbilly Jim. King Kong Bundy. Junkyard Dog. Greg "The Hammer" Valentine. Brutus "The Barber" Beefcake. Roddy Piper. Adrian Adonis. The Hart Foundation. The British Bulldogs. Butch Reed. Koko B. Ware. Tito Santana. These were just *some* of the marquee names that wrestled in the lead-up to the Intercontinental Championship that night.

Other than a six-man tag team match that took almost nine minutes, none of the other matches were longer than eight minutes. No titles changed hands. No match dragged on too long. The fast revolving door of stars was the ideal warm-up for the ninth match of the night: Savage versus Steamboat.

After a few hours of entertainment, it was the first WrestleMania III match with a belt on the line and the first one featuring a remarkable physical comeback. Fans knew it *meant something*. And for the two men who had dedicated the last three months of their lives to this performance, it was "go" time.

"I remember standing backstage with George Steele before going out on the cart," Steamboat said. "At the last second before they hit my music, I'm going through the match in my head. I was so stressed out. I guess I burned up a bunch of nervous energy behind the curtain. But what I do remember is, we came through on the cart, and the first thing was, I completely forgot about all the stress. I was in awe of all the people in the stadium. And then I had to gather myself and sort of have tunnel vision."

While Steamboat waited to be driven to the ring, the fans in the arena and at home watched the Macho Man's pre-match message for Steamboat:

"Oh yeah, Dragon! I am the lord and master of the ring! And you're gonna find that out! One athlete to another! Right now! You can't be with me! No! History beckons the Macho Man. Yeah!"

Then the millions at home watched as the Macho Man and Miss Elizabeth drove down the aisle to resounding cheers. Yeah, he was the bad guy. Yeah, they loved him anyway.

Macho Man wore a resplendent, shining, red-white-and-blue robe and Elizabeth wore a light pink dress. They waved to the fans like they were royalty.

On the television feed, the WWF cut to Gene Okerlund's pre-match interview with Steamboat, where the Dragon issued his final warning to Macho Man before the fight:

"Randy Savage. The day has finally come. The minutes. The seconds. We have reached our moment. As you and I climb in the ring, we clash like two titans. But there will only be one winner. One winner, Savage. This dragon is breathing fire. This dragon will scorch your back. I will come away with the championship belt! And see new horizons!!!"

The feed then cut to Steamboat entering the arena. The crowd exploded like it was the first song of a rock concert. Steamboat, wearing a red headband and white gi, soaked it all in with laser focus.

Steamboat is back!

"It was really a moment in time as far as going down that aisle and all that energy," Steamboat said. "It's something that you can't even explain . . . when you have 93,000-plus in the Pontiac Silverdome. That was incredible. It can never be equaled as far as a rush going down to the ring."

When the match began "the place just exploded," Okerlund said. "The preparation that Randy had, he would get tighter than a tick in the time leading up to a match. He was more intense. So about the time that the bell rang and it was time for him to go, he was ready to be shot out of a cannon."

Ding! Ding! Ding!

After a brief lock-up the two men slammed into each other like bighorn rams, and *it was on*. The pace was unrelenting. Irish whips. Hip tosses. Throwing wrist locks. Savage and Steamboat didn't look like the wrestlers that had come before them that night. They looked like two outside linebackers. They were jacked and agile and athletic. If they had gloves on they could easily have been mistaken for heavyweight boxers.

Unlike many of the cartoonish matches that resembled brawls or beat-downs, this match had the feel of a brutish, uptempo ballet. Everything was fast, fast, fast. Even the counts and pins were quick.

At one point early in the match they had a two-count kick out, clothes-line, then another two-count kick out in about 1.5 seconds. It was dazzling.

"Steamboat! Steamboat! Steamboat!"

The more the crowd chanted the more Macho Man took over, just as they'd planned. They weren't wrestlers on this night. They were conductors, directing the audience in and out of certain sequences with emotion and power and pain in a wrestling symphony.

In the heart of the match, for about six solid minutes, Savage rag-dolled Steamboat and absolutely kicked his ass. He unleashed his entire wrestling repertoire: clotheslines off the ropes. Backbreakers. Suplexes. Elbows to the head. Macho took him down for two-count after two-count, but Steamboat kept getting up.

"Macho Man throwing everything but the kitchen sink and can't keep the Dragon's shoulders down!" commentator Gorilla Monsoon shouted.

"I don't know how," Jesse Ventura chimed in. "He has given him three or four moves right now that would have beat any average man."

Then, right on cue, when the fans thought the Dragon was out of fire, it happened. Ricky dug deep. Recharged. Began to fight back. One punch and one chest slap at a time.

"This is beyond wrestling ability. This is guts personified!" Monsoon shouted.

And yet . . . they were toying with the audience. With every Steamboat swing the crowd grew louder, and just as they were ready to blow the roof off the Silverdome for Steamboat, Savage raked his eyes and gave him a hip suplex and tried to pin him.

Once again Steamboat escaped.

The viewing experience had now moved past a wrestling match. It had transcended to a higher plane of entertainment, more akin to a Broadway play — drama and action happening live with two men giving the performances of a lifetime.

After twelve minutes, both men were exhausted.

The audience was in a frenzy.

How is the Dragon still standing?!

What does Macho have to do to finish this guy?!?

Steamboat mounted a comeback. He was Sisyphus, willing the boulder to the mountaintop. When he leaped off the top rope and landed a flying karate chop, the Silverdome sounded like the Detroit Lions had just won the Super Bowl. Steamboat was getting his revenge! He pinned Savage!

One . . . Two . . . . Thr— ohhhhhhhh!

Almost.

Then the Dragon tried to pin the Macho Man again. And again. And again. Now it was the Macho Man who wouldn't go down.

"Savage in a whole heap of trouble!" Monsoon yelled.

The audience had no clue which way the match was headed at this point. They'd been toyed with and tormented for too long. Anything was possible.

After an "accidental" collision knocked referee Hebner down, Macho Man crushed Steamboat with an elbow off the top rope, but now there was no referee physically able to make the count.

With Steamboat lying unconscious and Hebner groggy, Savage hopped out of the ring and grabbed the bell from the timekeeper, coming full circle with how the rivalry began. It was poetic. Perfect.

He climbed the top rope to once again destroy Steamboat with the bell, and just as he was about to leap, George "The Animal" Steele saved the day. He shoved Savage, who injured his back as he fell to the mat.

In pain, Savage body-slammed Steamboat, but before he could go for the pin, the Dragon reversed the move and put the Macho Man in a small package pin.

ONE!

TWO!

THREE!

STEAMBOAT WINS!

"History is made here in the Silverdome!" Gorilla Monsoon shouted.

While Steamboat was applying the pin, Randy took a split second to admire their work. Waiting for the crowd's reaction, he whispered, "We got 'em, Dragon."

In a fifteen-minute match, they'd squeezed in twenty-two false finishes — that's just about one every fifty seconds. They'd done everything they set out to do. It was glorious.

"When you go back and look, after George Steele pushed Randy off the rope, Randy got up and reached for his back," Lanny said. "He put his hand on his back because that's where he took a bump. The audience needed to remember that before the simple finish. He was an artist."

When it was over, many of the biggest names in wrestling instantly believed they'd just witnessed the greatest match in the history of the sport.

"It was as perfect as you would ever get for a match," Jesse Ventura said. "For pure wrestling excitement and what happened in the ring, Macho Man and Steamboat was the greatest match I ever saw."

"Macho Man and Steamboat raised the bar," Jimmy Hart said.

Standing in the Dragon's Den after reliving the event, Steamboat takes a deep breath and contemplates that night all those years ago.

"You have two guys who wanted to wrestle to perfection on the biggest day of the year," Steamboat said. "And we put this match together. It ended up being the match of the night, the match of the year and the match of the decade. Thirty-five years later, fans still talk about our match at WrestleMania III."

CHAPTER 23

You Are the Master of Your Destiny

"**H**acksaw" Jim Duggan, the two-by-four-wielding patriot and wrestling everyman, joined the WWF in 1987 at the dawn of Macho Madness. He'd spent nearly a decade in the territories, performing all over Georgia, Alabama, Texas and the mid-South. When he got the call from Vince McMahon, he was ready to make the leap to the big time, but he'd been working seven days a week for years and didn't keep up with the WWF roster. Other than a few of the territory guys, he didn't know many people — although one guy stood out.

"I was down there for years wrestling with [Junkyard] Dog and when you go up to the WWF as the new guy you find your corner and stay in it," Duggan said. "I'd been encapsulated in the mid-South, but one of the first guys you notice is Macho. When I'd travel I'd put a big hat over my head so I wouldn't be recognized. Not Mach. He'd walk through the airport in full gear."

Duggan, like Randy Savage, had been a legitimate athlete before pro wrestling. He was a four-sport letterman in high school (football, basketball, wrestling and track) and was New York state's high school wrestling champion in the heaviest division. Standing 6'3" and weighing nearly 275 pounds, Duggan was also the prototypical offensive lineman for the run-heavy 1970s college football scene. He received offers to play at powerhouses like Ohio State, but opted to play at Southern Methodist, where he became team captain and was eventually drafted by the Atlanta Falcons before an injury ended his career.

"I knew Lanny well and my wife, Debra, traveled with me then," Duggan said. "Her and Liz became friends. Then Mach and I became pretty close friends before we really started working together."

With most wrestlers, when you're friends outside of the ring it means that you both drop your gimmick and hang out as real people. For instance, "Hacksaw" and "Macho Man" would be left in the locker room while Jim and Randy grabbed a beer or watched a baseball game.

Not so with Savage. When you were friends with the Macho Man, *you were friends with the Macho Man.*

"He called me 'Hacker,'" Duggan said. "In that voice of his. 'Hey, Hacker.' What you saw on TV was the way he was in real life. He was wound pretty tight. We'd go into McDonald's and in that voice he'd say, 'I'll have French friiiess and a burger. Oh yeah.'"

Duggan also got to see the cerebral aspect of Savage that few understood. Behind the neon clothes and shiny costumes and under the wild hair and sunglasses was a deep, complicated and contemplative man.

He was educated and well read. He enjoyed learning and games of strategy.

In Duggan, who had a college degree in applied plant biology, he found someone he could battle wits with occasionally.

"He was a very good chess player," Duggan said. "I played chess in high school and a little bit in college. I could usually beat most guys in the dressing room but he was good. He was up on me in games when we stopped playing."

It was during this early period of their friendship that Macho Man lost the Intercontinental Championship belt to Ricky Steamboat, which left a lot of options on the table for Vince and company to consider.

Would Macho try to recapture the Intercontinental title?

Would Macho challenge Hulk Hogan for the Heavyweight Championship?

Everything was on the table.

"He was very professional," Duggan said. "Business-wise, he was extremely competitive. A lot of people don't understand what it's like to be up on that level. He was one of the best and he stayed on top of his game for a long, long time."

That being said, in the immediate aftermath of WrestleMania III Randy Savage was a bit . . . lost.

"My brother wanted to have the match of his life with Steamboat and he did," Lanny said. "Everybody said it was the greatest match they'd ever seen. He did it. But there was a question of, 'What do you do next?'"

In Savage's mind, his first order of business was to regain respect. Even though he had just put on the most incredible performance in pro wrestling history, he lost. Yet in the loss, he saw an opportunity to claw his way to the top and — in a stroke of genius — turn babyface for a run at the heavyweight championship.

A month after WrestleMania III, Savage did an interview with the *South Bend Tribune* promoting a Black Tuesday event and he completely let his guard down. It was one of the rare interviews where readers got a glimpse of the man behind the Macho Man, or at least a healthy mix of the two.

"I have to re-prove myself all over again," he said. "I need to start beating people right away. There's only one spot on the top of the mountain. I'm a better athlete than Hulk Hogan, but that's barroom talk. He's there now and that's what counts . . . But I've paid my dues. You can underline that and put it in capital letters. I wish I could bottle the intensity I've had since I got into wrestling. You have to want to be the best with all your heart."

Then he got deep.

"I've lived inside this tormented body and mind all my life," he continued. "I've been so intense. If I won the WWF heavyweight title from Hulk Hogan I don't think I'd have a letdown. I have too much desire to be the best."

And then, for the first time breaking character, Randy Savage admitted that perhaps his days of being a heel were done. He'd become so popular, and so many people cheered for him even when he openly acted like a jerk, that it might be high time to embrace it.

"I can't afford to lose again," he said. "The public is fickle. I want people to dig me. That's why this South Bend match is so important to me. I'm at a critical point in my life."

The writer who conducted the interview, Al Lesar, noticed he was dealing with a different Macho Man — a deeper, more vulnerable version.

"Don't let it get around the world of professional wrestling, but Randy 'Macho Man' Savage isn't such a bad fellow," Lesar wrote. "In a sport often accused of being a fraud, 'Macho Man' could be one of its genuine personalities. His trademarks — the low-toned gravelly voice, bulging biceps and beautiful manager Elizabeth — were there, but the 'attitude' wasn't. He spoke as a thirty-four-year-old athlete who, while on the verge of reaching the pinnacle of his profession, saw his world momentarily crumble."

Yes, the outcome of the Steamboat match was staged. And yes, his future in the WWF would be a result of creative decisions instead of pure wins and losses like baseball or football. However, for a perfectionist like Savage, *how* those decisions were made and the *way* his future would be mapped out were of equal importance to the decided outcomes.

Of course he wanted to take Hogan's spot. Everyone did. But after his defeat to Steamboat, the path to get there was a little fuzzy. That's why his goal for the rest of 1987 was to pick up the pieces and get some much-needed professional clarity.

In a short December profile in his hometown *Tampa Tribune*, he discussed the level of focus he thought was necessary to become champion, which began, as always, by finding dedicated time in the gym despite having a "helluva schedule."

"I'll either train in my gym here at the house or find a place to work out," he said. "It's a twenty-four-hour-a-day deal. It's a matter of how committed you are."

When *Tribune* journalist Jimmy Nasella asked about potential burnout, Savage scoffed.

"That's only an excuse. You are the master of your destiny. Whatever you have to do [to keep going] you do. That's the bottom line."

During the conversation, the subject of retirement came up. Again, Savage had no time for it. He was in his prime.

"Money-wise I could get out today, I'm happy to say," he said. "What bothers me about retirement is losing the competitive edge. I've always been *real hyper*. When I was twenty I was the hungriest person alive and now I'm trying to stop the young whippersnappers. I have a lot of pride and have had a super-competitive life. I really don't know how I'll deal with that. Now, though, is the time to bear down, it's not the time to get soft."

If you're wondering why the WWF didn't milk the Savage vs. Steamboat chemistry for a trilogy like Muhammad Ali and Joe Frazier, the answer is that the Dragon is a dedicated dad.

"My son was born in 1987 and I asked for time off," Steamboat said. "I've only got one child and didn't know back then if I would have more. But I'm glad that I decided to be there when he came into this world. You only get that one shot."

Vince McMahon didn't believe in time off or belts going unchallenged for a long period of time. His mentality was, "Steamboat's out. Next man up."

"When you tell Vince that you want to take a vacation because your son is being born, he says okay, but you have to lose the belt," Lanny said.

Enter the 6'1", 243-pound Elvis impersonator/wrestler, the Honky Tonk Man, aka Wayne Farris. Farris, incredibly, happened to be Jerry Lawler's cousin, and after starting his pro wrestling career with his training partner Koko B. Ware and wrestling as "Dynamite" Wayne Farris, he reinvented himself as Honky Tonk Wayne in Calgary, Canada, for Stampede Wrestling in the early 1980s.

When he left for the WWF in 1986, he dropped the "Wayne" and introduced himself to the nationwide audience as the "Honky Tonk Man," complete with Elvis Presley–inspired hair, sideburns, clothes and guitar. He even brought Jimmy Hart on board to be his version of Colonel Tom Parker.

The gimmick took off — along with Honky Tonk's finishing move, the "shake, rattle & roll" — establishing Farris as a top heel inside of a year. Then, a fortuitous encounter in a WWF hallway with Hulk Hogan and Vince McMahon changed everything. While the top two men at the WWF were discussing the future of the Intercontinental Championship, they caught sight of Honky.

"I just happened to walk by while they were standing in the hallway and Hogan looked and said, 'What about him?'" Farris said. "That's how it happened because Butch [Reed] was going AWOL or M.I.A., which happens sometimes . . . I walked by and they said, 'What about him,' and I said, 'OK.' Vince pulled me aside and told me what he wanted to do."

After Honky Tonk heard that Steamboat was taking a break and that this might be his shot to establish himself as a star on the roster, he pushed all his chips on the table.

"If you have a championship belt, you don't go home and spend time with your wife and children," he said. "You have to be on the road and [Vince] said, 'This guy wants to go and do this and I got to have the belt in a town.' I said, 'Listen, if you give me that belt, I don't want a day off.' And I ran with that belt for sixty-four weeks."

This run coincided directly with Savage's babyface turn, meaning the Honky Tonk Man needed an angle against the Macho Man. So it was time to break out the now-established Randy Savage Feud Playbook, which consisted of two easy, proven steps:

Step 1: Talk shit to Macho Man.

Step 2: Disrespect Elizabeth.

In the Honky Tonk Man's promo video before *Saturday Night's Main Event XII*, which aired on October 7, 1987, the wannabe Elvis nailed both with a flourish:

"Number one, I'm gonna shake, rattle and roll you, Macho Man and leave you curled up in the ring like a pretzel. Number two, I'm gonna steal your woman. I know she likes a Honky Tonk Man. She wants to be with me. She likes the way I walk. She likes the way I talk. She likes a winner!"

The event was taped at the Hersheypark Arena in Hershey, Pennsylvania, in front of a sold-out crowd of 9,000 fans. None of them knew they were about to witness wrestling history — a moment so monumental it would have ripple effects for years, lasting all the way to WrestleMania V.

"I remember that was my first *Saturday Night's Main Event* in Hershey," Bruce Prichard said. "That Hershey arena was so special. It was an old hockey arena that went straight up and it was great for television tapings. It was a magical moment."

We'll get to the magic Prichard is referring to shortly, but what you need to know right here is that the original plans for the night were killed when the Honky Tonk Man claims he did the unthinkable: deny a direct order from Vince McMahon and refuse to drop the belt to Macho Man.

"It wasn't really about dropping the title," he said. "It wasn't the fact of losing the belt or anything of that nature . . . I had a deal with WWE and Vince, a handshake deal. There were no contracts back then. 'I'll do anything you want if you give me an opportunity. If I do good, pay me. If I don't do good, I'll pack my bags and move down the highway.' All I said was, 'Treat me good on TV. Take care of me on television.' Back in the old days, us old guys always believed that if they destroy you on television, you're pretty much destroyed."

At the time of the Hershey event, the Honky Tonk Man had only held the belt for about four months. He felt he was finally getting into a groove with his character and connecting (as a heel) with fans. He was getting over. He believed that it was his time for a run. When he found out the WWF wanted to go in another direction, he wasn't having it.

"When they mentioned the destruction of the Honky Tonk Man on television and going with 'Macho Man' . . . I said, 'No. I'm not going to do this on television,'" he said. "'You want to do it, I'll do it anywhere else. I'm not doing it in front of thirty-five million people.' I had to protect my business too. My business was the Honky Tonk Man."

Meanwhile, the WWF had put the internal wheels in motion months earlier for a program with a massive, game-changing storyline: Hulk Hogan joining forces with the Macho Man.

"The tide was turning so much with Randy being really popular at the time," Prichard said. "This just solidified his superstar babyfacedom. With Hulk coming out and sprinkling the Hulk dust and getting him involved and the beginning of that formation."

The formation he's talking about is the Mega Powers, a tag team and shocking partnership between Hulkamania and Macho Madness, with Miss Elizabeth as the centerpiece. The end result of Phase 1 of the planned mania/madness merger would be Randy Savage as the WWF

World Champion with Hulk by his side at WrestleMania IV. That was the first half. Phase 2 was the eventual blow-up of the Mega Powers with a must-see showdown between the two at WrestleMania V.

Yeah, it's a *lot*, and we've only covered the Hulk and Macho angles.

The chess moves that had to be made for all of the above to happen over a fifteen-month period involved a half-dozen other wrestlers with a dizzying array of storylines and feuds to keep track of:

- The Honky Tonk Man vs. Macho Man
- The Hart Foundation vs. Macho Man
- Hulk Hogan vs. the Hart Foundation
- Hulk Hogan vs. Andre the Giant
- Hulk Hogan vs. "The Million Dollar Man" Ted DiBiase
- Andre the Giant vs. Macho Man
- Hulk Hogan & Macho Man vs. Andre the Giant & "The Million Dollar Man"
- Hulk Hogan vs. Macho Man

"The plans for Randy Savage to win the championship at WrestleMania IV were in the works long before October of 1987," Prichard said. "We had all that shit with Hulk and Andre set up to do the tournament. The whole point of that angle was to bring Savage and Hulk together. We created the Mega Powers for them to explode."

This is why pro wrestling is a soap opera with body slams, a drama with DDTs. From a creative standpoint, if you know that the conclusion of your story arc is a Hulk Hogan–Macho Man face-off in WrestleMania V, but you're planning everything a few months after WrestleMania III, when the two hate each other, you need to create two inciting incidents — one to bond them and one to separate them — with a common emotional lynchpin you can tighten and then let loose to blow them apart.

That lynchpin was Miss Elizabeth.

And Act I, Scene 1 of this Shakespearean tragedy with turnbuckles took place that night in Hershey, Pennsylvania.

———

OPEN ON: The Macho Man, tanned, sweaty and fighting for his life in his signature pink trunks under the hot arena lights. He's battling his opponent and emotion. Every chance Honky gets, he winks at Elizabeth. Shakes his Elvis-inspired hips at her. Gyrates towards her. With each lewd gesture the audience's rage at the Honky Tonk Man builds. They couldn't hate him more if the WWF flashed a sign on the Jumbotron that read, "You Should Hate the Honky Tonk Man."

From outside the ring, Jimmy Hart berates Elizabeth with his famous megaphone.

After a headbutt off the second rope leaves Macho Man helpless, the Honky Tonk Man exits the ring and corners Elizabeth with Jimmy Hart. She's stuck between them. Scared. Trapped.

Macho wakes up just in time. He sprints outside the ring and drops the Honky Tonk Man with an elbow. Then he scampers up to the top rope and leaps to the floor outside, nearly ten feet down, crushing Honky with a double axe handle. The tide turns. Macho Man tries to unleash hell on Honky but Jimmy Hart will not stop interfering.

He climbs to the top rope and Hart grabs at his feet.

He goes for the pin and Hart pulls his hair.

He goes for another pin and Hart grabs Honky's leg.

The fans are infuriated. Macho is infuriated. He's had enough. He grabs Jimmy Hart by the hair, pulls him into the ring and raises his right hand for a punch.

The crowd responds: *"Do it!"*

Macho Man lowers the boom with a straight right to the forehead, knocking Hart clear out of the ring to a near standing ovation.

Now things really pick up.

The Hart Foundation (tag team partners Jim "The Anvil" Neidhart and Bret "The Hitman" Hart) show up to defend their manager.

It's now three-on-one: the Honky Tonk Man, The Anvil and The Hitman against the Macho Man.

Keep in mind as you're reading this that you know what is about to happen, but the nearly ten thousand live fans and the estimated thirty-plus million watching at home have no clue that their minds are about to be blown.

The three-on-one quickly gets out of hand, with camera cuts to Elizabeth, crying, helpless, watching her man take a monster beating. They're punching him. Slapping him. Humiliating him.

There's nothing she can do? This is awful!

The scene culminates with the Hart Foundation holding up a barely breathing Macho Man in a crucifix for the Honky Tonk Man to punish. Honky grabs his weapon of choice (his guitar) and lines up Macho Man to be smashed over the head with it.

Just as he's about to swing, Elizabeth dashes into the ring, putting her body in harm's way to protect Savage. The crowd's collective jaw drops.

Did she just do that?

Honky Tonk Man is livid. He yells at her. Tells her to get out of the way. Then he does the unconscionable. He shoves her!

Nine thousand people gasp at once.

Elizabeth slides out of the ring and runs down the aisle, seemingly fleeing the scene. With her gone, Honky Tonk reaches back with his guitar, takes aim, and blasts Savage in the head with it.

"Booooooooo!"

You've never heard such loathing for a performer as Honky Tonk heard after his Gibson connected with Macho's forehead. As Honky laughs and the Hart Foundation continues to kick Savage while he's down:

We suddenly hear a low smattering of cheers.

Then a few hundred more fans chime in.

Then the entire arena roars as they see what's taking place.

Elizabeth didn't run to the locker room to escape . . .

No . . .

She ran to the locker room to get . . . *Hulk Hogan.*

As the crowd explodes she drags a bewildered Hogan down the aisle to the ring. Once he catches sight of what's going on — a three-on-one, unfair demolishing of Macho Man — the greatest babyface of them all will not stand for the injustice.

He puffs his cheeks, runs into the ring and proceeds to clean house!

While Hogan's smacking around the Hart Foundation, Macho Man comes to and joins in, clocking Honky Tonk, The Hitman and The Anvil. Both men wreck shop, and as the final Hart Foundation member is tossed over the ropes, the two fired-up titans — in a choreographed moment that belongs in the Louvre — back into each other and turn with rage.

If you were, let's say, six to twelve years old, this is the precise moment that your brain, jacked up on adrenaline and sensory overload, experiences an atomic bomb–level explosion.

Hulk Hogan! Randy Savage! In the same ring! Are they gonna fight?! Wait, don't fight! Hulk saved Savage! But they hate each other! Arrghhhh . . .

The two men stand there, fists up, wings up, ready to throw down. Elizabeth clutches her heart. *This isn't what she wanted.* Macho Man catches sight of her. He realizes that the man he's hated from the moment the ink dried on his WWF contract just saved his ass and protected his woman.

A pause.

He lowers his fists and raises his arms to the side in peace. Then, astonishingly, he extends his hand. Hulk Hogan's eyes dart around the ring, milking the moment, letting the audience help him decide what to do.

Should he embrace his enemy?

The crowd wants it. So bad. They cheer louder and louder and louder and then . . .

Hulk shakes Macho's hand, and in the truest sense of the phrase, the crowd goes wild.

END SCENE.

If you just read the above and are old enough and lucky enough to have witnessed the scene live or on television in real time, then you likely have goose bumps. This was, in no uncertain terms, one of the biggest sports and entertainment moments of the late 1980s. It was the thing *everyone* at school was talking about on Monday. The thing you couldn't escape on the playground or in the fraternity house or out with your buddies. It was the handshake heard round the world and it had been planned and executed to perfection.

This is how Hulk Hogan, in character, put an exclamation point on the night in an interview with "Mean" Gene Okerlund shortly after the match:

"Well you know, 'Mean' Gene! We really don't know what we're dealing with here! And I'm just a little worried about locking up here! We might just blow the whole planet up! Everybody knows that Hulkamania is the strongest force in this universe! But when I hit that ring and I saw what the Madness was all about, I realized! There was a whole other universe out there! A whole other frontier! And the power of the Madness and the Mania just blew my 24" guns out, man!"

Then Macho Man joined in:

"I'm still in a state of shock right now! In fact I don't think I'm gonna be coming down for a loooong period of time! Yeah! Reckless abandon is what I used to be! Yeah! But I've opened up my eyes. Yeah! The big man! The big man here, yeah! He endorsed Macho Madness and it gave me direction! Yeah! Reckless abandon it used to be. But now! With direction! With the mega . . . yeah . . . the mega . . . yeah . . . the Mega POWERS! Yeah! Mega Powers! Yeah! I feel the power right there, big man. Yeah!"

Back to Hulk:

"I'm just worried about where we're going from here! Is it the stratosphere? Is it the ionosphere? With the Madness and the Mania as one guiding force we could go ahead and take the whole WWF!"

With that, Phase 1 of the Mega Powers saga was underway.

CHAPTER 24

Hulk

"The only other person that I could call at three or four o'clock in the morning to talk about wrestling and would even answer their phone is Vince McMahon," Hulk Hogan said. "And that's how Randy was. Except Randy called me. 'Hey, brother. Got an idea.' So when you go in bed with Randy, you were in it for the long haul. Good or bad, brother. He's going to drag you through the mud whether you like it or not. And it was intense, because Randy was such a passionate person, and he was so in love with Elizabeth. Dude, I'm telling ya, the lines were so blurry with business."

This quote, from Hogan's interview with the WWE celebrating the 25th anniversary of the Mega Powers, encapsulates what every wrestler who had an angle with Randy Savage learned quickly: there wasn't a business side of the Macho Man and a personal side of the Macho Man. *There was only the Macho Man.*

When it comes to describing the relationship between Hogan and Savage, the word that pops up most often with people who knew them is "weird."

"They had such a weird relationship," said Eric Bischoff, the longtime wrestling executive and producer for both WCW and the WWF. "Hulk was pretty consistent ... He's a very easygoing guy. Business-wise, he can be a real challenge. But on a personal level, he's so easy to get along with.

And it would be up and down between those two. One minute they'd be thick as thieves and the next minute they'd be at each other's throats. Usually it was Randy who was pissed off about something."

This inherent weirdness stemmed from Randy's paranoia about Elizabeth and his natural intensity about . . . you know . . . everything.

"He and Hulk always had such a love/hate relationship," wrestler Kevin Nash said. "One month they were cool drinking beer, the next month Randy was exiled in another locker room. But if you drank Hulk's beer you were on his list."

"Randy had a 'fuck you' list a mile long," Lanny laughed when hearing this. "He had a long memory."

"Mean" Gene Okerlund often found himself in the middle of the two stars with live on-camera interviews and backstage planning.

"When the Mega Powers did come out, it was kind of scary for me," Okerlund said. "Because now you're dealing with some internal problems but they're supposed to be facing someone else."

The funny part about all of the tension is that Hogan and Savage's friendship started off so innocently. Just two guys whose wives met and wanted to hang out.

"One night [Randy] came into our dressing room and he asked for Linda [Hogan's ex-wife] to help [Liz] with her hair," Hogan said. "Once we all realized we lived in the same area we thought we should all get together. We'd go shopping or hit the beach. It was great."

Pretty soon, Hogan and Savage were not only working in the ring together but working out together too. They'd hit the gym, grab food and have barbecues at each other's places with their wives. Hulk and his wife Linda even spent time with Judy and Angelo. It was a wrestling Camelot.

"Hulk would have these big parties," Jimmy Hart said. "And Terry [Hogan] would lay it all out, Randy would throw in ideas. Then they'd talk about the angles."

Things were excellent — until they weren't.

Savage's paranoia about Elizabeth sometimes created bizarre scenarios for the wrestlers who had a firm grasp of fiction versus reality.

On several occasions Macho Man acted like the storylines they'd created out of thin air were really happening. Just as he'd blown up on

George "The Animal" Steele's hairy dunce character for trying to steal his wife, he'd go off on Hogan for similar staged events.

If Hogan was supposed to grab Elizabeth and bring her into the ring, Macho would take issue with how hard he held her wrist. If Hogan had to lift Elizabeth up, Macho would give him hell about where he touched her and how. For Hogan and many of the other wrestlers, navigating around his hair-trigger temper wasn't easy.

"You knew you were going to have tremendous matches. You knew you were going to get great physical interviews. But he was so hard to read. Very difficult sometimes to work with," Brutus "The Barber" Beefcake, an old WWF nemesis, said. "You never knew who you were going to get with him. Very unpredictable."

Backstage his jealousy about Elizabeth shrouded everything.

The wrestlers in the locker room saw a lot. Some stuff they dismissed as a guy being an overprotective husband; other stuff they chalked up to "Mach being crazy."

There are stories of Savage locking Elizabeth in certain rooms to keep her away from the boys, though Lanny swears that never happened.

"He got Liz her own locker room so she wouldn't have to change with all the boys," he said. "Any woman who came to town changed with Liz. Cindy Lauper, anyone."

There are other stories of Savage challenging guys to a fight the second they looked at Liz the wrong way. That one's a slight exaggeration, but everyone from Hulk Hogan to Jake "The Snake" Roberts has confirmed that Randy wouldn't tolerate even the slightest sign of disrespect towards her — both real and imagined.

Roberts, who attempted to travel with his wife on the road, understood how difficult it was to be together all day every day.

"I had my wife involved," he said. "It's tough."

Jimmy Hart tried to talk sense into Savage on more than one occasion, telling him, "What are you worried about? How can she be with someone else? You're with her 24/7."

Randy wouldn't hear it.

To limit her exposure to the other wrestlers, on the road Savage and Liz rarely went out with anyone.

"She went to the dressing room, to the ring, then back to the dressing room and they were gone," Ted DiBiase said.

For all of Macho Man's energy and charisma when the cameras were rolling, after the shows at the peak of his fame he was . . . boring.

"I traveled with Randy a lot. They didn't go out and party," Bruce Prichard said. "They went back to the room and went to bed."

That was the real life of Randy and Liz, just a late-1980s married couple working together, traveling together, eating and exercising and arguing together, and deciding whether to watch *Miami Vice* or *Dallas* on a Friday night in a Marriott before bed.

Boring.

But their fictional life, the life of the Macho Man and Miss Elizabeth inside the WWF universe?

That life was on a rocket ship to staggering fame and celebrity.

The sports and entertainment landscape of the late 1980s and early '90s was ruled by all-time greats. Magic Johnson, Larry Bird and Michael Jordan were the NBA's superstars, with the Celtics, Lakers, Bulls and Pistons duking it out in the playoffs every year. The NFL was riding high with Joe Montana and the San Francisco 49ers, John Elway and the Denver Broncos, and soon Troy Aikman, Emmitt Smith and Michael Irvin with the Dallas Cowboys. The future of baseball, megastar Ken Griffey Jr., was just getting going in the Major League.

Wayne Gretzky sat atop hockey with the LA Kings. Andre Agassi and Pete Sampras's rivalry was in full swing. Mike Tyson was flattening guys until he ran into Buster Douglas. Bo Jackson *and* Deion Sanders were playing two sports, with Bo starring in his famous "Bo Knows" Nike commercials.

Major League and *Field of Dreams* brought sports fans to the movies. The first *Batman* with Michael Keaton hit theaters. We had sequels to *Rocky*, *Terminator* and *Die Hard* all within twelve months. *Cheers* and *Roseanne* ruled television.

This was the backdrop to Macho Man's rise to the top spot in the WWF.

And if you're thinking that pro wrestling was some minor sideshow — a mere distraction for kids while adults watched *real* sports — think again.

Outside of the 1989 Super Bowl between the 49ers and Broncos, which drew a typically massive 73.9 million viewers, the WWF's *Saturday Night's Main Event* cards in 1988 and '89 either beat or were comparable to the numbers put up by the big four sports in their signature events.

Game 1 of the 1989 NBA Finals between the LA Lakers and Detroit Pistons drew a 14.0 rating. Game 1 of the 1989 World Series between the Oakland A's and the San Francisco Giants drew a 16.2 rating with 25 million viewers.

Placing the Stanley Cup Finals in this group isn't really a fair fight in the United States, but the matchup between the Calgary Flames and Montreal Canadiens drew lower than a 5.

And forget any of the golf and tennis majors — compared to the above events nobody watched them. Even the 1990 U.S. Open between heated American rivals Andre Agassi and Pete Sampras drew only a 4.

What about wrestling?

Glad you asked.

The *Saturday Night's Main Event* on February 5, 1988, featuring the rematch between Hulk Hogan and Andre the Giant from WrestleMania III, drew a 15.2 rating and a viewership of 33 million people. For nearly all of 1988 and 1989 the WWF's signature show drew a rating between 9 and 12, far outperforming average regular season and early playoff round NBA, MLB and NHL games. On national TV only the NFL could compete with wrestling.

This is why the WWF's storyline ending with Macho Man as champion had such high stakes. They weren't simply maneuvering Savage to place him at the top of the WWF — they were simultaneously anointing him as one of the biggest stars in sports and entertainment, period.

With millions of eyes on the WWF week in and week out, the road to WrestleMania IV and Macho Man's title was paved with angles upon angles upon angles, all of which had to play out just right to set up a rarity in the pro wrestling world: a vacated title.

Since the creative storyline ended with Macho Man and Hulk Hogan facing off in WrestleMania V, that meant they were still allies as part of a unified and indestructible Mega Powers in WrestleMania IV, which further meant they couldn't have Macho Man beat Hogan for the belt at that time.

The solution was to roll in the simmering, ongoing feud between Hulk Hogan and Andre the Giant. In early January 1988, Andre and Hogan sat across from each other at a desk, with the WWF World Heavyweight Championship belt on the table, and agreed to have a rematch at the *Saturday Night's Main Event* in February.

Andre "won" the match even though Hogan clearly got his shoulder off the mat during the pin. Later, it was revealed that the referee Dave Hebner's twin brother, Earl, officiated the match, tipping it in Andre's favor. After winning the belt, Andre "sold" it to "The Million Dollar Man" Ted DiBiase as part of his feud with Hogan as well.

"The whole setup for WrestleMania IV was brilliant," DiBiase said. "The rematch with Hogan and Andre from WrestleMania III, and it was the first time that wrestling was on live network television since the 1950s. And the story is of Hogan and Andre but the real story is me having Andre selling me the belt after he beats Hogan, setting up WrestleMania V."

This was the catalyst for WWF President Jack Tunney's "decision" to vacate the title completely, declaring that it wasn't won in a sanctioned match. This set up a single-elimination, fourteen-man tournament at WrestleMania IV to determine the new champion. (Hogan and Andre both received automatic byes to the second round.)

And *all of this* was put in motion to pave the way for the Macho Man to be victorious without having to defeat his Mega Powers partner Hulk Hogan in WrestleMania IV in Atlantic City, at the Trump Plaza Hotel and Casino, in front of 19,199 fans and millions more around the world on television.

Deep breath.

Got it? Don't worry if you didn't. During WrestleMania IV the WWF hired *Lifestyles of the Rich and Famous* TV show host Robin Leach specifically for a segment to outline all the storylines in the tournament to help casual fans and newcomers catch up to what they were witnessing.

For our purposes, Savage defeated Butch Reed, Greg Valentine and the One Man Gang to reach the finals. Andre and Hogan conveniently got a double disqualification, leaving a final matchup for the world championship of the Macho Man versus the Million Dollar Man.

"You can cut the electricity with a knife!" Gorilla Monsoon shouted in the lead-up to the final matchup. And you could. Not only was there going to be a new champion, but this was the first time since the WrestleMania series began that Hulk Hogan wasn't wrestling in the final match.

Of course, he was still part of the show.

When Savage vs. DiBiase begins, Andre the Giant is looming in DiBiase's corner. From the moment the bell rings, he begins interfering with the Macho Man, and you know the rules: you mess with one member of the Mega Powers, you mess with *both* members of the Mega Powers.

For about five minutes, Macho tries to fend off DiBiase by himself, but every time he's about to finish the Million Dollar Man, the giant stands in his way. Eventually, he's had enough.

Playing the crowd like a fiddle, Savage heads over to Elizabeth and gives her instructions. She quickly disappears down the corridor.

Everyone on earth knows what's coming, and it's glorious.

No sooner does the audience start cheering "Hogan! Hogan! Hogan!" than the Hulkster makes his entrance to back his boy Randy. Now you've got Andre the Giant in full, pissed-off Andre mode shouting at the referee and helping DiBiase on one side of the ring, and a concerned Hogan urging Randy on with Elizabeth on the other.

Meanwhile, Macho and Million Dollar continue to kick the crap out of each other. After several false finishes and a missed elbow off the top rope by Macho, DiBiase puts him in his patented sleeper hold, the Million Dollar Dream, and things look bleak. When Macho tries to put his hand on the rope to fend off the move, Andre smacks his hand away.

"Booooooo!"

The referee admonishes Andre with his back turned. *Big* mistake.

Hogan seizes the moment, grabs a chair, hops into the ring and flattens DiBiase with a blow to the back. Both men go down. The crowd is apoplectic.

"Get up, Macho! Get *up*!!"

Macho stands up, sees DiBiase laid out, notices the referee's focus is back in the ring and rallies the entire arena behind him. He raises his hand, twirls his finger, races to the top rope and jumps an incredible two-thirds of the way across the ring with his flying elbow! Lands it! And . . .

One!

Two!!

Three!!!

The Macho Man is your (cue Howard Finkel) newwwwwww undisputed champion of the World Wrestling Federation!

Lights flash. The crowd leap to their feet. "Pomp and Circumstance" plays. Hogan grabs the belt from the announcer's table, sprints into the ring, helps Savage to his feet, hands him the belt . . . and finally . . . finally . . . finally . . .

After nearly two decades in pro wrestling . . .

After thinking of nothing else from the moment his baseball career ended . . .

Randy Poffo aka Randy Savage aka the Macho Man is the number one wrestler in the world.

He raises the belt in triumph, sweaty and exultant. Elizabeth follows him around the ring, emotional. Hulk Hogan fends off Andre and DiBiase with a chair. As the two bad guys exit, Hogan grabs Macho Man's right hand and Elizabeth's left hand and raises their arms in victory.

"This is Macho Man's finest hour!" Gorilla Monsoon shouts. "An unprecedented four victories. And now the Macho Man is the undisputed World Wrestling Federation Champion! Macho Madness! Hulkamania! And the lovely Elizabeth!"

It was a lovefest.

It was a dream for WWF fans.

Hulk Hogan and Macho Man had built an unprecedented partnership between the company's two biggest stars. All had gone as planned. Now it was time to tear the whole damn thing down.

CHAPTER 25

The Tower of Power

Randy Savage stands in front of a room full of reporters at a press conference. Lights pop. Cameras roll. He's wearing a bright bandana, his vintage white-rimmed Macho Man shades, a sleeveless shirt with white laces up the collar, and leather pants with a leopard print on one side and white swirls on the other.

The centerpiece of his gear is the shiny new WWF Championship belt around his waist. On the table in front of him are two more large bright belts with the WWF logo and a major brand sponsor featured underneath. There's also a giant banner with the brand logo in the backdrop.

Miss Elizabeth stands behind him, smiling, as he holds court with a microphone in his new role as the face of the WWF *and* as the lead in a new $12 million advertising campaign. It's a huge day for the WWF, for Randy and for their marketing teams.

If you're expecting Randy to shout "Snap into a Slim Jim!" through the microphone, think again, because before Savage's iconic beef jerky partnership, he spearheaded the efforts of another nationwide brand's foray into wrestling: Mountain Dew.

"I vow to all of you right here! Yeah! Right now! In front of the world . . . Oh yeah! That I'm gonna win the very first Slam of the Night competition for Mountain Dew! Ooohhh yeahh!!"

The brand-new Featured Slam of the Night segment was a direct rip-off of Budweiser's Player of the Game baseball promo, but instead of showcasing the player with the best stats or highlights, Mountain Dew was going to give the Slam of the Night to the best body slam during a live WWF taping.

"Wrestling's charged-up action fits in with Mountain Dew's image of rowdy fun," PepsiCo vice president Don Uzzi said.

And nobody in wrestling was more charged up in 1988 than the "Macho Man" Randy Savage.

Since winning the title on March 27, Savage had been on a whirlwind worldwide tour in his new role as champion, superstar and number one pitchman for the WWF. His routine was relentless.

In one stretch in early May, he was in Minneapolis on a Tuesday night taping promos after the show until 3 a.m. At 7 a.m. Wednesday he flew to Winnipeg, Canada, for a show on Thursday, then to Omaha, Nebraska, on Friday, cramming in phone interviews during every layover. As champion, Savage was slated to work nearly 300 nights a year and command upwards of $10,000 per show.

"My schedule has actually tripled," Savage said at the time. "Not as far as wrestling dates but as far as being world champion. You're in demand. The press conferences, special appearances, interviews, all mixed together. It's a twenty-four-hour-a-day thing, but I can handle it. It's something I'm excited about."

This was not a position he took lightly. He believed being a champion required a consistently strong mind and body. He also believed the way to maintain peak performance was through a commitment to his old standby: fitness. No matter how packed his schedule got, he never wavered from the meathead path.

"You have to be in shape mentally as well as physically," he said. "Durability means a lot. That's the number one thing on my mind when I get into a city. The Gold's Gym and the arena, that's all I usually see. I like to work two hours a day in the gym, then there is running, biking, swimming . . ."

All those years on the road in the ICW, piling up hundreds of thousands of miles in his dad's old car, driving overnight, cramming into hotels, hitting the weight room on one hour of sleep — that was all paying off now.

"It's not like a baseball team where you have a four-game or an eight-game home stand," he said. "We go from one city to the next, night after night. You see guys come in and after two weeks on the road, you see changes in them."

Not with Savage. He was built for this.

"I want to stay up as long as I can," he said. "Some people are overnight successes. I had to pay my dues. I dedicated my whole life to athletics. Now this means everything."

As Vince McMahon's top dog, Savage was called upon to represent the WWF for everything. Major things. Minor things. Nonsensical things.

When the *Cincinnati Enquirer* was putting a wish list together, asking celebrities which holiday VHS tapes they'd like as presents, they asked Macho Man — along with a slew of other celebrities from the era like Estelle Getty and Jerry Mathers — which tape he'd like to receive as a gift.

Estelle Getty chose her favorite movie, *Brief Encounter.* Jerry Mathers wanted an original copy of *King Kong.* And what did the Macho Man want? His answer won't surprise you.

"Oh yeah! *WrestleMania IV*," he said. "Because it shows me winning four matches in one day to win the WWF Championship Tournament and become World Wrestling Federation Champion. And my manager Elizabeth likes it too."

Anything and everything falls under the scope of your responsibilities as the new face of a financial juggernaut. In a deep dive on the WWF's balance sheet in the middle of 1988, the *St. Louis Dispatch* attached some eye-opening numbers to the pro wrestling powerhouse.

In 1988 alone, the WWF staged about 1,000 events and had three TV shows on 260 stations, reaching 96 percent of U.S. households. When the final numbers were tallied, WrestleMania IV crossed $40 million in total revenue, and that was just the tip of the iceberg.

The World Wrestling Federation made $200 million from merchandising alone. There were sixty wrestling videos in the federation's catalogue.

Music albums. Pop hits. Videos. There were all manner of toys, lunch-boxes, T-shirts, and even $20 Miss Elizabeth beach towels.

With Savage on top, there was pressure to maintain the standard Hogan had set. Incredibly, Macho Man surpassed it.

"Randy Savage, the few times he has wrestled since he won the title, he's drawn really good crowds," Bill Apter, senior editor for *Pro Wrestling Illustrated* at the time, said. "He is drawing 8,000 and 9,000 in arenas where they were drawing 4,000 or 5,000 fans before."

When asked for comment, Savage said, "I've been blessed. I have to thank that big Macho Man in the sky."

Secretly, some competitors and executives were worried that without Hogan as champion, there would be a dip in ratings and the number of people attending live shows.

"There was a lot of jealousy and resentment," Jimmy Hart said. "He got to travel first-class with his wife, and they got treated like royalty. I remember the sentiment in the dressing room when he became champion was, 'Watch now — Randy's not the guy. He won't be able to carry the load. You'll find out Randy can't draw.'"

In fact, the opposite happened. In some places, as Bill Apter pointed out, the new champion beat the old numbers. In many other places, ticket sales remained strong.

"Everyone was surprised that attendance never dropped," Jimmy Hart said. "He proved to be the rightful king of the company."

For those paying attention, however (and Randy *always* paid attention), Hulk Hogan didn't exactly slink into the shadows. In fact, he was more visible than ever, giving off the idea that he was just letting Randy borrow the belt for a little while until he won it back. This was all scripted, of course, but still, Randy was the WWF Champion and yet the WWF didn't hold Hogan back at all.

"Randy wasn't the 'A' guy," Kevin Nash said. "There was one [Hogan]. Randy was 1A. The promotion was based more on Hulk. I think there was some animosity from Randy's standpoint."

We've established that Savage could be unreasonable and suspicious at times, but in this case, he had a right to be. Take the issue of WWF's *Superstars III* magazine that showcased Macho Man for the first time as champion.

Savage is on the cover, resplendent in a shimmery multicolored cape with the gold championship belt around his waist. Nothing abnormal there; he's the champ. Then you flip it open and the first photo is of Hogan standing dead center in the ring, clapping. Off to the left is Savage raising his index finger in victory.

Fine, maybe that was the best camera angle. So what if Hulk is the center-piece of the picture? Surely the first big spread is on Macho Man.

Nope.

Turn the page and the opening spread is a two-pager on Hogan. Then there are two more full spreads on the Hulkster, making it six straight pages of Hogan before we get to the WWF Champion, the Macho Man.

This didn't go unnoticed.

Wrestling Magazine, which covered the sport like *Us Weekly* covered entertainment, ran a story in their August '88 issue on this very topic. The cover focused on a large image of Hogan's head with Savage superimposed off to the side, and the headline read: "What Randy Savage Must Do to Escape the Shadow of Hulk Hogan."

Add to all of this the actual creative storyline where the Mega Powers were meant to slowly unwind, and you have a powder keg of fiction mixed with reality mixed with resentment ready to explode in the ring and in the locker room leading up to Wrestlemania V.

If we had to choose the apex of the Hulkamania–Madness partnership, it was during the inaugural SummerSlam event at Madison Square Garden on August 22, 1988, in front of 20,100 fans and tens of millions watching via pay-per-view.

The night was promoted as "the Mega Powers meet the Mega Bucks," which was a tag team match of Hulk Hogan and the Macho Man versus their rivals Ted DiBiase and Andre the Giant.

The precise peak of the Mega Powers' power is easy to spot. It happens about fifteen minutes into the match when both Hogan and Savage find themselves sprawled out on the floor outside the ring after taking a beating from Andre and DiBiase.

What happens next is forever seared into the minds of every teenage boy who witnessed that night. Here goes . . .

With Andre and DiBiase in the ring hollering at Hogan and Macho, and Bobby "The Brain" Heenan and Virgil harassing guest referee Jesse "The Body" Ventura, Elizabeth decides to do something to buy her men time to recover.

Does she shout at them? Does she pretend to cry? Does she fake being hurt?

No, nothing like that.

Instead, she decides that the best course of action to steal everyone's attention is to, ahem, *rip off her skirt*.

Yes, standing on the edge of the ring, the wholesome, lovely Miss Elizabeth, in front of the whole world, tears off her dress and reveals her bottom half covered in nothing but a small pair of red panties.

Andre's jaw drops. DiBiase's jaw drops. Virgil's jaw drops. Jesse's jaw drops. Millions of teenage boys around the country pass out.

(If only they knew the original plan. In a rare radio interview out of character, Elizabeth said the original plan for that moment was to have her take off her entire dress and have a bathing suit underneath. "But I wasn't comfortable with that," she said about opting for the red underwear.)

As Elizabeth parades along the side of the ring drawing all the eyeballs, Hulk Hogan and Macho Man get up. Just as the camera cuts to them, they give each other a mega handshake, sneak back into the ring and then put a hurting on the Mega Bucks that ends with an all-time, crowd-pleasing finish.

With Hogan's boot on DiBiase's neck, Savage hits him with a flying elbow off the top ropes. Then Hogan hammers DiBiase with an atomic leg drop and dives on top for the pin. The Mega Powers are victorious!

That, right there, was *it*.

The pinnacle would last about fifteen seconds.

As Hogan's theme song (not Macho's) blares and the Macho Man stands on the edge of the turnbuckles and pumps his fist to the crowd, Hogan, behind his back, scoops up Elizabeth to celebrate. When Macho turns around mid-celebration, his face goes from excitement to confusion.

Why is Hulk Hogan holding my woman up in the air? What the hell?

Hulk ignores the look and continues to pump up the crowd. Savage, for his part, puts on an Academy Award–worthy performance, switching in and out of joy and pain. He's happy and humiliated. He doesn't know what to do. One moment he's flexing for the crowd and the next he's spreading his arms out in a *What are you doing, Hulkster?* gesture.

The drama ends with the two titans hitting twin double-biceps poses for the fans — but the storyline's seeds of discontent have now been sowed.

Let the unraveling begin.

"It was just a play off real life," Hogan said. "It worked so well because Randy was the ultimate protector. To take that into WWE and turn it into entertainment. It was real. Because it did spill over on a personal level that made it much more intense in the ring."

Every promo, match and on-camera scene for the rest of the summer and into the fall featured hidden moments and Easter eggs that fed into the audience's growing belief that maybe, *just maybe*, Hulk Hogan had something going on with Elizabeth. This was all by design. There was nothing *really* going on. It was on-camera innuendo and teasing, a fake romantic entanglement on a reality television show.

First Hogan hugged Elizabeth at SummerSlam. Then he brought her out solo as his manager and looked at her with eyes that said she was more than a manager. Then he lifted her into the ring a little *too* casually. It was curious. It piqued the fans' interest. It drove the real Randy Savage crazy.

At the Royal Rumble in Houston on January 15, 1989, things almost came to a head when Hogan accidentally (on purpose) tossed Savage out of the ring to eliminate him.

Feeling double-crossed, Savage dove back into the ring to confront his "partner." He was livid. He screamed at him. Shoved him. Poked him in the face. The only thing stopping him from decking Hogan was the timely arrival of Elizabeth to physically get between them and force Macho Man to calm down.

The crisis was averted.

For two weeks.

At the Main Event II on February 3, 1989, Act III of the Hulk Hogan vs. Macho Man saga (that was planned in the summer of '87) comes to fruition, and with it the line between fact and fiction is completely obliterated.

The top draw of the night is a tag team match pitting the Mega Powers against a duo dubbed the Twin Towers — the Big Boss Man and Akeem. At one point during the match Savage is tossed out of the ring, and as he goes over the ropes he slams into Elizabeth, taking her down to the ground. A mat was laid over the concrete ahead of time for this exact moment, but what Hogan sees, and nobody else sees, is that Elizabeth's head misses the mat and bangs into the hard floor.

While Savage, Akeem, Boss Man and Ventura (commentating) stay on script, Hogan is concerned that Elizabeth might actually be hurt. He rushes over to her and bends down to see if she's okay.

On cue, as Macho Man comes to from the fall he sees Hogan tending to Elizabeth and interprets the scene as another betrayal by Hogan. Before he can do anything about it, he's dragged back into the ring.

This is where real life and ring life get turned inside out.

In the ring Savage is taking on Big Boss Man and Akeem two-on-one, according to plan. But his real-life paranoia takes over as Hogan carries his wife down the aisle to place her on a stretcher.

Where are Hogan's hands? Why is he touching her like that?

The next few minutes of the broadcast are intercut with Hogan, emotionally leaning over Elizabeth on her stretcher in the first-aid area, and Savage fighting the two behemoths by himself. The number of unanswered questions for the viewer at this point has reached mind-boggling proportions:

Is Elizabeth really hurt? Is Savage really mad? Did Hogan have to leave? Does Hogan love Elizabeth? Is Hogan coming back? Is the match going to continue? Are the Mega Powers about to crumble?

When Hogan returns to the ring, Macho Man refuses to tag him in while he dispatches the Twin Towers by himself. Then, during a break in the action, instead of tagging Hogan's hand, he *slaps him in the face.*

Whoooaaaahhhhhh!!!

The sold-out crowd at the Bradley Center in Milwaukee, Wisconsin, and the 19.9 million viewers at home are collectively stunned. Even more incredibly, the match is still going on. But it's going to go on without the Macho Man.

Filled with rage, Savage grabs his belt, points at Hogan and leaves him high and dry in the ring, making a lightning-quick, 180-degree heel turn.

After Hogan wins the match solo he heads to the locker room and encounters the real-life, really pissed-off Randy Savage on live television.

"You're outta line!" Macho shouts. "Let me tell you why you're outta line! You got jealous eyes! You're looking at me with jealous eyes because you're a former champion! I'm not number three in the Mega Powers! I'm number one! You guys got me in the back seat! Man to man, you've never asked me for a title shot! You know why? You know why, Elizabeth! Because you can't beat me! . . . Those eyes! They lust for Elizabeth! I can't even stand to look at ya! You turn my guts in two!"

Randy Savage's skin is a dark crimson. He's trembling with fury. He's got his finger right in Hogan's face. It all feels real, *because it is.*

Hogan, for his part, is watching two movies at once. He's got the scripted element that's leading into WrestleMania V, where he has to fight the Macho Man, but he's also got one of his good buddies standing in front of him accusing him of lusting after his wife.

It's genuine madness.

"Try and talk some sense into him," Hogan says to Elizabeth, for the benefit of the audience and their real-life friendship.

There's no talking sense. Instead Savage hurls himself at Hogan and smashes him in the face with the championship belt, knocking him to the ground on top of the medical equipment. While Elizabeth screams, he jumps on top and pummels Hogan in the face (not quite real hits but realer than normal).

We are now in the eye of the fiction/reality hurricane, because prior to Savage jumping on Hogan, the two were really arguing in the middle of the segment, with Savage furious about Hogan's hand placement as he carried Elizabeth away from the ring.

"During that segment in the back when we went to commercial break, I happened to remember looking to Dick Ebersol to count us in — you know, 10 . . . 9 . . . 8 . . . — and Randy and I were arguing about something," Hogan said years later in an interview for the WWE. "[He said] I was too close to her breast or something real crazy or some insanity that was going on. I looked at him to give me a 10 and he goes, 'We're already in!' It was crazy. It was insane."

Now Hogan is trying to keep the scripted part of the segment alive for the viewers while also navigating his friend/enemy's split with reality and his concern for Elizabeth.

"During the match, Randy came flying through the ropes and he crossbodied Liz," Hogan said. "She missed the mat and her head hit that concrete floor out there. I saw that. That freaked me out. And then to get in the back and get in an argument with this guy. Every time he'd point his finger in my face, I thought he was going to stick his finger in my eye. That's how close he'd get. He used to freak me out."

Years later, Elizabeth confirmed that there was a mat mishap and she really had hurt her head.

"Randy came crashing out of the ring and knocked me over and there was supposed to be another mat there," she said. "That was the only time I ever got hurt and Hulk carried me out."

By the end of the segment the Mega Powers were officially done and the real-life friendship between Hogan and Savage was on the outs.

"I can remember Hulk carrying Elizabeth back to the dressing room after she got knocked down," Bret Hart said. "The things that bothered Randy about Hulk and his apparent affection for Liz. How he carried her or how he picked her up and things like that. He had some issues with that jealousy thing and sometimes it would filter into the match."

Eight weeks.

That's all that was left in Macho Man's planned run as champion heading into WrestleMania V. It was tumultuous. It was torturous. It was time.

"That's what a year with 'Macho Man' was like," Hogan said. "It was intense. When you're wrestling with Randy, you better be ready, because it was the greatest time, but it was really, really intense."

"Why Savage rebelled against his friend's generosity is anyone's guess. Some would say, like too many athletes before him, he couldn't deal with having it all. Others contend that Savage made a wise choice, turning on Hogan to recapture the hunger and adversity which characterized his claim to the top spot in the wrestling world. In less than seventy-two hours, the world will know the judiciousness of Savage's decision, after 'Macho Madness' faces its toughest challenge in the form of 'Hulkamania.'"

The above copy appeared in the *New York Daily News* three days before WrestleMania V. It was one of hundreds of pieces running nationwide in the lead-up to the headlining match of wrestling's Super Bowl. The buildup for Randy Savage vs. Hulk Hogan had captured the nation and crossed over into the mainstream. Stories on their rivalry ran in sports sections right alongside columns about the NBA and baseball's spring training.

Alan Raskin, the longtime wrestling columnist for the *Philadelphia Inquirer*, thought WrestleMania V might be the most-watched event yet.

"By the looks of it, this weekend's fifth edition [of WrestleMania] at the Trump Plaza Hotel and Casino in Atlantic City, will be as popular an event as ever. Only limited seating, at $150 per, remains. So if you don't already have one of the 21,000 tickets, the best way to take in the fourteen matches is either by pay TV or at one of the five humongous-screen closed-circuit locations in the region."

Raskin, like the rest of the wrestling diehards and casual fans, was captivated by the clash of the rivals-turned-friends-turned-heated-rivals.

"Savage has recently accused Hogan of 'constantly grabbing the spotlight' and having 'lustful eyes' for their co-manager, Elizabeth, with more than a 'business relationship' in mind," Raskin wrote.

With the "Mega Powers Explode!" tagline splashed across every newspaper, billboard, *TV Guide* and magazine in the United States all spring, the stage had been set for the culmination of the Hogan-versus-Savage saga and the general public was all-in.

On the night of the event, there were 767,000 pay-per-view buys, smashing the WWF's previous record and setting the standard for a decade (the mark wouldn't be beat until the WWF's Attitude Era in 1999 with "Stone Cold" Steve Austin as the headliner).

In no small part, the reason was the over-the-top, blood-and-guts rage of the Macho Man's promos heading into the event, many of which are used as popular memes across social media to this day.

His most famous from this period begins with an extreme close-up of a sweaty, maroon-faced, enraged Macho Man growling so hard into the camera it sounds like his words might shatter the glass and the veins in his neck might burst.

> Ooohhhh Hulk Hogan, yeahhh! You say you don't know where the Macho Man is coming frooooom . . . You're right! You don't know anything about the Macho Man Randy Savage and where I'm coming from . . . Because it's MIND BOGGLIN' TO YA! Yeah! How one man! Could make it to the top of the World Wrestling Federation mountain, yeah! All by myself. No pukesters helping me to the left! And no pukesters helping me to the right! Didn't need 'em then! DON'T NEED 'EM NOW! And another person I don't neeeeed . . . is Elizabeth either, yeah! Because I'm a champion by myself! ALL BY MYSELF! You don't know where I'm comin' from, Hulk Hogan . . . But I know everything about Hulk Hogan, YEAH! I know what makes you tick! You've got the audacity, yeah! To say that at WrestleMania V! That Hulkamania's gonna survive! I'm gonna tell you one last time! For all the pukesters before Sunday afternoon! Hulkamania! Is DEAD!

Out of context, Savage comes off like a deranged serial killer who may in fact murder someone. In context, Savage comes off like a deranged serial killer who may in fact murder someone. It's a mesmerizing two minutes and it helps explain why everyone bought the match despite knowing there was a 90 percent chance Hulk Hogan was going to win. And then the whole thing almost didn't happen.

In the days before the big event, Savage's bursa, the thin, fluid-filled sac on the bony tip of the elbow, became painfully infected with a serious case of bursitis. The night before WrestleMania, it was swollen, red and hot to the touch, meaning that the infection was worsening and would require surgery. In advanced cases, the sac can open spontaneously, spew pus and cause serious, life-threatening illness.

Despite the relatively simple surgery required to fix the issue, the recovery takes from three to six weeks, time the Macho Man didn't have.

"[His] bursa sac was broken and infected with Staph. He should have had the bursa sac removed and everybody told him to do it. The doctors told him, 'It can rot the bone, the bacteria.' But Randy, being a total pro, said, 'Ooohhhh, not Randy Savage, brother. I'm wrestling Hogan.'"

Turning down surgery, Savage opted to wrestle with his elbow wrapped in a heavy white bandage to blunt some of the searing pain that was going to occur during the match and to hide the injury from fans.

"That's what I remember," Hogan said. "Him just being in so much pain and having that crazy elbow of his swollen and infected, and still going through all the craziness we went through that night and not complaining, moaning or whining, but just really being a pro."

When the main event finally got underway, both men received monster ovations entering the arena with Savage's being a mix of boos and cheers. Miss Elizabeth also got her own entrance (to Macho Man's music) and decided to sit in a neutral corner. But once again, Savage was openly slighted by the WWF.

In his first title defense at a WrestleMania, rather than being introduced second as is the tradition for the champion, Savage was introduced first and the challenger, Hogan, entered second. If there was any doubt about who was going to win this match, that was perhaps the final tip-off.

Once the match began, Savage set the pace with his speed and athleticism and pummeled Hogan, even cutting his eye, while receiving thunderous boos. Regardless of Savage's popularity, the WWF universe was not yet ready to cheer against their beloved hero Hogan. After Elizabeth interfered on behalf of both men and got tossed, Savage went to work on Hogan, giving the impression he had a shot at victory.

"I gotta believe, Gorilla, that pukeamania is running out," Jesse Ventura said on the broadcast. "It's only time now."

It wasn't time.

Randy set up Hogan's comeback with everything he had, including a choke out followed by a flying elbow off the top rope that, Ventura said, "nobody has gotten up from!"

Savage went for the pin, but Hogan kicked out, hulked up, hit him with the boot and then laid the leg drop on him. One. Two. Three.

"This crowd has become unglued!" Gorilla Monsoon shouted as the lyrics to "Real American" filled the air.

To many, the belt was back where it belonged — with Hogan.

To Macho, it hurt.

And to the other men on the roster, it felt . . . not unfair, but maybe a little unfortunate, because Savage was able to carry the company. That much was clear.

"I remember when he lost the belt, I told him how proud I was of him," Jimmy Hart said.

Bret "The Hitman" Hart agreed.

"When he lost the title, I went to his locker room to thank him," he said. "I made a point of telling him what a great champion he'd been."

CHAPTER 26

Royalty

Miss Elizabeth needed a break.
She was wiped out.

When Hulk Hogan spent time with his wife Linda after a match, he took off his red bandana and his yellow Hulkster shirt and transformed back into her husband, Terry Bollea.

When the Macho Man spent time with Elizabeth after a match, he took off his shades and his cape and . . . was still the Macho Man.

"Being married and working twenty-four hours a day and traveling was very hard on our relationship," Elizabeth said in a rare candid interview years later.

During the height of their Mega Powers entanglement, Savage's scripted jealousy didn't end when the segment was over, often bleeding into real life. This made their marriage difficult and their working relationship nearly impossible.

"He became fixated on one irrational thought," Elizabeth told *WWF Magazine* during an interview that was half in-character and half foreshadowing the future. "He convinced himself that there was something going on between the Hulkster and me. Really, it was a very unpleasant time.

"Looking back, I understand that Randy was just insecure, and that this was the way he dealt with it. But back then I was shocked, hurt and yes, pretty angry. When I tried to jump in between them [Hulk and Randy], Randy shoved me out of the way. So I was forced to make the most painful decision of my life. Although I loved Randy Savage, I had to walk away from him. I couldn't stay with a man who did things like that."

This entire quote was given over two years after the events unfolded at WrestleMania V. It was with the WWF's own magazine and certainly wasn't an off-the-record piece of objective journalism, but as with all things involving the Macho Man and Elizabeth, it didn't matter if the answers were scripted or not because they applied to both the WWF's storyline and their real lives.

"He's the most complex person I've ever met," she said, recalling her decision to stand in Hulk's corner during their feud. "I guess, in a way, I wanted to teach Randy a lesson. I was proud of the Hulkster when he won the belt back. But I never stopped feeling the pain."

This pain is what caused the couple to finally give each other some space. On the home front, they'd decided that it was time for Elizabeth to take a break from the road for a while. On the work front, they'd made a similar decision, opting to use her interference on Hulk's behalf and the entire Mega Powers storyline to have Macho Man choose a new manager, while Liz sporadically showed up in Hulk Hogan's corner.

This was obviously setting the stage for a massive, crowd-pleasing reunion between the two, but that was down the line. In the immediate aftermath of the Macho Man losing the championship belt, he'd turned heel and leaned in hard, dropping the First Lady of Wrestling for his new manager, Sherri, played by "Sensational" Sherri Martel.

Martel was a wrestling star in her own right who cut her teeth in Verne Gagne's American Wrestling Association. She joined the WWF in 1987 and defeated the Fabulous Moolah to win the championship belt early in her tenure, before becoming Savage's manager after WrestleMania V.

From a character standpoint, pairing Macho Man with Sherri after Miss Elizabeth was the ultimate turn to the dark side. It was like going from Dorothy to the Wicked Witch of the West. Where Miss Elizabeth was classy and looked like every small town's homecoming queen, Sherri's gimmick was that of a dark mistress. She had big, dark hair and often sported spiderweb makeup as eye shadow. Rather than shy away from her sex appeal like Liz, she was forward and seductive. Her entire demeanor was a complete reversal of how Miss Elizabeth comported herself.

This accomplished three things.

One, it gave Savage a partner in crime as he explored the depths of his bad guy turn. Two, it gave Miss Elizabeth, who was still "managing" Hulk, her own rival. Three, it kept a lingering question in the minds of WWF fans:

Will Macho Man and Liz ever get back together?

But adding Sherri wasn't the only new post–Mega Powers wrinkle to the Macho Man gimmick. In order to counterbalance Hulk as the company's benevolent ruler, they went all-in on elevating Savage to the WWF's number one heel by giving him an evil crown of his own. Literally.

There is a long and storied history of the King of the Ring tournament that began with its debut in Foxborough, Massachusetts, in 1985, where Don Muraco defeated the Iron Sheik. From there, several wrestlers won the tournament and crowned themselves "king," most notably "King" Harley Race, "King" Haku and "King Hacksaw" Jim Duggan.

Duggan's reign lasted all of three months before losing it to Randy Savage on August 30, 1989. Savage then quickly renamed and rebranded himself as "the Macho King" and anointed Sherri his "Sensational Queen."

"When he beat me to become King of the Ring, I had Harley Race's old cape and crown," Duggan said. "It was like a bushel basket. It was old and beat up. Then they came out with a whole new crown and cape."

Not only that, the WWF created an entire coronation ceremony on *Superstars of Wrestling*, properly announcing the new "royal couple," that aired in September of 1989.

Savage, wearing all gold and black with his shiny crown, entered the arena with Sherri to an avalanche of boos before making his way to the ring, where almost the entire WWF roster awaited the ceremony: Mr. Perfect. The Honky Tonk Man. Greg "The Hammer" Valentine. Akeem. Jimmy Hart. Mr. Fuji. Ted DiBiase. Dino Bravo. It was like a "We Are the World" recording but with wrestling stars milling about.

And to top it all off, in a fitting gesture, Lanny "The Genius" Poffo was present to recite a poem for the occasion:

> Behold, this humble entourage,
> Their heads are bowed in reverence,
> At the very slightest whisper of one name
>
> Exalting in his splendor,
> Which is altogether fitting,
> Of the people and the land from whence he came
>
> False monarchies are commonplace
> As kingdom's rise and fall
> But I The Genius call of glory and renown
>
> Say the Macho Man is everything
> That everybody everywhere
> Would ever, ever want to wear a crown . . .
>
> We witnessed the dethroning of one
> Jim "The Hacksaw" Duggan
> Whose crown and robe are in a stage of ravage
> I now remove my mortar board and place it near my heart
> And thus proclaim you Macho King Randy Savage!

To further cement Savage's place atop the palace of heels, the Million Dollar Man presented him with a solid gold scepter, and the two old rivals shook hands. Now in full Macho King regalia, which included a crown that said "Macho" on it, a brand-new cape that read "Macho King," his scepter and his new "queen," Savage strolled out of the ring to begin his reign.

"Not much changed personality-wise," Paul Roma said. "I don't think Randy changed as far as who he was when he did the Macho King move."

Without Elizabeth as a constant source of drama on camera for him, the vibe was different around Macho on the road and backstage.

"I traveled with Sherri a lot," Roma said. "I loved Sherri. Her favorite song was 'Love Shack.' I always remember that."

Hacksaw Jim Duggan's feud with the Macho King continued for a short time and he remembers it fondly — for the most part.

"My wife and I became friends with Sherri," Duggan said. "I remember one time we did a match where Macho hung me over the apron and Sherri was on the floor. She was supposed to take a big swing and missed me by a quarter of an inch. I knew the second was coming and she was going to overcompensate and she decked me. Macho leaned in and said, 'I didn't do it. She did.'"

But Savage and Sherri's main feud continued to be with Hogan and Elizabeth.

At SummerSlam the Macho King joined with Hogan's *No Holds Barred* co-star Zeus to take on the Hulkster and Brutus "The Barber" Beefcake. Savage had Sherri in his corner and Hogan had Elizabeth in his.

When the match was over, Miss Elizabeth smacked Queen Sherri with a purse and then she, Hogan and Beefcake cut the queen's hair.

It was an interesting and odd time for Savage. Hogan was still in his crosshairs, but the Hulkster was in the midst of a new storyline with the Ultimate Warrior. Savage was also still married to Elizabeth, but their appearances had grown sporadic and their relationship was fraying by the day.

Unlike the two-year program that ended with WrestleMania V, things were in a state of limbo towards the end of 1989 and into 1990. While the Macho King gimmick got over with the fans, it never felt as if it were an endgame. It was more like a way station to see how things played out with Hulk and Warrior and Vince McMahon and Elizabeth. Even his appearance during WrestleMania VI, where the king and queen of evil fought in a mixed tag team match against Dusty Rhodes (with a little Elizabeth interference), felt empty as the main event of the night featured Hulk Hogan losing the championship to the Ultimate Warrior.

At the same time, however, Randy Savage's star power was reaching new heights. He was a main-eventer in wrestling and an A-lister in entertainment. He was everywhere.

CHAPTER 27

Mainstream Macho

The 1989 Cincinnati Reds were putrid. By September they were almost twenty games behind the division-leading San Francisco Giants and in the final weeks of the season, they were mired in a ten-game losing streak.

"Face it. The Reds haven't been terrific entertainment lately," columnist Paul Daugherty wrote. "Watching them is like watching the shower scene in 'Psycho' every day for a month."

They were that bad.

Unless you were a member of the Eric Davis fan club or you bet a friend that you'd watch all twenty-nine of Kal Daniels's hits on his way to batting .218 for the season, there was simply no reason to be at Riverfront Stadium.

Except on September 21, 1989.

Why?

Because in the bottom of the third inning, one-time Cincinnati Reds minor leaguer and current WWF superstar Macho King finally made it to the major league — as an announcer.

Clad in gold pants, a purple and gold sleeveless vest and his new crown, Macho King joined Marty Brennaman and Joe Nuxhall in the radio booth.

"Give me a bat!" Macho shouted, before tearing down a picture of Hulk Hogan they'd put up to antagonize him.

"Oh yeah! This is what I'm gonna do to *youuuu*, Hogan," he said.

Once word got around the stadium that there was royalty in the booth, the Reds players came out of the dugout to get a look at Macho. Eric Davis even hit him with a double biceps pose and Macho flexed back.

The fans erupted. It was the most fun they'd had all year.

"It was, without a doubt, the highlight of the Reds season," Daugherty wrote.

Sourpuss and terrible person Marge Schott, the Reds' maligned owner, hated it. She admonished the announcers after the game for bringing a wrestler into the booth.

"If a celebrity like Macho Man can't go into the booth, who can?" Davis asked. "It's entertainment. She's always saying she wants to entertain the fans. Well, they shoulda *paid* the Macho Man to come here today."

Everywhere Savage went, crowds and attention followed. He was crossing completely over into the mainstream, passing the proverbial "does your mom know who he is?" test: if your mom knows a sports or entertainment star, they've climbed out of their niche into general celebrity.

For Savage this meant that on a daily basis, non–wrestling fans were becoming aware of him for the first time at ballparks, celebrity signings, mall appearances and even on late-night television shows.

Imagine, for a moment, that you'd never heard of Randy Savage or the Macho Man or the Macho King. The name Hulk Hogan is familiar, but you couldn't pick him out of a lineup. You didn't know people even watched wrestling.

So you're settling in to watch some late-night television in the late '80s or early '90s. You're flipping through your TV guide and you see that Macho Man is on *The Arsenio Hall Show*.

What is a Macho Man? you ask yourself and turn on the show.

If you're reading this, you likely became enthralled with the Macho Man as a kid. But what if you were an adult in 1989 and you just . . . came across him on television? What would that be like?

The spotlight slides to the right, flashing a bright ring on the entrance to the stage of *The Arsenio Hall Show*. The maroon columns and symmetrical rectangles and curves carved into the purple glass shine like the Manhattan skyline. Audience members bang their hands together, louder and louder, adding whistles and shouts as the seconds pass. Heavy electric guitar licks kick in from the band. The song is familiar, but if you aren't a World Wrestling Federation fan you can't quite place it right away.

As your brain fires billions of neurons and synapses to locate the name of the song, an iconic figure struts into the beam of light. He is resplendent from top to bottom. On his head sits a cowboy hat unlike any you've ever seen. It's wrapped in giant black stars on a white background with the underside of the lid displaying the opposite, white stars on jet black.

The top half of his face is covered with a wraparound pair of sunglasses that resemble the windshield of a Corvette.

His jacket is like a merger of football pads, a Liberace piano and a shower curtain from *Boogie Nights*. The black sleeves shimmer and the white stars down the forearms shine. As the man spreads his arms out wide to soak up the adoration, a hundred strips of black-and-white leather hang from each sleeve like upside-down zebra skins.

The crowd roars.

The man's skintight leather pants (one leg black, one leg white) are also covered in stars of varying sizes. As he spins so the crowd can get a full look at his ensemble, he reveals a giant patch on the back of his jacket with "Macho Man" spray-painted right below his shoulders in a dazzling, slashing white script.

As Arsenio applauds, the guitar licks reach a crescendo and you can finally place where you've heard the song before.

Is that the graduation song? The one played at every high school and college graduation ceremony each spring?

Why yes, yes it is.

What the hell are they playing that for?

For starters, the graduation song isn't actually called "The Graduation Song." And it's not really a song. The "song" is a series of marches composed for orchestras by Sir Edward Elgar. Elgar was an English composer born in Worcester, England, in 1857. During an illustrious career composing symphonies, choir works and chamber songs, he was appointed Master of the King's Musick in 1924.

His most enduring work, to the extent that a modern American would recognize it, is the "graduation song," which Elgar grandiosely titled *The Pomp and Circumstance Marches*. He chose the title in honor of Act III, Scene 3 of Shakespeare's play *Othello*:

> Farewell the neighing steed and the shrill trump,
> The spirit-stirring drum, th'ear-pierce fife
> The royal banner, and all quality,
> Pride, *pomp and circumstance* of glorious war!

I realize you didn't expect to be reading Shakespeare in this book, but here we are. And the thing is, it's a perfect passage to describe Randy "Macho Man" Savage, whose entire stage persona exuded pumped-up pomp and bending circumstances to his will.

In fact, that's why Macho Man chose it as his WWF ring entrance music.

To those not tuned into Macho Man's career, this is new information. To die-hard Macho Maniacs, it's all part of the total package. And it's awesome.

But what would the Great Bard and the Master of the King's Musick (a man fond of stiff, gray, single-toned three-piece suits) think of this display — a 6'1", 240-pound wrestler preening to a march? What would they think of the ego and the arrogance and the . . . pomp and circumstance of it all?

They'd love it.

Shakespeare was a showman. Elgar was too. More importantly, they were both artists. And they both would have had to marvel at Randy Savage's all-in, unbeatable live spectacles. Make no mistake about it, Randy Savage's creation, Macho Man, was performance art at the highest level. From the voice to the vibe, he invented a character that transfixed audiences and mesmerized fans.

Case in point: as Savage crosses the stage in front of Arsenio towards his seat for the interview, his sheer size and the mass of his outfit blocks out the host entirely. It's like a lunar eclipse — a Macho Moon eclipse, if you will. And before Arsenio can even speak, just as the crowd's clapping quiets down, Savage senses the moment and launches into a short, nonsensical (but nonetheless captivating) rhyme to focus the room's attention. The first exchange of the interview is really everything you need to know about Savage's unique magnetism:

Macho Man: "The tower of power, too sweet to be sour, I'm funky like a monkey, sky is the limit and space is the plaaaaaaaace!!!!"

Arsenio: "Hellllloooooooo . . ."

The interview fills two full segments and while Arsenio–Macho Man didn't quite reach the rarefied air of a Howard Cosell–Muhammad Ali exchange, their appreciation for each other is palpable — so much so that Arsenio delved deep into Savage's psyche, covering "macho" talking points and serious ones.

On the heavy side, they discussed anabolic steroid use, a topic that was previously taboo but was slowly making its way into mainstream conversation. We were still a half-decade before Mark McGwire, Barry Bonds and Sammy Sosa all doubled the size of their craniums, forearms, and home run totals, but rumors of athletes and entertainers "juicing" were rampant.

Macho Man took them head-on, admitting that he'd used 'roids, but that they made you much less "macho." He then looked right into the camera through his sports car shades, pointed at the audience and warned, "I did them a long time ago when they were legal but I don't do them anymore. It's like putting poison in your body. Pluuuuuuus, it gave me one hell of a case of PMS!"

With this anti-steroid Public Service Announcement out of the way, Arsenio cruised to some lighter fare: asking Savage if he ever cried (sometimes), whether he was always the Macho Man (no, first he was a Macho Baby!) and finally, was he going to beat the Ultimate Warrior?

To add to his question, Arsenio took out a wrestling doll of the Ultimate Warrior and wondered out loud, "I don't know if you can beat this guy." With both arms on top of the couch behind him, as relaxed as ever, Savage replied, "Only one person can be at the top of the mountain at this particular time and I'm sorry to say that he's gonna lose and I'm gonna win . . . I'm gonna beat him one, two, three in the middle of the ring. If he beats me I'll shake his hand, but he better not turn his back after that or I'll nail him."

CHAPTER 28

The Warrior
and the Wedding

"**H**ulkster told me you can make me some clothes."

These are the words renowned fashion designer Michael Braun hears when he picks up the phone in his shop on a random weekday. He can barely understand them. They sound like they're coming from a choking grizzly bear. Plus, the guy didn't even say hello.

"I get a call from somebody I don't know," Braun said. "I pick up my phone and I hear this voice. I held the phone out, like, *Who the hell is this?* I have no idea who this person is . . . I say, 'Come by tomorrow, we're here noon-to-six.' The next day Randy comes in with Elizabeth. He's got little shorts with three stars across the front and two-inch lettering on the tush that says 'Macho Man.'"

This was the first impression that Randy Savage made on Braun, a legendary designer who made clothes for everyone from Jimi Hendrix and Bob Seger to Aerosmith, the Temptations, Sonny and Cher and Gladys Knight and the Pips.

So there's Braun, standing in his factory, staring at these Speedo-like wrestling trunks and thinking, *Is this guy serious?*

"I said, 'Dude, I'm not making shorts. And I need real estate. I need from the ground to up past your head,'" Braun remembers. "You're asking me to make clothes. I'll make you some clothes."

"I need capes," Savage growls. "I've made a lot of money like this."

"Dude, I'm not a cape guy," Braun fires back.

After some back and forth, Braun agrees to make him a few outfits to get him started.

"Any idea what you want?" Braun asks.

"Make anything you want," Savage says.

"This is the kiss of death!" Braun says. "To say to a creative, do whatever you want? And to not even put a price on it?"

Regardless, Braun accepts the challenge and puts together five full outfits. Wild colors. Zany designs. Outlandish patterns and fabrics and add-ons.

Savage picks up the outfits and takes them for a test drive. He wears each outfit to a different show and a month later returns to Braun with a story.

On the last night of the trip he put on his final new outfit, a purple suit with chains all over it. When he's all decked out, he walks out of his smaller dressing room into the main room where all the wrestlers are sitting around, playing cards, shooting the shit. They stop dead when he strolls in.

"Where did you get that?"

"That's great!"

"Love that, Mach!"

Then Macho leaves the dressing room and as he's on his way to the ring he bumps into Vince McMahon, who stops him and says, "Wow! This is great. Where did you get it? Who made it?"

When Savage gets to the ring and the spotlight hits him, the room pops.

"'I really got over, brother!' he tells me in that voice," Braun says. "Then he tells me that was the outfit he liked least. After that, he just said go for it. Soon I was making forty-five outfits a year for him."

The wardrobe rebrand was part of Macho's overall plans to level up. Worldwide domination was beckoning. The capes and sleeveless T-shirts and bandanas had taken him to the upper reaches of wrestling stardom. Now he was ready to make his permanent mark on pop culture.

Randy Savage's time as the Macho King was fruitful. It carried him through the post–Mega Powers years as the top bad guy in the company and kept him in the spotlight as a counterweight to Hogan.

The final match of his early '90s saga with the Hulkster was an enormous success. Main Event III in 1990 with Queen Sherri in his corner drew an impressive 12.9 rating and 20.9 million viewers, topping the numbers from the event in 1989 featuring the Mega Powers implosion — and still dwarfing most of the playoff numbers for the NBA and MLB.

Originally, the match was supposed to be guest refereed by boxing legend Mike Tyson, but instead featured Buster Douglas, who'd defeated him in a historic upset a few weeks before. Now, with the Hogan–Savage feud fizzling, the Macho King began a new program, going after his next worthy opponent, the Ultimate Warrior.

Portrayed by ex-bodybuilder James Hellwig, the 6'2", 280-pound Ultimate Warrior was the thickest, most muscular stud on the whole roster. After making his WWF debut in 1987, Warrior ran through the company like a cannonball through a glass window. He was a one-man wrecking crew, a true force of nature.

He had massive arms, a concrete chest and a freight train–sized back. He was also an electric performer — a human energy drink mixed with lightning.

With his painted face ready for war and neon strings tied around his arms to make his biceps bulge, Warrior bolted to the ring for his matches in a dead sprint, lighting crowds up to unheard-of levels.

"Shit, I gave more in my ring entrance than most people gave in the whole match," Hellwig said. "And the fans got more out of my ring entrance. If I wasn't blown up and exhausted by the end of the match, then I didn't think I gave the people their Ultimate Warrior money's worth."

The character was beyond unique. He was a unicorn. A creature from parts unknown who spoke of gods and spirits and charging elephants. He violently shook ropes, screamed into the sky, stomped his feet and charged around the ring like a stick of dynamite exploding over and over again.

To kids the world over, he was instantly captivating.

His signature move, the Gorilla Press, involved hoisting even the largest WWF stars like Hulk Hogan clear over his head and then letting them slam to the ground. He was a sight to behold, a rightful heir to Hogan and rival for the Macho Man.

"I did the clothesline, the gorilla press, the splash and then I shook the ropes," Hellwig said. "Then I'd go back again and do my power shake. I did more in my finish than most people did in the whole match."

In many ways, Hellwig and Savage were the same. They cared deeply about the fans and the gimmick and they had the same dedication to the gym.

Like Macho, Warrior used the weight room as his anchor, building his entire travel schedule around finding time to lift, even at ungodly hours.

"There were guys that came to the WWF with bags and bags and bags of wrestling moves, but none of them made it like the Ultimate Warrior character," Hellwig said. "The charisma is the most important part. If you don't have the charisma none of the other stuff matters. The charisma is what made the body work. The charisma is what made me go to the gym at two o'clock in the morning because that is what I have to do to be the Ultimate Warrior."

You can easily imagine Randy Savage, who was impressed by Warrior, saying the same exact thing.

"My big thing is coordination and quickness," Savage said. "I'll never be 300, 400, 500 pounds. Now somebody like the Ultimate Warrior who is 290 pounds . . . I didn't know people like that were born."

The feud between the two stars was standard creatively: match interference, distractions, threats . . . the usual WWF fare. However, in the middle of the program, things got a little personal (as they always did with Savage) when he purposely knocked Warrior clean unconscious during a match with Sergeant Slaughter. This time, though, the retaliation wasn't over Elizabeth.

It was over the thing Savage loved second most in the world: money.

A few months before the knockout, Warrior hit Savage so hard during a match that he broke Randy's hand and injured his arm.

"Randy was out six weeks, or whatever it was, and wasn't getting a paycheck," Sergeant Slaughter said. "That was like taking money out of his pocket, which, other than breathing, the biggest thing in Macho Man's life was making money."

While Savage and Slaughter game-planned for the match at the 1991 Royal Rumble, where Slaughter was set to become the WWF champion over Warrior, Savage had an idea to use one of his Macho King props as a weapon.

"Randy and I came up with the scenario where he hit Warrior with the scepter," Slaughter said. "When it happened in the match I heard this ungodly sound of glass shattering — Randy had hit the Warrior right between the eyes with that scepter. It was obliterated. It didn't go in the ring, but it was all over the floor. After that Warrior was supposed to be lying in the ring, but when I went over he was still sprawled over the second rope."

Savage had wielded the scepter in matches before and he'd figured out just the right way for the impact to look devastating without causing any harm. Of course, in this case, he was looking to do a little damage — perhaps too much.

"I tried to pull [Warrior] back in but he was deadweight," Slaughter said. "He was completely knocked out. I finally got him off the rope and threw him into the ring, and I saw glass sticking out of his head like a spear. It was an incredible sight."

There were ten minutes left in the match along with a planned finish involving some more interference, but all of that was now off the table because Warrior was unconscious.

"I thought, *What do I do? He's knocked out,*" Slaughter said. "'I don't want to just cover him and that be it — the heat is going to go on Randy.' I figured Warrior wasn't moving, so I would just drop an elbow on him and hopefully that would wake him up and he'd kick out of it. So I dropped the elbow and covered him — I didn't even grab his leg because I thought he was going to kick out.

"And I heard, 'One,' so I grabbed his leg; 'two,' I was still waiting for him to kick out and he didn't kick out; 'three.' The match was over and I was like, *What the hell?* So I celebrated — I was the new World Champion."

Warrior's run as champion had been short-lived, but in his mind, it led to a storyline with Savage that was equal to his previous rivalry with Hulk Hogan.

"You don't get to a place in the business like that unless you're willing to drop the belt," Hellwig said. "It's not good business for them to just have you drop a belt and not have you ready to go into another program. I dropped the belt, Randy came to the ring, hit me with the scepter and that led to what I think was a match that belongs in the same category as my match with Hogan in WrestleMania VI."

The match he's talking about is the famous Retirement Match in WrestleMania VII, which was billed as the first "Career vs. Career" match, meaning whoever lost had to retire.

I realize that when you read this as an adult, you smirk, knowing that neither the Macho Man or Ultimate Warrior was going to hang up their wrestling trunks for good and never enter a ring again if they lost.

But . . .

If you were around ten years old at the time (like I was) you were genuinely concerned that you'd never see one of your two favorite wrestlers again. Laugh at it if you want, but for millions of kids in 1991, this was our reality.

Add in the fact that the Hogan vs. Sgt. Slaughter face-off held little appeal in the way of backstory and buildup, and what you have is a majority of fans tuning in as if the Ultimate Warrior vs. Macho Man match was the main event.

That was how Savage viewed the match (all of his matches, really) and that was Hellwig's mindset as well.

"Me and Randy both have A-personalities," he said. "Typically when you have two people like us there's a clashing, but there wasn't between us. We had really good chemistry. And I liked Randy as a person. He was a really stand-up guy."

Where some may have felt threatened to face off in back-to-back WrestleManias with the company's two biggest stars (Hogan and Savage), Hellwig was inspired.

"I've never been envious of people that had talent," he said. "They make me work harder."

Savage, for his part, also had an ace up his sleeve. He knew that following the match, his two-year heel run was likely over because the WWF was closing the loop on one of the longest-running stories they had going: his relationship with Elizabeth. After keeping the couple apart since the Mega Powers split, it was time to give the people what they wanted — a reunion of Macho Man and Miss Elizabeth.

But first, the Retirement Match at the Los Angeles Memorial Sports Arena in front of 16,158 people.

Two things stand out about the beginning of the Ultimate Warrior and Macho King's battle at WrestleMania VII. The first is that instead of his usual dead sprint to the ring, the Warrior slowly walked in, soaking up the applause and giving off the impression that this was the biggest match of his life.

Second was the Ultimate Warrior's size. As we've established, Savage wasn't the biggest wrestler. He regularly gave up several inches and often twenty or more pounds to his rivals. Usually, fans hardly noticed. Hogan, for instance, was much taller and beefier than Savage but somehow it felt like Randy took up similar space in the ring.

Not so with Warrior.

When the Macho King and the Ultimate Warrior circled each other on the mat, Warrior looked like he was a different species than Macho. A monster. When they slammed into each other off the ropes, Macho bounced off him like he'd run into the side of a building.

About six minutes into the match, Warrior picks up Savage in a choke slam with the ease of a dad lifting his two-year-old. Then he tosses him to the ground like a crumpled-up piece of paper. In fact, Savage spends the first third of the fight being flung around like a stuffed animal that a kid was wrestling. Every punch by the Warrior lands with a thunderclap.

The beating looked so brutal and real because Savage was a lights-out seller. He knew the harder the hits looked, the more visceral the feel for the audience. So he jumped on every lift to make himself seem lighter. He ricocheted himself off of every slam and punch. It was a master class.

As the match wore on and Macho King finally turned the tide, he went for the finish, hitting Warrior with five straight flying elbows off the top rope, each time with the Warrior on the ground, still and lifeless. It appeared over.

We could be seeing the end of the Ultimate Warrior!

But when Macho went for the pin, with the audience screeching, Warrior kicked out. Savage sold the moment with everything he had, spreading his arms out, bewildered as to how a human being could survive his finishing move nearly a half-dozen times.

He's in shock!

As the audience cheers, they bring the Ultimate Warrior slowly back to life. In no time, he's high-stepping around the ring and then mopping the floor with Savage. *Boom. Boom. Boom.* He drops him with three straight clotheslines, lifts him three feet over his head for a Gorilla Slam, hits his splash, pins him and . . . Savage kicks out.

All of a sudden the cameras cut to Miss Elizabeth in the audience.

What is she doing there?

She has a worried look on her face. She's concerned for Savage.

Now it's Warrior's turn to be confused. He cries out to his warrior gods. He talks to his hands. He looks up at the sky, acting as if his talent had betrayed him. Then, after nearly getting his throat smashed by a Savage double axe handle off the top rope outside the ring, he makes his comeback while the audience gets more shots of an increasingly distraught Miss Elizabeth.

After three monster spears, Warrior drags Savage to the center of the ring and doesn't even bother with a pin. He simply puts his boot on Savage's chest for the three count and wins.

Now the action really starts.

With Savage down and out, and his career seemingly over with forced retirement after losing, Queen Sherri enters the ring and begins to humiliate Savage. She yells at him and kicks him while he's down.

With every punch, they cut to Elizabeth watching from her seat.

We see the pain on her face.

In her eyes.

Does she still love him?

What's she going to do?

Suddenly, she's out of her seat! She climbs over the barricade, slides into the ring, grabs Sherri by her hair and tosses her out of the ring.

The crowd erupts in cheers!

Lying on the mat face down, Savage has no idea what's going on. Each time Elizabeth reaches for him, he brushes her away, thinking it's Sherri. This is a brilliant bit of storytelling, drawing the moment out, delaying the pleasure of the audience for as long as possible.

Then . . .

He pulls himself up on the ropes and turns with his fists up, thinking it's Sherri (who betrayed him) . . . but . . . it's his first love, Miss Elizabeth. She puts her hands to her face. Savage sees Sherri screaming at him from the floor and being escorted out and it dawns on him what happened.

Miss Elizabeth came to his rescue.

Not a single person in the arena is in their seat.

The cheering starts slowly at first, growing to a monster ovation.

Elizabeth is crying. Macho King is spinning.

"Tears are flowing! What a heart on that lady!" Gorilla Monsoon shouts. "She loves him. She's loved him from the beginning! And I think he loves her!"

Savage runs his hands through his hair.

Should he trust her?

Can he trust her?

Yes!

He opens his arms and she dives into them! There's not a dry eye in the house. As he lifts her off the mat in a massive bear hug, "Pomp and Circumstance" begins to play. For wrestling fans, it's better than any ending in any Hollywood movie.

"Look around us!" Monsoon shouts. "Everyone is crying! . . . What a woman! And what a man!"

Every pan to the audience shows fans clapping and crying and giving the couple a standing ovation. Savage lost the match and he doesn't have a belt, but he's back on top as a good guy — a brilliantly executed creative move.

As a final gesture, Savage holds the ropes for Elizabeth to leave the ring, reversing the roles from her tenure as his manager.

"He's turning into a big softie," Bobby "The Brain" Heenan says.

"He entered the match with·twenty thousand people booing him. He lost the match. His career's over, but he got Elizabeth back. This is his farewell," Monsoon says, summing up the evening.

Oh, right, you forgot he was "retiring" after this.

Not so fast.

Most couples take a year or more to plan their real wedding. The WWF gave Macho Man and Miss Elizabeth five months to map out their fake one. And that included a televised "proposal."

The timeline went like this:

Savage and Miss Elizabeth reunited at WrestleMania VII on March 24. On June 17 at a *Superstars of Wrestling* taping, Savage, decked out in a purple and yellow suit, met "Mean" Gene Okerlund and Elizabeth in the ring to get down on one knee.

"I've got something to say to the zillions of people around the world! And I've also got something to say to Elizabeth. Elizabeth! Elizabeth! Elizabeth! I love you! . . . Will! You! Marry! Me!"

"Ohhhh yeahhh!" Elizabeth says, causing the audience to howl in delight.

Shortly after, a wedding date was announced for August 26, 1991, at SummerSlam in Madison Square Garden. The nuptials would be broadcast live on pay-per-view.

For the next two months, the WWF launched an advertising campaign that "cordially invited you to the wedding of Randy Savage and Miss Elizabeth." At nearly every show the couple made appearances and signed autographs to build momentum.

To counter the lovey-dovey feel of the broadcast, the WWF billed the event as "A Match Made in Heaven," which was the wedding portion, and "A Match Made in Hell," which promoted the main event of the night, a handicap tag team match with Hulk Hogan and the Ultimate Warrior joining forces against Sergeant Slaughter, Colonel Mustafa and General Adnan.

For the rest of the summer, the WWF marketing department became an offshoot of *Bridal Guide*, featuring the couple in radio ads, newspaper spreads and the coveted cover of *WWF Magazine*.

In the magazine's feature story, "Miss Elizabeth: A Woman of Devotion," Liz explains why she's "marrying" Savage.

"Another woman would have written him off long ago," she said. "But another woman has never gotten as close as I have to the Macho Man. I've come to realize that, beneath all his bluster, he's like a little boy who wants to be held and told he's good. Underneath all the boasting there's a warm side that has invited me in and let me become a part of his life . . . Yes, we've had our hard times, but show me a couple who hasn't."

There is nothing fictional about this statement. It's true in both the WWF storyline and Randy and Liz's real marriage. And for a brief moment, planning the fake, public SummerSlam wedding at MSG in New York City papered over the harsh, serious issues that had affected their marriage since they first said "I do" in Frankfurt, Kentucky, in December of 1984.

"They were like two kids planning their wedding," Linda Bollea, Hulk Hogan's ex-wife, said.

When the big day finally came, the event felt like something planned for a royal monarch.

"Their marriage at SummerSlam was one of those great weddings," Okerlund said. "Talk about pomp and circumstance."

With Miss Elizabeth in a white lace wedding dress and Savage wearing a white and gold suit with a white and gold feathered cowboy hat and white and gold sunglasses, the two stood on a podium at the center of Madison Square Garden and gave their vows.

Savage, when asked if he'd honor Miss Elizabeth "so long as you both shall live," delivered an all-time "Oooohhhh yeahhh!" Liz stuck with the traditional "I will" and then they kissed a "kiss seen around the world!" according to Gorilla Monsoon.

Roddy Piper, also commentating, said, "That's what it's all about! That's America! Beautiful! You did it, Macho!"

Thousands of balloons were released from the Garden's rafters and the couple waved to the twenty thousand fans in attendance.

"It was done so well in the context of what we'd become: sports entertainment," Ted DiBiase said. "It was like watching the prince and the princess get married on television."

There would be no honeymoon.

CHAPTER 29

Snake Bitten

"You're gonna do *what?*"

Lanny Poffo, like many little brothers before him, was pretending to sleep in the back seat of his older brother's car on a road trip. Up front, Randy and Elizabeth were arguing about something Randy had volunteered to do that sounded insane: let a venomous, ten-foot king cobra bite him clean on the arm.

"Let's just say Elizabeth was against the idea," Lanny said.

Elizabeth tried to talk Randy out of it the entire drive through Indiana on the way to a *Superstars of Wrestling* taping just before Thanksgiving of 1991.

"Randy knew it would be good business," Lanny said. "It would push their feud to the next level. And he told Elizabeth that Jake [Roberts] said the snake was de-venomized."

Elizabeth wasn't convinced and her concern was giving her husband pause.

So how did we get to the point where Randy Savage was willing to let half-inch fangs pierce his skin to shock a live audience? For that we have to go back two months to the wedding reception after the ceremony at Madison Square Garden.

Shortly following the nuptials, the newly married couple headed to a staged reception emceed by "Mean" Gene Okerlund with a band and a few tables of "guests." With the cameras rolling, Okerlund toasted "Mr. and Mrs. Macho" and they breezed through all of the normal wedding moments in about forty-five seconds.

They drank champagne with their arms intertwined. They had their first dance. They cut the cake. Liz threw the bridal bouquet. Then they began opening presents.

They got a new blender, a pair of shiny silver candlesticks, a silver ice holder and . . . uh-oh . . . hiding innocuously in a pink box, a *king cobra* courtesy of Jake "The Snake" Roberts! This horrifying reveal was followed by an ambush attack from The Undertaker and Roberts himself, knocking Macho Man to the floor and scaring the crap out of Liz.

This wedding "gift" kicked off the storyline for Macho's next feud with Roberts, but there was still the matter of his forced retirement after the Career vs. Career match with the Ultimate Warrior.

Over the course of the six months since WrestleMania VII, Savage had only been doing commentary, but that didn't stop Jake from dogging him every chance he got. The near-constant slew of insults towards Macho Man was supposed to culminate in Indiana, where Jake would goad Macho out of the booth and attack him with the cobra.

By the time the car with Lanny, Liz and Randy arrived at the old Market Square Arena in Indianapolis, Savage was good and fired up, ready to confront Jake about this ludicrous idea. Making matters worse, all the boys in the locker room knew about the planned snakebite and decided to mess with Macho.

"We're all back there playing cards and Albert the snake guy shows up," Hacksaw Jim Duggan said. "He throws the snake on the ground and this cobra stands up three feet in the air. We're all like, 'Holy shit.' Albert went to grab the cobra and it bit his hand and we all ran out. Then DiBiase goes over to Macho and says, 'You know, Mach, I don't think they can get all the poison out.'"

"What do you mean?" Macho asks.

"I think they can only get 99 percent out," DiBiase says, screwing with him.

Macho can't take it.

He storms over to Jake with a firm demand.

"Your cobra's gonna bite me, okay, you got that?" Macho said. "But here's the fuckin' proooblem, yeahhh . . . There's a lot of people around here that'd like to take the Macho Man OUT. You know what I'm sayin'? And you might be one of them."

"What are you talking about?" Roberts replied.

"I want to fuckin' know . . . If the thing's got the fuckin' gimmicks out."

"Randy, it's not poisonous," Roberts said.

"Ah-huh! Good, so you say. Then you don't mind if it bites you FIRST. If you don't let it bite you, then it tells me it hasn't been fixed, yeah!"

Jake is backed into a corner. He knows his snake has had the venom taken out. He also knows it hurts like hell to get bitten and isn't in the mood for it. But he has no choice. He walks with Savage into the locker room, rolls up his pant leg, takes out the snake and lets the cobra sink its teeth into him.

"I had to pull my damn pant leg up and let that son of a bitch bite me," Roberts says.

"Ooohhh kayyy," Macho says. "Just sit down right there, Snake Man. Don't take no antidote or serums or nothin'!"

Thirty minutes later Macho Man comes back.

"How you doin', Snake Man? That botherin' ya?"

Roberts has been sitting there pissed off for a half-hour with fang marks in his leg. But he isn't dead or sick. This satisfies Randy. Sort of.

"Ahh, okay," Macho says. "But make sure it's the same snake in the ring. I don't want no snakes changin'!"

Roberts is worn out.

What have I gotten myself into? he thinks.

Hours later, Roberts lures Macho out of the announcer's booth and into the ring, according to plan. Once he gets Savage tied up in the ropes, he goes for his snake bag and there's a collective "holy shit!" among the audience.

Is Jake gonna let his cobra loose on Macho Man?

Yep.

But not a calm snake — a furious snake.

"I paintbrushed the shit out of that snake," Roberts says, referring to smacking the snake bag before taking it out. "That snake was ready!"

With Savage's arms stuck in the ropes, Roberts picks up the snake and drops it right onto his chest, steering its mouth towards Macho Man's left bicep, and then *SNAP!*

The snake latches on and gnaws through Savage's flesh while he writhes in pain. This is no gimmick. There is no trick photography. There is no way to fake this.

It is a real, live king cobra chewing the shit out of Randy Savage's arm.

It was so graphic that kids in the audience cried, and when it aired they put a huge red *X* over it on the screen, which made the entire scene even more provocative.

"Then that snake wouldn't let go!" Roberts says. "It went on forever. Elizabeth came running down to tell me to get the snake off of him. At first I couldn't get it off. It shocked people."

That was exactly the point.

"Our feud generated a lot of interest after that angle," Savage said. "Even though they couldn't show it on national TV. It was too graphic ... My arm blew up like a balloon for days. About five days later, they had to rush me to the hospital with a 104-degree fever. It's unbelievable to walk into the hospital and tell a doctor it's a snakebite. Finally, the fever went down. They gave me antibiotics, and luckily, the snake WAS de-venomized, but twelve days later the snake died."

This made Savage laugh.

"He was de-venomized, but maybe I wasn't!" Savage joked.

After the snake stunt, Savage petitioned WWF President Jack Tunney to reinstate him into the company so he could face Jake in the ring. Tunney granted Savage's wish, setting up a match between the two at the new *This Tuesday in Texas* pay-per-view, which Savage won. When the match was over, Roberts hit Savage with multiple DDTs (his finishing move) and shoved Elizabeth, leading to a rematch at *Saturday Night's Main Event XXX* in early 1992. Savage won that too, closing the program.

"We worked our asses off to build that storyline," Roberts said. "Randy and I were just naturals. He was a good listener out there in the ring, and he would let me lead him. He was a raw ball of energy ...

"The WWE rushed the whole thing because it was just too powerful. It didn't fit their timeline, and that was stunning because we could have wrestled each other for years. It was supposed to lead into WrestleMania but it didn't."

Instead, Vince McMahon placed Savage in a feud with the new WWF champion, the recently acquired legend from the WCW, Ric Flair. Once again, Elizabeth took center stage in the conflict as Flair claimed to have had a prior sexual relationship with her that Savage didn't know about, going so far as to produce doctored photos.

This led to a match between the two icons at WrestleMania VIII for both the World Championship and Elizabeth's honor. Unfortunately, it also ran parallel to the unwinding of Randy and Elizabeth's real-life marriage. What followed from the end of 1991 to the end of 1992 was a mix of incredible career joy and excruciating emotional pain that played out publicly for Savage, nearly breaking him as a person and a pro wrestler.

While the feud with Flair heated up and Savage continuously proclaimed his love for Elizabeth as part of the WWF's fictional storyline, the facts of his life were the polar opposite: he and Liz were separating.

Things came to a head one night in Miami while Hulk was on location shooting the movie *Mr. Nanny*. The trip began innocently enough, with Liz driving down solo to hang out with Linda and their kids. At some point, after Liz stopped answering calls from Randy and wasn't in her room when Linda went looking for her, things escalated quickly.

Randy, concerned and paranoid, flew down to Miami that night and arrived wild-eyed and angry.

"Where's Liz?!" he shouted when he showed up at the Hogans' room.

"Randy, I don't know!" Linda said, really not knowing.

"Where do you think she is? Who was she with last? What did you guys do?"

Linda had never seen Randy like this and wasn't sure what was going on. She was also unaware that Liz was trying to avoid Randy.

"I'd never seen them argue or fight at all," Linda said.

"When Liz showed up, I didn't know that Randy and her had broken up," Hogan said. "He was so intense. He was thinking that my wife and I led her astray and that wasn't the case."

But there was no changing Randy's mind. Once he found Elizabeth they decided it was over between them. Then Savage decided it was over between him and Hogan. Two of the most important relationships in his life — done in a matter of days.

Now here's the insane part.

While all of that was going on in the real world, Macho Man and Miss Elizabeth still had to pretend to be in-love honeymooners in the WWF universe, *and* Randy was about to become the World Champion again at WrestleMania VIII.

Can you imagine how much this would mess with your head?

You're losing the love of your life in real life, but in your fictional life you're happy newlyweds. Your marriage has hit rock bottom, but you're about to reach the mountaintop of your profession. Your fans love seeing you and Elizabeth back together, but you're about to divorce for good.

It was like psychological bumper cars for Randy, with one emotion smashing into the next on a daily basis.

"Randy was crushed by it because he wanted to make it go no matter if it was going or not," his mom, Judy, said.

On April 5, 1992, the Macho Man and the Nature Boy met in the ring in front of 62,000 fans at the Hoosier Dome in Indiana for the eighth WrestleMania. By this point, Savage was thirty-nine years old and Flair was forty-three and both were near the end of their physical primes, but their stage presence was electric. The two men had known each other since the mid-1970s, when Savage had just finished playing for the Reds, and they got a kick out of working together.

"Randy was still playing baseball when I first met him," Flair said. "I was there in his corner during his infancy in the business, saw him blossom and become so much better. I was proud of him, and wrestling him at WrestleMania was awesome."

The two clicked and clearly appreciated what each other brought to the table.

"When you have that kind of chemistry and respect for each other, it doesn't take a lot of thought process to go out there and make music," Flair said.

The match had everything. It was two masters at work, one playing the hero (Savage) and the other playing the villain (Flair). The moves were expertly timed. The selling was off the charts. Flair, who was new to those in the WWF audience who hadn't followed him at the WCW, drew heat like nobody else. Savage, now beloved, fought back with guts and gusto.

The two men battled all over the ring, hitting each other with Irish whips, tosses, clotheslines, suplexes, small packages, false finishes and more. The drama was laid out like a screenplay, with Flair pummeling Macho early, then Macho coming from behind and hurting Flair, who then came back and "injured" Macho's knee.

We had blood. We had punishment. We had Mr. Perfect interfering on the outside for Flair and Elizabeth clutching her hands as always for Macho.

The turning point in the match was when Flair "ruined" Savage's knee in a figure four leglock. That became the audience's hook. Every time Flair punished the knee, the fans went deeper in the tank for Savage. This set up our climax, where a limping Macho Man suddenly blocked a Flair punch and whipped him to the ground for the pin. *One . . . Twoooo . . . Threeeeee!*

The crowd went apoplectic.

The "Macho Man" Randy Savage (the "King" slowly disappeared throughout 1991) had just won his second World Championship.

"Curt Hennig [Mr. Perfect], God rest his soul, managed me," Flair said. "And Liz managed Randy and we gave them a hell of a show. Wrestling him in that spotlight was awesome, but it was a difficult point in time on a personal level for Randy. Emotions are difficult, and personal lives are difficult to deal with. There was so much tension at that time between Randy and Liz. As a matter of fact, that was the last time they were together. They split the next day."

On April 19, fourteen days after WrestleMania VIII, Miss Elizabeth made her final appearance with the WWF.

For a time, Savage continued duking it out with Flair minus the Miss Elizabeth storyline. He had title defenses against Flair, Shawn Michaels, and a match with the Ultimate Warrior at SummerSlam in front of 80,000 people at a sold-out Wembley Stadium in London. After finally dropping the belt to Flair, Savage joined the Ultimate Warrior to form the "Ultimate Maniacs" tag team.

Unfortunately, the busyness of being champion wasn't enough to block out the pain Savage was feeling in his heart. He had truly and madly loved Elizabeth, and by the end of the fall of 1992, their marriage was officially over. Her absence had been conspicuous throughout the summer, and once the divorce was made official on September 18, Savage released a statement in *WWF Magazine* addressing the news:

> It is a fact that Elizabeth and I are divorced, and I would like to go on record right now and say that this is nobody's fault. It's just one of those things that didn't work out.
>
> The next thing I want to say is: Elizabeth, I know you're out there and reading this. Please remember that in my heart, I will always love you.
>
> — Randy Savage

Despite staying in the ring through the fall, by the start of 1993 the drama and the public split with Elizabeth had taken its toll. Even the always-ready, never-tired Macho Man needed time to regroup and recharge.

"I went through that divorce and I didn't feel like I could give 100 percent," he said afterward. "In fact it was far less than 100 percent. A lot of times in your personal life you gotta take a step back to go forward."

The steps back he's referring to were both literal (in the ring) and figurative (in his life). Rather than take a break from the WWF entirely, Savage hung up his trunks for a while and worked as a color commentator for much of that year.

Along the way a funny thing happened.

Somehow, without actively wrestling, his popularity grew. With all the amazing angles and epic battles and unforgettable promos and the marriage and the Mega Powers and the divorce, Savage had been at the top of the WWF for the better part of a decade. Time and talent and tenacity had done their job. While he worked the commentator booth, something became clear to everyone in wrestling. The Macho Man had moved beyond heel and babyface status and transcended to a higher plane of superstardom: icon.

Without planning it, by stepping away from the ring he found himself with not only the time but the inclination to become the official ambassador of the WWF to fans, companies and philanthropies around the world. Even better, he enjoyed the hell out of it.

"One of Randy's guiding philosophies was that he always wanted to use his fame to bring enjoyment to others," Lanny said. "He was very sincere in this. And after the break with Elizabeth and from the ring, he had the time to embrace that."

He also had time to plan his next career moves and explore his role as celebrity pitchman, forming one of the all-time great brand partnerships.

CHAPTER 30

Snap into It

"**C**an you do one more?" a soft voice asks meekly off-camera.

"I've got thirty more in me, brother!" Randy Savage says.

The Macho Man is standing in front of a green screen filming a Slim Jim commercial. After the company couldn't secure their first choice for a new brand pitchman, comedian Sam Kinison, and they weren't thrilled with their second choice, the Ultimate Warrior, Randy Savage stepped into the role and never looked back. Actually, he didn't step into the role — he snapped into it.

Andrew Modlin, the former senior marketing manager for Slim Jim, tells the story of how on the very first commercial shoot — where Savage would debut the line, "Need a little excitement? Snap into a Slim Jim!" — they thought they lost him due to a stupid injury on a set they'd built to resemble a library.

"The first commercial shoot we did, there was a mishap," Modlin said. "And the books came down and then the door came down and he ran out on the door and he slipped and fell. And we were very concerned that he was going to walk off the set at this point."

But they didn't know Savage very well. First, he's not a prima donna in the work ethic department. Second, he's not walking off any set with money involved.

"He gets up and in his voice says, 'Let's do that again!'" Modlin said. "He wanted to be perfect for you, because of what you were looking for."

The ad campaign was aimed at Gen Xers in the early '90s. High school kids. College kids. Twentysomethings. And Macho Man was the embodiment of what they were after.

"What we were looking for was a rebellious attitude," Modlin said. "Randy was a perfect match for what we were trying to achieve both on and off camera."

From the look to the voice to the attitude, Savage somehow made plastic-wrapped sticks of mechanically separated chicken, beef, lactic acid starter culture, dextrose, salt, sodium nitrite and hydrolyzed soy cool. He also printed money for the brand.

Starting in 1993, the famous Slim Jim commercials, where Savage would destroy kids' boredom with his catchphrase and cured meat, were everywhere. They'd show up during wrestling matches and NFL games and sitcoms. Ads were in every sports and entertainment magazine you could find. Macho Man display cases decorated the cash registers in every 7-Eleven, convenience store and gas station around the country. It got so that the second you saw that dark red and yellow coloring, you knew Slim Jims were close. The results blew away anything the brand could have hoped for.

"When we started our advertising campaign and then expanded it nationally, within about a three to four year period we had doubled sales of the business because of Randy," Modlin said.

By the year 2000, Slim Jims' revenue topped $150 million.

With sales soaring through the roof, Savage's pop culture status continued to grow. Being a pitchman for the beef jerky brand gave him a level of visibility no other wrestler, not even Hulk Hogan, could match.

The Macho Man was no longer limited to being seen on pay-per-views and main events and the new *Monday Night Raw*. He was at NASCAR races, grand openings and NFL games. His voice and face were ubiquitous — to the point that some people weren't aware of his legendary career in the ring.

"[Slim Jim] has been great for me," he told a young Jeff Pearlman of *The Tennessean*. "I never imagined doing the Slim Jim ads would bring so much recognition. A lot of people know that before [they know] I'm a wrestler."

While the last quote was certainly true, it also gnawed at Savage a bit.

After his divorce, his time spent commentating, working with brands and making appearances for charities was rewarding. He loved it. It helped heal his soul.

That was one side of the coin.

On the other side were his age and ambition. He was barely forty years old, far too young to simply never wrestle again. After twelve months on the sidelines, he felt a strong inner pull to get back in the ring.

"Randy did fine," Ted DiBiase said of Macho's time in the booth. "But being in the ring as a competitor was his first love."

Publicly, throughout most of 1994, Savage said all the right things about his position within the WWF. When asked in the fall how he felt about retirement and how some athletes can't walk away, he said, "That's a very good question. Ego does have a lot to do with it. I've even seen other athletes go and compete in leagues where there's less competition, just to be the big fish in a little pond . . .

"I'm very comfortable with what I've done in the World Wrestling Federation, so I don't have a problem with that. Whether I'm broadcasting or not broadcasting, or in Florida riding my surfboard, it doesn't matter to me."

This was, in no uncertain terms, complete and total bullshit. Wrestling again *did* matter to him — more than anything.

"Randy wasn't happy at all being behind the desk," Kevin Nash said. "Randy wanted to be in the action. Randy still thought he had a lot to give."

That was exactly how he felt.

"Okay. I did it. I stayed out for about a year or year and a half and now I'm ready to throw my hat back in the ring," Savage said. "I made a commitment to myself. I'm a survivor. And I'm ready to go again."

Randy being Randy, he didn't want to return to the ring aimlessly. He wanted to come back with a plan — an epic program that would allow him to wrap up his illustrious career in style with a huge, headlining match at a WrestleMania. He even had the perfect opponent selected and got so excited about it, he woke up his brother, Lanny, well after midnight to share the idea.

"He's getting bored and he's noticing that Shawn Michaels is emerging — not just as a tag team wrestler, but the greatest talent in the business at the time," Lanny said. "He calls me up at two in the morning and he says, 'Can you find some breakaway champagne bottles?'"

Lanny asks why and then hears the idea. It's good.

"His plan was to drink to Shawn Michaels's career," Lanny said. "Pour him a glass, they would drink, they would toast, and then Randy would smash the bottle over Michaels's head, starting a two-year feud — like the Hatfields and McCoys — ending in WrestleMania, where Michaels loses his hair if he loses and Randy retires to the announcing table if he loses."

For five years Savage had been chasing the opportunity for a match to rival his famous bout with Ricky "The Dragon" Steamboat at WrestleMania III. He believed he had the storyline and the talent to do it with Shawn Michaels.

Sounds amazing, right? What a finish! What a way to go out!

Not happening.

"Pat [Patterson] says, 'Randy, we're having a youth movement and the best thing you can do is stay on the microphone,'" Lanny said.

Vince McMahon felt the same way.

Savage was devastated.

"Randy had planned to pass the torch to Michaels and lose right in the middle of the ring, as he did at WrestleMania III, because he was not selfish. He wanted to do what was best for business. And they wouldn't let him," Lanny said. "That's why he went to the WCW."

Savage explained this decision years later.

"They wanted me to do the commentary thing, but I just wasn't ready to take off my boots at that point," Savage said. "I'm glad I didn't. It wasn't anything but an attitude, or a direction which the WWF was going [in], and they proved me to be 100 percent correct in where they were going, because they had a vision.

"But at the same time, it didn't work for me at that time. And I'm glad I made the move that I did, looking back, because I just wasn't ready to do that. I have to do things because I want to, not because I have to."

The decision to leave the WWF was an earthquake for the company. It was like announcing that Mickey Mouse was leaving Disney. All the guys looked up to him by that point. He was a mainstay. A cornerstone.

"It was a big blow to a lot of us in the locker room. He was a hero to most of the guys," Bret Hart said. "We always respected Randy. When I was in WCW he still had some misgivings about how he left the company. A little bitter. Felt he'd been betrayed. I sensed the same thing on the other side with Vince."

From the moment Savage joined the WWF he'd bonded with Vince McMahon and in fact was asked about him in the December '94 issue of *WWF Magazine*, where Macho was featured on the cover.

"I have always been able to tell Vince McMahon just how I feel — it could be negative or positive. He's a fighter, he's a tough guy and I'm not talking about physically," Savage said. "He's very aggressive about staying positive and attacking the situation. He doesn't lie back. I respect him, and I respect his whole family, and there's a reason for that. They're leaders."

The respect Savage had for McMahon made his decision to leave all the more difficult. But in Randy's mind, ultimately there was no decision. If the WWF wasn't going to let him wrestle, then his run was over. Time to go where he was wanted.

On November 7, 1994, Vince McMahon shared the news of Savage's departure with an emotional statement on *Monday Night Raw*:

> At this time, obviously conspicuous by his absence is the "Macho Man" Randy Savage. And I'd like to announce, unfortunately, that Randy Savage has been unable to sign a contract with the World Wrestling Federation — not unable to, rather to come to terms with the World Wrestling Federation for a new contract. But Randy, I know you're out there listening, and on behalf of all us

here in the World Wrestling Federation, all of your fans and certainly me, the number one fan, I'd like to say thank you for all of your positive contributions to the World Wrestling Federation. Thank you, Randy Savage, for all the wonderful memories for so many years here in the World Wrestling Federation. We wish you nothing but the best. Godspeed, and good luck.

CHAPTER 31

Revived and Reunited

A thick, menacing steel door that belongs in front of a nuclear warehouse splits open from the middle. A red warning light flashes above. Heavy, thick white steam billows out.

Then a familiar voice echoes over the loudspeaker.

"Ladies and gentleman! Please welcome! The Macho Man! Randy Savage!"

Through the smoke a glittering gold and black cowboy hat emerges. Under the hat, wild sunglasses and a giant gold and black suit over a neon green shirt spin into frame. "Pomp and Circumstance" blares as Savage twirls and parades towards the source of the loudspeaker voice: "Mean" Gene Okerlund.

It's one month after Vince McMahon bid the Macho Man farewell on *Raw*, and this is Savage's debut, on December 3, 1994, on *WCW Saturday Night*.

World Championship Wrestling (WCW) was founded by television and media tycoon Ted Turner in 1988 after purchasing the assets of the National Wrestling Alliance and Jim Crockett Promotions. Turner's goal was to go head-to-head with the WWF for national pro wrestling supremacy.

After WCW had lost the battle to the WWF its first few years and been stuck with a regional audience in the early 1990s, Eric Bischoff took over as executive producer in 1993. To raise the profile of the company, one of his strategies was to take advantage of the WWF's stated "youth movement" by poaching talent they were no longer interested in supporting.

By the time Savage joined the WCW at the end of 1994, the company had built a roster that looked like an all-star team from the first five WrestleManias, including Bobby "The Brain" Heenan, Dusty Rhodes, "Mean" Gene Okerlund, the Honky Tonk Man, Hulk Hogan, Jesse Ventura, "Hacksaw" Jim Duggan, Jimmy Hart, "Mr. Wonderful" Paul Orndorff, Paul Roma and even Ricky "The Dragon" Steamboat.

When Macho Man joined, nearly all of the headliners from WrestleMania I through V were performing under the WCW banner, along with a few of their own stars like Ric Flair (back from the WWF), Sting, a young Triple H (Paul Levesque), up-and-comer Stone Cold (Stunning Steve Austin) and Diamond Dallas Page.

The move to bring in Savage was a no-brainer from a talent standpoint and was spearheaded behind the scenes by Hulk Hogan. Personal feelings aside, Hogan knew their battles meant something to wrestling fans of all ages, and having a Mega Powers reunion or rivalry would attract attention and further legitimize the WCW.

"Hulk Hogan was really the one to convince me Randy was a good asset," Bischoff said. "Hulk and Randy had a very on-again, off-again, hot-and-cold relationship. But when Hulk came to the WCW, he wanted to bring some of the biggest names he could. Despite what was then a relatively tense relationship between the two of them, Hulk was the one who kept after me to reach out to Randy."

When Randy was finally ready to leave the WWF for the WCW, his Slim Jim sponsorship, of all things, made it an easy transition. Bischoff explained the inner workings on his podcast.

> Randy's first contract was completely subsidized by Slim Jim. Randy came over, he was excited to jump over. Vince thought he was washed up and too old and beyond his prime. And Randy didn't feel that way. He was very motivated. He's a super-competitive guy. Randy had the

relationship with Slim Jim. That was not a WWE relationship. That was a Randy Savage relationship that WWE benefited from. So when Randy came over to WCW, that came over with him. And I negotiated a separate promotional agreement with Slim Jim, where the money went right into the WCW and the face value of that agreement was equal to or surpassed Randy's agreement.

This was one of the few business deals where everybody involved won. Savage was getting paid to wrestle again. The WCW was able to bring in a legend with no budget hit. And Slim Jim got a boatload of advertising, from placement on ring posts and ring aprons to Savage handing out Slim Jims to fans before matches.

It was everything Randy could have hoped for, but prior to joining the new company, he had one final question and it was the same one he had for Vince McMahon back in June of 1985: "Got room for my brother?"

The request was denied at first, but when Savage got around to renegotiating his contract, he made it clear that he was willing to take less money for his little brother.

"Randy, because he loved his brother as much as he did, until the day he died, wanted Lanny to have an opportunity financially and hopefully at some point an opportunity to perform in the ring," Bischoff said. "Randy came to me and said, 'I want you to hire my brother.' My response was, 'Randy, I can't. I can't justify it.' Randy made it clear that he would take less money. We had talked about that number. We were pretty comfortable with it.

"So of course I did it because just like bringing in Randy, because of the Slim Jim deal, bringing in Lanny had zero effect on my budget."

With the business out of the way, Savage came out swinging for Hogan — then the WCW Champion — from that very first *WCW Saturday Night* show and interview with "Mean" Gene. Then in a plot twist, during his first appearance at Starrcade, Savage bailed out his old nemesis Hogan against an attack by Avalanche and his crew, the Three Faces of Fear.

At this point there are two important things to remember about Savage's run in the WCW. The first is that it started when he was forty-two years old, with a wrestling body that was biologically close to ffity-five from the thousands of bumps he'd taken over twenty years in the ring. He was slower. He didn't jump as high. He couldn't toss guys nearly as far.

This isn't to say he didn't do many of the same moves from the peak of his career. He did. It's just that they were maybe 60 percent of prime Macho Man. One thing that did help him was that the WCW rings were smaller than the WWF rings, which he claimed made him look faster.

The second thing to remember is that most of the younger guys on the WCW roster idolized him.

"Randy Savage is one of the guys I looked up to," Steve Borden (Sting) said. "I loved him. He was so far out there with his character. There was something about it I could identify with."

Between the sponsorship money, his drawing power with the fans and his presence affecting the guys in the locker room, Savage was a game changer for the WCW.

"He gave the WCW incredible legitimacy," Lex Luger, a former rival and WCW Champion, said. "Everyone he worked with in turn was legitimized."

Lanny loves talking about this comeback because it shows the grit and determination he always admired in his older brother.

"My brother never needed a chip on his shoulder to be motivated," Lanny said. "But he never forgot how the WWF treated him at the end. When they said he was too old, he headed for a place that said he wasn't too old and he built himself right back up to become WCW Champion."

Savage won his first WCW Championship at World War 3 following a chaotic, borderline absurd, feast of muscles event called a sixty-man, three-ring battle royal. As the name suggested, it involved three rings of sixty men (twenty in each ring) wrestling for the championship belt.

Ironically, his old pal Hogan gave him the win after eliminating Sting, Lex Luger and "The Giant" Paul Wight together, before getting pulled out by The Giant under the bottom rope. That left Savage and another former WWF performer, One Man Gang, in the ring, and Savage eliminated him for the belt.

SuperBrawls. Bashes at the Beach. Halloween Havocs. World Wars. Starrcades. Stampedes. Clashes of Champions. Savage did 'em all.

Hogan. Sting. Flair. "Stunning" Steve Austin. He wrestled 'em all. Once they even managed to bring Angelo Poffo into the storyline for a Slamboree match.

Savage's crowning achievement in the WCW, though, from a storyline and rivalry perspective, was his last great program with Diamond Dallas Page (DDP).

In 1996, the WCW introduced a gimmick called the New World Order (nWo) with Scott Hall, Kevin Nash and the dark-bearded, newly branded villain "Hollywood" Hulk Hogan. The angle was that the nWo was a group of outlaw wrestlers, unaffiliated with the WCW, who were trying to infiltrate and take over the company.

The concept of a group of rogue badasses messing up the "corporate" WCW was brilliant. They used guerrilla marketing tactics, broke into broadcasts and shows and brought a ton of attention to the WCW overall, propelling their *Monday Nitro* show into a ratings war with WWF's *Raw*.

In early 1997, the Macho Man, who had dropped his famous neon colors and started wearing all-black outfits including black bandanas and black sunglasses, joined the nWo and began his feud with Diamond Dallas Page by spray-painting "nWo" on his back after a sneak attack on an episode of *Nitro*.

There were other added wrinkles as well, including one where Savage and the newly returned Miss Elizabeth (Savage invited her to the WCW once they were on good terms) "outed" the fact that Kimberly, DDP's Diamond Doll valet, was his wife in real life.

The program lasted nearly eight months and included matches at the Spring Stampede, the Great American Bash and a tag team match at Bash at the Beach. Bear in mind that DDP was forty-one years old and Savage was forty-five during their run. The two had excellent chemistry together and the feud was notable for launching Page into another level of stardom.

"Two years before we actually worked together, he [Savage] pulled me aside in a nightclub, and we talked about psychology and about the character Diamond Dallas Page having too many gimmicks with the sunglasses and the cigar and the gum . . . he was like, 'Brother, ya need to knock it back,'" Page said.

Knowing that he was getting solid-gold advice from an all-time great, Page took everything Macho said to heart. It took him time to refine the gimmicks he wanted to keep and drop the deadweight, but it worked. Eventually, he got the Diamond Cutter hand sign over as his signature. Savage was impressed and asked to put a program together with Page, who hadn't done a pay-per-view yet.

"So here we are in Florence, South Carolina, this place is sold out, people are hanging from the rafters, and Arn Anderson walks into the dressing room, and he says, 'So Mach . . . what do you wanna do for the finish tonight?'" Page said.

Savage, who controlled his own booking and had full control over how these things go, says, "Hmmm . . . I think I wanna take the Diamond Cutter tonight."

DDP couldn't believe it.

"I'll never forget it," Page said. "Arn was shocked. He says, 'Diamond, you realize what an honor this is?' I'm like, uh, yeah! Are you kidding?"

Savage and Page put on an incredible show, and just as Macho Man was about to slam Page, he reversed it, spun Savage down and hit the Diamond Cutter.

"The roof blew off," Page said. "The ref slid down: One! Two! Three! And the place erupted. While we're lying there, Randy said, 'We got our finish for Spring Stampede.' . . . When he put me over at Spring Stampede on April 5, it was my 41st birthday."

The latter Spring Stampede match was a turning point in Page's career. It made him a top guy in the WCW and a main event pay-per-view draw. That was the power of the Savage mystique. He was a kingmaker at that point.

Later that year, on Thanksgiving, DDP is getting calls from some people he helped get jobs, thanking him. It's that time of year. The holidays. Everyone is taking time out to be grateful. It puts Page in a reflective mood and he begins to think about who he is grateful for. Jake "The Snake" Roberts helped him out. Dusty Rhodes was his mentor . . .

Then he thinks, "I should call Randy Savage." When he dials the number, Randy doesn't pick up, so he leaves a message.

"I go, 'Randy, I know you're probably gonna think this is a little corny, but I just gotta tell you, man, without you, I'm not sitting in this spot in life right now. And I want you to know, for what it's worth, I really appreciate it, man. I hope you have a really great Thanksgiving.'

"And that was it. Two weeks go by, I didn't even see him, and I forgot about it. The next TV taping, he comes up to me. 'Diamond! C'mere!' He was just as intense behind the scenes, y'know? He pulls me aside, and I'm like, *Oh man . . . what'd I do?*"

"I got your message," Savage says. "I gotta tell ya. I played it for my dad. I said, 'Dad . . . did you ever get a message like this from one of the boys?' He replied, 'Randy, I've never even HEARD of anyone getting a message like this from one of the boys.'"

Then Savage pulled Page in and gave him a huge bear hug.

"I want you to know," Savage said. "It meant everything to me."

Before Savage's nWo run was over, he beat Sting for his third WCW Championship (on a torn ACL) and continued feuds with longtime colleagues Roddy Piper, Bret Hart and, as always, Hogan. In one of his final in-character splits from the new "Hollywood" Hulkster, Savage joined a rival nWo faction called the nWo Wolfpack.

Eric Bischoff, who spent a lot time with both Savage and Hogan during this period, said things were solid between the two of them in the late '90s.

"They got along great," he said. "Oftentimes I'd go down and hang out at Hulk's on the weekend or if I had business to do I'd stay at Hulk's for three or four days and Randy was there all the time. They worked out together. They trained together. Ate sushi together. Drank beer together. They were very, very friendly at this point."

Miss Elizabeth, for her part, was still chugging along as a wrestling manager, joining the nWo and also going with Randy to the nWo Wolfpack. By this time, Savage wore more black than Johnny Cash and nearly all of his gear had ditched the "Macho Man" wording in place of the single word "Madness" written in jagged letters on everything. Liz wore all-black outfits as well.

The images and videos of Macho and Elizabeth backstage and entering the ring with WCW are in stark contrast to a decade earlier — from fluorescent neon capes and bright fabric and classy cocktail dresses to black jeans and black leather skirts and shirts.

Elizabeth sumed up their time in the WCW best.

"It's still fun," she said. "You just can't explain it. It's a shock to me to think that the whole microcosm of people who were involved in wrestling that many years ago in the WWF are still on top: Hulk, Randy, Roddy, Mean Gene. It's amazing."

CHAPTER 32

Dark Macho

This was not the Macho Man you grew up with. This was some old guy who used to be Macho Man. This was a version of Macho Man that your brain couldn't reconcile.

Imagine going to the mall to see Santa Claus but instead of having snow white hair, a fluffy beard and a billowing red suit, the St. Nick you encounter is trying to be a hard-ass: his beard's trimmed tight, and his hair's slicked back Pat Riley–style into a ponytail. He's wearing black leather pants and a black shirt. He's got tight silver chains around his neck.

What the hell is this? you'd think.

For kids who grew up watching vintage Macho Man in the 1980s, the man appearing before them on WCW in 1999 was unrecognizable — jarring even. Sure, there were plenty of wrestling fans who had continued to follow Savage throughout his WCW run and had watched the slow evolution from pomp and circumstance to pissed off and crazy . . .

But . . .

For the tens of millions of fans who grew out of pro wrestling when they got to high school or college, or lost touch for a bit because they started families of their own, or were twelve at the time of WrestleMania III but were now twenty-five, this final evolution of the Macho Man was hard to wrap your head around.

By this time Randy Savage was almost fifty. He was on some concoction of chemicals and supplements and hormones that made his muscles look puffy and about to burst. And, as part of his new Team Madness gimmick, he'd surrounded himself with not one, not two, but three barely dressed women half his age: Gorgeous George, Madusa and Miss Madness.

Now, this isn't to say it didn't work for the die-hard fans who'd kept up with him. It did. Team Madness got over with the WCW followers of the late '90s, for the most part. But it was such a massive departure from the once-beloved character that when a majority of those late '80s and early '90s Savage fans happened to catch sight of this version of Macho, their first thoughts were:

Is that Randy Savage? and *I didn't know he was still wrestling.*

The charisma was still there and the essence was still there and the voice was mostly the same, somehow even gravellier, but the joy appeared to be long gone.

"He could no longer compete with the young wrestlers athletically," Lanny said. "So he got creative. He surrounded himself with as much gimmickry as he could."

This was an angrier, darker Randy Savage, who — when he said things in promos like "I'm the baddest dude on the planet!" — came off like an old man shouting nonsense rather than the iconic Macho Man from a decade earlier.

From his perspective, the turn was understandable.

He was trying to adapt. Trying to stay relevant. Trying to stay cool and hardcore, which was the theme in wrestling and entertainment in the late '90s. The WWF built their entire Attitude Era around this concept. The problem was that Savage was a half-century old and couldn't ably perform in the ring anymore. You can't be the baddest dude in wrestling if you wince climbing to the top rope.

Once considered the sun of the entire pro wrestling solar system, he had become a sideshow. An afterthought. And it was tough to watch for so many millions who were nostalgic for the former WrestleMania headliner. He made his final WCW appearance in May of 2000, and after a few years returned to the public eye for the pinnacle of this Dark Macho era with the release of his 2003 rap album, *Be a Man*.

Like nearly every important relationship in Randy Savage's life, this one began in a gym. He was working out with a few boxers in St. Petersburg, Florida, when he ran into Big3 Records chairman Bill Edwards. Edwards was managing one of the boxers and the two became fast friends. During their conversations, Savage shared that he listened to LL Cool J, Eminem and Run-DMC and that he'd be interested in making some music.

Edwards was not about to turn down a "Macho Man" Randy Savage rap album produced in his studio.

"Randy liked it," Lanny said. "One of the most annoying things about Randy, even though he was two years older than me, he would call me up and always introduce a brand new word I didn't know. He would say 'true dat,' and I would say 'what is that?' He kept up with the lingo.

"Randy put a lot of himself into it and practiced everything he possibly could to learn the craft. He was not a halfway kind of guy. He did something or did not do something, all or nothing. He was invested thoroughly."

The album was produced and co-written by a group called Da Raskulls and Savage managed to get DJ Kool of "Let Me Clear My Throat" fame on a track. Like everything else in his life, Savage tried to find a place for Lanny on the album, originally asking him to write a song dissing Hulk Hogan. His younger brother declined that idea.

"I didn't want to be part of a CD that insults Hulk Hogan. I love my brother, but I also love Hulk Hogan. In a twenty-one-year career, the guy who gave me the best four months of it was Hulk Hogan, and I'll be damned if I'm going to blaspheme him on some music," Lanny said.

Instead, he had a better idea, and co-wrote a song as a tribute to Curt "Mr. Perfect" Hennig for the last track on the album. While the title track was a classic early 2000s diss aimed at Hulk Hogan, the tribute to Hennig was the most well-received song on the CD.

"Just like everything else, it takes a little bit of adjusting, but I caught on pretty quick," Savage said at the time of the album's release. "Right now I'm all about it. This is everything to me. Music's been a part of me. Now I'm going to put the power on. We're going to rock the country; we're going to rock the world."

Savage's first live show in his hometown was . . . encouraging.

"People felt good about it," he said. "We had a lot of energy. I've never been humble about anything in my whole career, so I'm not going to start now. Once again the madness is running wild."

Truthfully, the promotion of the album generated more buzz than the album itself. Over a decade removed from his prime stardom and several years removed from the ring, most in the media used the album as a touchpoint for "Where are they now?" pieces on Randy Savage because, let's be honest, the news that the Macho Man was rapping in 2003 was met with a collective "Seriously?"

But there Macho Man was, appearing at MTV's Video Music Awards radio forum. There he was again, getting praise from Lil Jon; and again on camera with 50 Cent. To drum up publicity for the project, Savage went on a nationwide tour that included record stores, strip malls and even the Mall of America.

Longtime wrestling writer Scott Fishman covered Macho Man's media tour as his first assignment during a college internship with the *Miami Herald*.

"It was at a Walmart autograph signing," Fishman said. "Before he went out to do the signing I talked to him for a couple minutes in the break room. All the workers were surrounding me and listening to our conversation."

Fishman grew up a Macho Man fan and couldn't believe he was sitting face-to-face with one of the all-time greats. As they talked, Fishman took stock of the fifty-one-year-old Savage, who wore an all-black outfit with sunglasses.

"He was very soft-spoken and down to earth," Fishman said. "He was definitely in shape still. Like his WCW run towards the end. Height-wise, he was probably a little smaller than you'd think."

The most memorable appearance of the tour came when Savage co-hosted Nickelodeon's *Slime Time Live* with Dave Aizer.

"I was always a big WWF kid growing up," Aizer said. "He was great. Everything we wanted to do or the kids wanted to do he would roll for. Sometimes you meet some people and you're disappointed. This was not the case."

The album, as you may have guessed since you likely never heard of it, did not do well. It sold roughly 15,000 copies. Far less than Savage would have liked.

"He was also having a bit of delusions of grandeur," Lanny said. "He thought he was going to sell 15 million CDs . . . and then, he was doing it as a comeback. He hadn't been on television in years. It was like reinventing himself."

In the end, *Be a Man* didn't accomplish Savage's goal of regaining the public spotlight. There was, however, one final role in a major Hollywood movie that did just that: Bone Saw McGraw.

CHAPTER 33

Bone Saw

He appears thirty-seven minutes into director Sam Raimi's 2002 *Spider-Man*. Long dark hair. Thick beard. Muscles like they were pumped up using an air compressor.

To many in the audience, he looks familiar.

Then he talks.

Then we get a close-up.

Then, collectively, at the same exact time across hundreds of seats in a darkened room, everyone thinks, *Holy shit! Is that Randy Savage?*

Yes, yes it was.

The role of Bone Saw McGraw was being played by none other than the Macho Man.

"He didn't have an agent. People contacted him directly," Lanny said. "He had to audition for the *Spider-Man* movie but he didn't know if he was up against anybody."

"Let's face it, the part was written for me," Savage said. "Bone Saw is a cocky, colorful professional wrestler who likes to surround himself with attractive ladies. My character is basically Macho Man with hair extensions."

When Savage was offered the part he hadn't been in the limelight for a while. And he hadn't wrestled in years. He was in good shape, but not wrestling shape. And he didn't have nearly the size of someone who was going to be manhandling Tobey Maguire around a steel cage.

"He had six months to train while he grew his beard and hair out," Lanny said.

Over the course of that half-year, Savage put on an incredible (and unhealthy) fifty pounds of muscle through diet, exercise and some combination of unconfirmed growth hormones and God knows what else.

When the movie opened, even his old wrestling buddies barely recognized him.

"I saw the movie and didn't realize Randy played Bone Saw," Paul Roma said. "I couldn't believe that was him. He was so swollen."

Looks aside, Randy had the time of his life on set. And as with everything else in his career, he didn't film his scenes on cruise control. He gave everything he had, even asking people to call him Bone Saw on set to get into character.

He worked closely with the stunt coordinator to make sure the wrestling scenes were accurate and he peppered Sam Raimi with questions about directing. Raimi, looking like a dad cruising Home Depot in search of light bulbs, learned the finer points of double axe handles and chair smashing. When he wasn't talking to Raimi or other cast members, Randy was banging out push-ups between takes to look as pumped up as possible.

"The action sequences were real intense and the crowd was into it big time when we filmed it," Savage said.

About those action sequences . . .

"He was offered a stunt double, but of course, Randy being the Macho Man, he wouldn't accept that," Lanny said. "He did his own stunts."

While this sounds tough on the surface, it almost had disastrous consequences. During his fight scene with Tobey Maguire, about two minutes after delivering these lines . . .

"Hey, freak show! You're goin' nowhere! I got ya for three minutes! Three minutes of play time!"

. . . Savage was almost paralyzed.

You have to watch the scene closely to see it, but once you do, you can't miss it. Towards the end of his battle with Maguire, he's tossed across the ring and is supposed to bounce off the ropes upside down. He got the upside-down part right, but the bounce didn't go as planned and Savage landed on his neck. Everyone thought he was seriously hurt. He was, after all, not a young guy anymore.

After he got up, Raimi asked if he could do another take and Savage, of course, obliged. In fact, they did ten more.

"He fell on his head doing that monkey flip," Lanny said. "And he continued to do take after take. He loved those people. The next morning he couldn't get out of bed. I never saw him turn his neck after that. He'd turn his whole shoulder and body. For years I'd ask, 'How's your neck?' and he'd say, 'Never better.'"

For those on set who grew up fans of the Macho Man, it was a surreal experience, especially when they learned that he was a nice, hard-working guy.

"He was awesome. He was amazing. He was fabulous," Lisa Danielle, who played one of Bone Saw's Bone-ettes, said. "It was very fun. He took direction like the rest of us and knew his lines. He improvised the line 'It's play time,' which was great."

The wrestling scene was shot over the course of three long days, from 7 a.m. to 7 p.m. or later, which meant the cast subsisted on craft services, energy bars, caffeine and whatever they wanted to bring on their own. Savage, always focused on his physique, took it one step further.

"I remember he carried a whole pack of grilled chicken breast with him in a Tupperware container for his protein," Danielle laughed.

Danielle said he was very low-key on the set and blended in whenever he could. He was aware that a lot of the crew had grown up watching him and he talked to everyone, even obliging a few signature requests after shooting.

As a general rule, asking for autographs and personal photos isn't permitted on or around the set, but Danielle managed to grab one for her collection.

"When you're on set you don't ask for pictures," she said. "But I took a picture of Bone Saw and the Bone-ettes and had everyone sign it. It was too big of an opportunity to pass up."

The same went for Savage and the moviemaking process overall, as he soaked up every minute in front of the camera.

"Sam Raimi taught me so much," he said. "It was unbelievable . . . just following him around. Everybody knows he knows the deal. It's the opposite of wrestling, where they send you out there on your own. Here it's live at five!"

"He was very happy," Lanny said. "He'd been out of the limelight for a while. He thought being a superhero would make him kind of immortal."

Spider-Man opened in 3,615 theaters across the United States in May of 2002 and made over $825 million around the world. It kicked off the modern take on superhero movies. Millions of fans filled seats to see Spidey, the Green Goblin, Tobey Maguire, Kirsten Dunst, James Franco and Willem Dafoe.

And all of them were treated to a surprise dose of the Macho Man.

CHAPTER 34

Serenity

Lanny was supposed to pick up a twelve-pack of Miller Lite on the way to Randy's house but the Publix supermarket was out. He checked every shelf of beer in the entire refrigerated aisle. Nothing. *Dammit*.

Reluctantly, he grabbed what he thought was the next best thing, Miller Genuine Draft. It was close, but it wasn't what Randy asked for and he knew he was going to get shit for it. Whatever.

A few minutes later Lanny pulled up to his brother's house, walked in with the MGD and put it on the counter. Randy looked at him and at the beer.

Here it comes, Lanny thought.

"Son of a bitch," Savage growled. "I send you for Miller Lite and you can't even get that right."

"Yeah, yeah," Lanny said as they both laughed.

This was on May 19, 2011, the night before Randy Savage died.

In the years prior to his brother's death, Lanny was convinced that Randy was experiencing some kind of cosmic and spiritual awakening. Whatever anger and intensity that had been driving him for so long, from high school baseball to the Cincinnati Reds to the ICW, WWF,

WCW and beyond, had finally dissipated. He didn't wake up and go to bed pissed off anymore.

He'd come to accept things as facts of life rather than focal points for frustration. He'd spent his middle-aged years ashamed and embarrassed about his graying hair and his bald spot and getting older in general. In his final half-decade he gave up the dyes and lotions and hats and came to peace with his white, thinning hair. That was who he was now. So be it.

He'd held on to so many grudges that he'd lost track. Big ones. Small ones. Perceived slights. Real backstabbing. It was time to let go.

A few months before his death he'd put to rest one of his longest-standing real-life feuds — the one with Hulk Hogan. The two hadn't spoken in almost ten years when they ran into each other at the doctor's office.

"He came up and grabbed Hulk from behind," Judy Poffo said. "Hulk turned around and he was so happy. Randy wasn't angry anymore."

"[We] were sitting on those little seats in the doctor's office in Tampa and all of a sudden the door opens and in comes Randy," Hogan said. "'Yeahh! Ohhh yeahhh! What's up, Hogan?' He had that gleam in his eye and looked really healthy. He gained his weight back and he had a wedding ring on."

The wedding ring was another layer to Savage's spiritual endgame.

There had been plenty of girlfriends after Miss Elizabeth, and when she died tragically in 2003, his heart ached even though they hadn't seen each other in years. Love wasn't on his mind much in his mid-50s until, once again, a conversation at the gym changed his life.

He was working out one day when a woman came up to him and asked, "Do you know Lynn Payne?"

Macho gave the lady an interested look and said, "Yeah."

The lady was Lynn's best friend and she asked if Macho would like to see her. Lynn and Randy had dated very early in his minor league baseball days (way back in 1973) and hadn't been in touch since. She had married and divorced and had kids and now was single. Randy was intrigued, so he drove 180 miles down to Fort Myers to catch up with Lynn.

"When he came back, the stars never shined so bright," Lanny said. "It was love at first sight, again."

"She made him so happy," Judy said. "So completely happy."

With Lynn in his life, Randy began thinking more and more about his legacy and what he wanted to do with the years he had left. On a day-to-day basis, he'd begun to make up for all the lost time on the road by spending more time with his parents, taking them to their doctor's appointments and having regular dinners at each other's houses. You know, just being a loving son who was around to help out.

He stayed out of the spotlight, mostly, though he continued to have time for just about any charity involving kids, especially his long-standing tradition of reading "The Night Before Christmas" at the Yankees/Steinbrenner Children's Holiday Concert for underprivileged kids in Tampa.

"Mr. Steinbrenner was a big fan of Macho Man and Hulk Hogan and other wrestlers in the area," Howard Grosswirth, the Yankees' VP of Community and Media Relations in Tampa, said. "He didn't want just someone to read 'The Night Before Christmas.' At one point he was thinking of who the next big thing is [that] the kids would love to see. Then we reached out to Macho Man."

What began as a single invitation became a standing invite year after year. The kids enjoyed it. Randy enjoyed it. And the community got behind it.

"Randy was larger than life," Grosswirth said. "The kids absolutely loved him. He spoke to the kids. We ask anyone who is doing the reading to say a few words to motivate them and put them on the straight and narrow. And he was wonderful. In the later years the kids knew him from *Spider-Man*."

There were plenty of other charities Savage found time for, and whenever anyone reached out to have him speak to kids, he accepted. One time, he even built them a weight room.

After a friend who was an assistant football coach at Admiral Farragut near Savage's home showed him around the school, Savage was bummed out about the team having a crappy weight room. So he built them a new gym, stocked it with weights and named it after his dad, Angelo Poffo. They placed a picture of Angelo doing sit-ups on the wall for good measure.

"I had just taken over the program," then head coach Mike Jalazo said. "It was my first year as head coach, period. And Randy came out to [football] practice to speak to the team. It was ninety-five degrees in Florida and we were on metal stands. He's in head-to-toe leather, doing the full Macho Man thing. He went on for forty minutes. We wound up going undefeated that year."

Jalazo remembers how the kids were captivated by him and how after the speech was done, Savage was calm and easygoing and stayed to talk to the kids. He told stories about wrestling and his father and perseverance.

By the time of Randy's marriage to Lynn, Angelo and Judy were both in their eighties and his dad was experiencing health problems. A few months before Randy's wedding date, Angelo Poffo, his personal idol, passed away.

"He was going to change the date, but we told him not to," Judy said. "Ang wouldn't have wanted him to change it. It was sad. He passed away in March and they got married in May."

The wedding took place on the exact spot that Lynn and Randy had met on the beach nearly forty years earlier. It was a small ceremony and, of course, Lanny wrote a poem for the occasion:

> *We are back on the beach where they met long ago,*
> *In honor of Randy and Lynn*
> *A beautiful couple that loved and lost*
> *But now they've both chosen to win*
> *"Nice Tan" was my brother's opening line*
> *"What?" was Lynn's thoughtful reply*
> *Surviving the time and the distance between*
> *Is the knot they have come here to tie . . .*

Other than the time of Angelo's passing, Randy appeared to Lanny and Hulk and others who spotted him around Seminole, Florida, as a relaxed, happy guy. He'd moved off of the beach into a secluded house on over an acre of property. The lot was surrounded by woods and offered total privacy. After decades of having fans shout "Snap into it!!!" and "Machoooooo!!!!" every time he stepped foot on his balcony, the quiet and zen of the surrounding trees was nice.

He'd found love.

He'd found serenity.

He was even potentially reconciling with the WWF, which he'd not had anything to do with since leaving for the WCW in 1994. Rumors. Gossip. There were plenty of theories as to why, but none were confirmed. What matters is that while Randy Savage was alive, he was not welcomed back into the WWF fold, nor did he push to get back.

But . . .

In 2010, at Comic-Con in San Diego, Savage showed up in a pretaped segment to promote an all-new Macho Man figure, even surprising the audience with a vintage "Ooohhhhh yeahhhh!"

On January 19, four months before he passed away, the WWE released a video showcasing what Macho's character looked like in their *WWE All-Stars* video game. He even let them shoot the promo at his house.

We can only speculate where this olive branch between Savage and the WWE was headed, however, because on the morning of May 20, 2011, he had a heart attack while driving and passed away.

He had just gone to breakfast with Lynn at their favorite spot, a Perkins restaurant near the house. He'd ordered his usual, an egg white and vegetable omelet, but had been complaining about not feeling well all morning. Lynn wasn't sure if this was the usual "I wrestled for almost forty years and my body always hurts" aches and pains — or something new.

When they left the restaurant, Lynn offered to drive because Randy appeared to be struggling. Being the Macho Man, he said he was fine.

A few minutes into the drive, just before 9:30 a.m., Savage slumped over the wheel, losing consciousness. Making matters worse, his foot was stuck on the accelerator. Thinking quickly, Lynn reached around Randy's body, swerved the Jeep out of oncoming traffic and hit a tree on purpose to stop the car. She undoubtedly saved the lives of people in oncoming traffic. Thankfully, she sustained only minor injuries. Randy was pronounced dead at Largo Medical Center.

Mark Boehme, who lived on the property where Lynn hit the tree, said Lynn was a hero.

"He'd come over the median and she steered the wheel this way," he said. "There was a fella on a motorcycle who said he had nowhere to go in oncoming traffic. He said he'd have been dead if she didn't turn the Jeep."

Boehme was teaching across the street that morning and in a short time, news media were all over his front lawn. As word spread about the tragedy, the locals mourned. Savage had been a long-standing, visible presence in the community.

"He was a character and we saw him often," Boehme said. "He was always willing to sign an autograph and pose for a picture. After the accident people loaded the tree with flowers and streamers and Macho Man figurines. They covered it with flowers. To this day, people pay respect by pinning Savage stickers and purple streamers and even Slim Jims on the tree."

Lanny was on a layover in Dallas from a flight he'd taken that morning. He'd landed shortly before 10 a.m. Central time. When he checked his phone he saw the hospital had called.

"They said, 'Randy has been in accident with his wife,'" Lanny said. "The way they said it, I knew . . . It was just devastating. I was a wreck. But I needed to be strong for my mother and daughter."

As the years passed, Lanny often thought about the last night he spent with his brother, grateful that it happened and sad it would never happen again.

"We laughed and we had fun," Lanny said. "Just like we always did."

Twelve years later, after missing his brother every day, Lanny passed away in February of 2023. His death, like Randy's, was sudden and shocking. He'd been the steward for the family's legacy. The torchbearer. Proudly representing all that he and his father and brother had accomplished in wrestling and in life.

We can only imagine him smiling now, reunited with the other Poffo men, laughing and having fun together, with (as Randy often said) that great big Macho Man in the sky.

ACKNOWLEDGMENTS

"Is that it, Dad?" my eleven-year-old daughter asked.

"I think so," I said.

We'd been in the car for four hours. West through the Everglades. North over Tampa Bay. West again on Park Boulevard in St. Petersburg towards Seminole, Florida, and our destination: a tree.

But not just any tree.

We were after a particular Florida fishpoison tree that sits just west of 113th Street across from the Bay Pines Evangelical Lutheran Church. There are thousands of these trees spread across Pinellas County, but this tree is special for one reason and one reason only: this was the tree Randy Savage crashed into after he had a heart attack while driving on the morning of May 20, 2011.

"Do you think people know that's the Macho Man tree?" she asked.

"We'll see," I said, pulling my car over to park on the side of the road.

There were plenty of stops I wanted to make on my Macho Man research road trip — Randy's house, his neighborhood, his condo, the memorabilia at Hogan's Hangout — but this one was the most important because I'd read that this tree had become the de facto public Macho Man memorial, a place for people to celebrate and mourn and remember the iconic wrestler.

"Look!" my daughter shouted, running to the tree.

During our ride I tried to explain to her how much Macho meant to millions of wrestling fans my age and why it wasn't silly or weird to visit this tree. No matter what I said, she was skeptical. After all, Randy Savage had died a dozen years earlier, and as she'd said while we were driving over the bay, "It's just a tree."

But then she saw the tree and, more importantly, what was on it: Macho Man stickers, Slim Jim wrappers, flowers, tassels, a bunch of faded purple ribbons wrapped around the trunk and, as if to seal the deal, two Macho Man figurines placed gently on the grass below it.

"Wow!" she said. "This is so cool. People still remember him. They care."

"Yep," I said. "That's why I'm writing the book."

Millions of us remember Macho Man.

And millions of us care.

First, I want to thank my daughter for going along on that road trip with me. As any author will tell you, writing a book is a largely solitary experience. Yes, you interview hundreds of people, but much of your time is buried in research: flipping through magazines and newspapers and books and watching or listening to interviews and, of course, writing. Lots and lots of late nights and early mornings and all-times-of-the-day solo writing sessions.

Any time you can spend working on a book while you're hanging out with someone, especially one of your kids, is great. Thank you, Reese. I'll cherish this book for a lot of reasons, but right up top will be that you were a part of it.

And to my son, Grant, who watched *all* of the Macho Man research with me. I mean all of the WrestleManias, all of the old matches and interviews on YouTube and all of the documentaries. I got to relive the magic of Macho through my ten-year-old boy's eyes as we perfected our "ooooh yeahhhh!" and "cream of the crop!" impressions together. What a gift.

On that note, my wife has had to listen to me and my boy shout "I'm the tower of power too sweet to be sour!" and "dig it!" for the better part of a year. She knew she married a macho man, but not *the* Macho Man. My favorite part of my boy falling in love with wrestling is when my wife goes into his room to kiss him goodnight and he sneak-attacks her and then rolls her up for a pin on his bed. One! Two! Three! So good. Love it all. You're a trooper, Steph!

In many ways this book has felt like a family affair because the Macho Man in particular and wrestling in general were such a huge part of my childhood. My brother, Craig, and I had every single wrestling action figure imaginable. We watched every pay-per-view. We wrestled nonstop, body-slamming each other on our beds until we got yelled at. (Side note: my kids, along with my niece and nephews Dean, Gus and Mallory, do the same thing and it's so cool to see.)

My dad, who worked for Toys "R" Us back in the day, even had Big John Studd at a grand opening and we got to meet him. Big shout-out to my mom for chronicling this (and all our other wrestling exploits). She kept meticulous photo albums of us with our plush toys, our Hulkamania shirts and more. It helped bring me back into the frame of mind I needed to write this book. My uncle, Ug, has been a huge Macho Man fan my whole life as well. So wrestling has been a part of my life — my whole life. And when I say I've wanted to write this book since I was a kid, I really and truly mean it.

Specifically, this book began during a conversation with my agent, Joe Perry. As we talked about potential ideas for a follow-up to my last book, *1996: A Biography*, I said, "It's time. Nobody has done the definitive Macho Man biography. I want to do it. I just need to find a way to get in touch with Lanny."

Joe's also a Macho Man fan and he agreed: it was time.

I shared the story of getting in touch with Lanny in the introduction of this book, but suffice to say, the biggest thank-you goes out to him. His green light to talk to me made this possible. But before I could get Lanny on board, I had to get in touch with him and I will be eternally grateful to JP Zarka of Pro Wrestling Stories for not only vouching for me to Lanny, but also for staying on him about getting back to me. You went above and beyond, JP!

After talking to Lanny, the next step was to find the right publisher and editor, and I wanted to make sure we found someone who not only understood Macho's place in pop culture but also got the weird and wonderful world of pro wrestling. We couldn't have found a more perfect partner for this book than Executive Editor Michael Holmes and his team at ECW Press. Shout out to David Marsh for a terrific copy edit, along with everyone else who I've worked with there. You've all been phenomenal.

Whenever I write a book I'm always amazed at how generous people are with their time when it comes to interviews. For this book, I spent time talking to people who grew up with Randy back when he was Randy Poffo, way before there was even a thought of the Macho Man, all the way up to his baseball and wrestling careers and his role in *Spider-Man*. That was a lot of ground to cover and just about everyone was game to chat.

And a big thank-you to all the people I spoke with, including these all-stars:

David Buehrer, Tom Bruno and Tom Bruno (yes, there are two), Chris Cirko, Lisa Danielle, "Hacksaw" Jim Duggan, Scott Fishman, Brian Gewirtz, Robert Gibson, John Guarnaccia, Howard Grosswirth (hat tip to all-time best friend Eddie Coblentz), Tim Gunn, Dr. Russ Holpuch, Sal Iacono, Mike Jalazo, Kevin Makely, Dutch Mantell, Bill Martin, Travis Orndorff, Rip Rogers, Bruce Ritter, Paul Roma, Tito Santana, Ricky "The Dragon" Steamboat, Bo Vespi, George Weingeroff, Craig Winter.

And thank you to my fellow authors Brian Solomon and Greg Oliver, who were both generous with their time and resources along the way.

And finally, I want to thank each and every one of you for going on this Macho Man journey with me. I hope you enjoyed reading this as much as I did writing it, and to paraphrase Jay-Z, you could have picked up any book in the world and you chose this one — I appreciate that.

SOURCES & REFERENCES

CHAPTER 1

Corben, Billy. *Macho Man: The Randy Savage Story*, WWE Home
    Video, 2014.
Husar, Big John. "Sits Up Like World Champion for 6,033 Times,"
    Chicago Tribune, Feb. 26, 1972.
Pazdur, Ed. "How Poffo Puffed Way to Record," *The DePaulian*.
Scheiber, Dave. "A Wrestling Dynasty," *Tampa Bay Times*, Dec. 27, 2001.

CHAPTER 2

Capouya, John. "King Strut," *Sports Illustrated*, Dec. 12, 2005.
Classic Wrestling Articles: Newspaper and Magazine Articles on the
    Sport of Professional Wrestling. classicwrestlingarticles.wordpress
    .com/tag/johnny-meyers/.
Gleason, Bill. Column on Ruffy Silverstein, *Chicago Sun-Times*, June 26,
    1979.
Harrison, E.J. *The Fighting Spirit of Japan and Other Studies* (London: T.
    Fisher Unwin), 1913, www.google.com/books/edition/The_Fighting
    _Spirit_of_Japan_and_Other_S/vOpAAQAAMAAJ?hl=en&gbpv
    =1&dq=inauthor:%22Ernest+John+Harrison%22&printsec=frontcover.

Hornbaker, Tim. *Legends of Pro Wrestling: 150 Years of Headlocks, Body Slams and Piledrivers* (Champaign, IL: Sports Publishing LLC), 2017.

CHAPTER 3

Johnson, Steven, and Greg Oliver. *The Pro Wrestling Hall of Fame: Heroes & Icons* (Toronto: ECW Press), 2012.

Legacy.com. "Outrageous, Gorgeous George," Mar. 24, 2012, www .legacy.com/news/celebrity-deaths/outrageous-gorgeous-george/.

Lexington Herald. "Angelo Poffo Booked as Tag Participant," Nov. 7, 1950.

Nannenga, Brittan. "The Great Zuma: A Mysterious Martian That Turned Out to Be a Blue Demon," DePaul University Newsline, May 1, 2020, resources.depaul.edu/newsline/sections/into-the -archives/Pages/The-Great-Zuma.aspx#:~:text=In%201950%2C%20 the%20world%20of,top%20that%20concealed%20his%20face.

CHAPTER 4

The Press Democrat (Santa Rosa, CA). "Roy Shire, a Wrestler Crowds Loved to Hate," Sept. 25, 1992.

University of Illinois Hall of Fame. "Ralph 'Ruffy' Silverstein," fightingillini .com/honors/hall-of-fame/ralph-ruffy-silverstein/104#:~:text=University %20of%20Illinois%20Athletics,-Main%20Navigation%20Menu&text =Ruffy%20Silverstein%20was%20the%201935,1935%20Big%20Ten%20 team%20title.

Wrestling Epicenter. "Carl Engstrom," www.wrestlingepicenter.com/ RIP/CarlEng.shtml.

CHAPTER 5

Barrasso, Justin. "Macho Man: Wild Road from Baseball Washout to WWE Hall of Famer," *Sports Illustrated*, Mar. 19, 2015, www.si.com /extra-mustard/2015/03/19/randy-macho-man-savage-wwe-hall -of-fame.

Cincinnati Post. "Poffo Winner," Jan. 24, 1959.

Gomez, Luis. "Macho Man's Road to WWE Hall of Fame Went Through Downers Grove," *Chicago Tribune*, Mar. 25, 2015, www.chicagotribune .com/travel/chi-macho-man-randy-savage-wwe-hall-of-fame-downers -grove-20150325-column.html.

Hornbaker, Tim. "'Cowboy' Bob Ellis Wrestling History," LegacyofWrestling.com, www.legacyofwrestling.com/BobEllis.html.

Lister, John. *Slamthology* (independently published, 2005), 219.

Posnanski, Joe. "The Baseball 100: No. 60, Pete Rose," The Athletic, Jan. 27, 2020, theathletic.com/1546407/2020/01/27/the-baseball-100-no-60 -pete-rose/.

Scinto, Maria. "The Truth about 'Macho Man' Randy Savage's Impressive Baseball Past," WrestlingInc.com, Jan. 26, 2023, www.wrestlinginc.com /964850/the-truth-about-macho-man-randy-savages-impressive- baseball-past/.

Shields, Brian, and Kevin Sullivan. *WWE Encyclopedia: The Definitive Guide to World Wrestling Entertainment* (Dorling Kindersley: New York, 2009), 121.

Terre Haute (IN) Tribune. "Mat Artists Perform Tonight," Feb. 16, 1959.

CHAPTER 6

Bensenville (IL) Register. "DuPage Cards Post Two Wins," June 9, 1969.

Berwyn (IL) Life. "Olympics to Play Tonight," June 6, 1969.

Chicago Tribune. "Louis Menchetti," www.chicagotribune.com/news/ ct-xpm-1993-11-29-9311290104-story.html.

Chicago Tribune. "W. Suburban League Has Co-Champions," May 23, 1971, chicagotribune.newspapers.com/search/?query=W.%20Suburban %20League&dr_year=1970-1979.

Daily Herald (Chicago). "Cards Soar, Sink in Weekend Games," Aug. 13, 1969.

New Wave Wrestling magazine. Interview by A.J. Almquist, February 1986.

Oshkosh (WI) Northwestern. "Chicago Orioles Win Three," June 22, 1970, thenorthwestern.newspapers.com/search/?query=chicago%20 orioles&dr_year=1970-1979.

Pearlman, Jeff. "Randy (Macho Man) Savage's Dream Was to Make It to the Majors," *Sports Illustrated*, May 23, 2011, www.si.com/more-sports /2011/05/23/macho-man.

Scinto, Maria. "The Truth about 'Macho Man' Randy Savage's Impressive Baseball Past," WrestlingInc.com, Jan. 26, 2023, www.wrestlinginc.com /964850/the-truth-about-macho-man-randy-savages-impressive -baseball-past/.

Twin City News-Record (Neenah, WI). "Chicago Orioles Face Macs," June 18, 1970.

CHAPTER 7

Bradenton (FL) Herald. "Cubs Open League Shutout Play," June 27, 1972.

Eck, Kevin. "This Minor League Flop Is a Big Hit in Wrestling," *Baltimore Sun*, June 13, 1994.

Schmidt, Neil. "'Macho Man' Is on Deck," *Cincinnati Enquirer*, Dec. 28, 1993.

Selman, Jim. "Bean Balls Fly, Expos Rock Tarps," *Tampa Tribune*, Apr. 30, 1974.

Story, Mark. "The Catcher in the Ring," *Lexington Herald-Leader*, May 29, 2011.

The Times and Democrat (Orangeburg, SC). "Cardinals Halt 15-game Losing Streak," July 8, 1973.

The Times and Democrat. "Meet the Cardinals," May 17, 1973.

Sarasota Herald-Tribune. "Two Arms Are Better than One," May 6, 1975.

CHAPTER 8

Cincinnati Post. "Ex-Ballplayer on Mat Show," May 10, 1975.

Hogan, Martin, Jr. "Meet the Pete Rose of Wrestling," *Cincinnati Enquirer*, Oct. 7, 1983.

Ludington (MI) Daily News. "Big Time Wrestling Coming to Mason County," Oct. 30, 1975.

Pearlman, Jeff. "Randy (Macho Man) Savage's Dream Was to Make It to the Majors," *Sports Illustrated*, May 23, 2011, www.si.com/more-sports/2011/05/23/macho-man.

CHAPTER 9

Poupart, Alain. "A Longshot Pays Off," *Miami News*, July 4, 1980.

Scheiber, Dave. "A Wrestling Dynasty," *St. Petersburg Times*, Dec. 27, 2001.

Selman, Jim. "Mean, Tough Randy Poffo, A Chip Off the Ole Block," *Tampa Tribune*, Dec. 18, 1976.

Warren, Jim. "Macho Man Is a Savage in the Ring," *Lexington Herald-Leader*, Mar. 8, 1984.

Wild, Danny. "Former Macho Outfielder Dies," MiLB News, May 24, 2011.

Wrestling Highlights Festival, *News-Journal*, Aug. 28, 1975.

Wrestling at Stark County, *The Tribune*, July 20, 1975.

CHAPTER 10

Charlotte News. "Two Main Events on Mat Program," Sept. 17, 1976.

Ledger-Enquirer (Columbus, GA). "Wrestling Update," Mar. 3, 1977.

Guzzo, Paul. "The Macho Mom: Judy Poffo, Mother of Wrestlers Randy Savage and Lanny Poffo Dead at 90," *Tampa Bay Times*, June 4, 2017, web.archive.org/web/20170605015528/://www.tbo.com/news/obituaries/the-macho-mom-judy-poffo-mother-of-wrestlers-randy-savage-and-lanny-poffo/2326147.

Mooneyham, Mike. "Hardcore Wrestling Pioneer Pampero Firpo: 'I Accomplished My Destiny,'" *The Post and Courier* (Charleston, SC), Oct. 6, 2018, www.postandcourier.com/sports/wrestling/hardcore-wrestling-pioneer-pampero-firpo-i-accomplished-my-destiny/article_aeobf1c6-c8a8-11e8-adc4-6bf86049c09f.html.

Pensacola (FL) Journal. "Their Stage," Jan. 19, 1976.

Selman, Jim. "Mean, Tough Randy Poffo, A Chip Off the Ole Block," *Tampa Tribune*, Dec. 18, 1976.

Macon Telegraph, March 6, 1977, page 25, advertisement.

CHAPTER 11

Bowden, Scott. "Tonight's Main Event: Scott Bowden vs. Dutch Mantell in an Oil Trough, Texas Death Match," KentuckyFriedWrestling.com, Apr. 5, 2010, kentuckyfriedwrestling .com/tonights-main-event-scott-bowden-vs-dutch-mantell-in-an -oil-trough-texas-death-match/.

The Tennessean (Nashville). "Angel Still Champ," Oct. 19, 1978.

The Tennessean. "Mantell Seeks Savage's Belt; Wynn Debuts," Mar. 22, 1978.

The Tennessean. "Pro Gridder Faces Savage in Headliner," Jan. 3, 1979.

The Tennessean. "Ross Team Takes Win in Feature," Dec. 22, 1977.

CHAPTER 12

Sherborne, Robert. "Took Fight Out of Ring, Police Say," *The Tennessean*, Nov. 25, 1978.

The Tennessean. "Wrestler Says Fight Report Not Entirely True," Nov. 30, 1975.

CHAPTER 13

Scala, Benny J. "Fan vs. Shooter: The Ill-Fated $1000 Sugar Hold Challenge," ProWrestlingStories.com, Jan. 10, 2023, prowrestlingstories .com/pro-wrestling-stories/sugar-hold-challenge/.

CHAPTER 14

Beifuss, John. "Jerry Lawler: 50 Years of Pinning Opponents and Running His Mouth," *The Commercial Appeal* (Memphis), Sept. 20, 2020, www .commercialappeal.com/story/news/2020/09/21/jerry-lawler-the-king -professional-wrestling-wwe-raw-memphis/5795501002/.

Clark, Kym. "5 Star Stories: Jerry 'The King' Lawler Celebrates 50 Years Inside the Ring," Action News 5 (Memphis), Nov. 11, 2020, www .actionnews5.com/2020/11/10/star-stories-jerry-king-lawler-celebrates -years-inside-ring/.

Classic Memphis Wrestling videos. "Promos for Lawler vs. Savage Cage Match," December 1983, www.facebook.com/watch/?v=2234107573392564.

Edwards, Don. "Rasslin' Grudge Match Expected to Be Big Draw at Rupp," *Lexington Herald-Leader*, Feb. 24, 1984.

Freedman, Lew. "Mark Sciarra Loved Being the Bad Guy," *The Tribune* (Seymour, IN), May 16, 2020, tribtown.com/2020/05/16/mark-sciarra-loved-being-the-bad-guy/.

Glasspiegel, Ryan. "Jimmy Hart Reveals Ruse to get Macho Man to WWE," *New York Post*, Sept. 2, 2022.

The Hannibal TV YouTube Excerpt – Jimmy Hart

Holder, James. "Jerry Lawler Recalls Crazy Randy Savage Story," ITRWrestling.com, Aug. 25, 2021, itrwrestling.com/news/jerry-lawler-recalls-crazy-randy-savage-story/.

CHAPTER 15

Lexington Herald-Leader. "Savage-Lawler Match No-Contest," Mar. 10, 1984.

Murphy, Ryan. "The 'Macho Man' Invades Memphis: Randy Savage, Jerry Lawler and the Battle for Tennessee," WWE.com, Feb. 26, 2013, www.wwe.com/classics/randy-savage-jerry-lawler-memphis-rivalry.

Snowden, Jonathan. "WWE Hall of Famer Jimmy Hart on Hogan, Wrestlemania I and Signing Randy Savage," BleacherReport.com, Nov. 19, 2013, bleacherreport.com/articles/1857503-wwe-hall-of-famer-jimmy-hart-on-hogan-wrestlemania-i-and-signing-randy-savage.

Warren, Jim. "Macho Man Is Savage in the Ring," *Lexington Herald-Leader*, Mar. 8, 1984.

CHAPTER 17

Braun, Michael. "How I Became Macho Man's Costume Designer," YouTube.com, May 29, 2021, www.youtube.com/watch?v=1Hh9xqSO7Qo.

Hammond, Randy T., Jr. "The Documented History of Wrestling in Poughkeepsie," Medium.com, Dec. 6, 2016, medium.com/thegroundhog/the-documented-history-of-wrestling-in-poughkeepsie-f470bd6dae8b.

Kokomo (IN) Tribune. "Roddy Piper," Feb. 25, 1999.

CHAPTER 19

Evans, Jim. "George 'The Animal' Steele Gives His Take on Randy Savage-Miss Elizabeth Angle," ThePostGame.com, June 24, 2013, www.thepostgame.com/blog/men-action/201306/george-animal-steele-jim-myers-wrestling-elizabeth-randy-savage.

Poupart, Alain. "A Longshot Pays Off," *Miami News*, July 4, 1980.

Steele, George. *Animal* (Chicago: Triumph Books), 2013.

CHAPTER 20

Campbell, Brian. "WrestleMania 3: An Oral history of Randy Savage and Ricky 'The Dragon' Steamboat," ESPN.com, Mar. 2, 2017, www.espn.com/wwe/story/_/id/18802068/oral-history-wrestlemania-3-randy-savage-vs-ricky-dragon-steamboat.

Santa Fe New Mexican. "Wrestle: Mania Hits," Mar. 28, 1987.

CHAPTER 21

Civilize the Savage, *The Dispatch*, Feb. 16, 1986.

CNYWrestling.com. "Jim Duggan," www.cnywrestling.com/ii/hof/halloffamer.php?id=174.

Giri, Raj. "Honky Tonk Man Talks Not Dropping the Title to Savage, Heat with Bischoff, Turning Down HOF & More," WrestlingInc.com, Apr. 8, 2012, www.wrestlinginc.com/news/2012/04/honky-tonk-man-talks-not-dropping-the-title-to-savage-551583/.

Lesar, Al. "'Macho Man' Tries to Gain Back Respect Tuesday," *South Bend (IN) Tribune*, Apr. 23, 1987.

Thomas, Jeremy. "Honky Tonk Man Explains Why He Didn't Drop the Title to Randy Savage," 411Mania.com, Apr. 9, 2012, 411mania.com/wrestling/honky-tonk-man-explains-why-he-didnt-drop-the-title-to-randy-savage/.

YouTube.com. "Bruce Prichard Shoots on The Honky Tonk Man Refusing to Lose the IC Title to Randy Savage," Sept. 14, 2020, www.youtube.com/watch?v=DMKVKYbcqEo.

WWE Network. "Hulk Hogan and 'Macho Man' Randy Savage Send a Message at WCW," 1995, www.facebook.com/watch/?v=3193061764073099.

CHAPTER 22

Guzzo, Paul. "Tampa Mansion That Once Doubled as a Fashion Factory for Stars Is for Sale," *Tampa Bay Times*, July 22, 2020, www.tampabay.com/life-culture/history/2020/07/22/tampa-mansion-that-once-doubled-as-a-fashion-factory-for-stars-is-for-sale/.

New York Times. "Fans lining up for Wrestlemania," Mar. 28, 1987.

Windsor (Ontario) Star. "WrestleMania, A Popular Disease," Mar. 28, 1987.

CHAPTER 23

Albuquerque Tribune. "Wrestling Federation Pumps Gold," June 11, 1988.

Benezra, Karen. "Pepsi Partners with Savage to Put Death Grip on Dew Foes," *Mount Vernon (NY) Argus*, Oct. 1, 1988.

Cincinnati Enquirer. "Celebrities Make Wish Lists," Dec. 25, 1988.

The Daily News (New York). "Randy Savage Jealousy," Mar. 30, 1989.

History of Wrestling. "WrestleMania V," May 5, 2017, historyofwrestlingblog.wordpress.com/2017/05/05/wrestlemania-v/.

Raskin, Alan. "WrestleMania Breaking out in Atlantic City," *Philadelphia Enquirer*, Mar. 31, 1989.

St. Louis Post-Dispatch. "Baseball Flop Turns to Ring," May 15, 1988.

CHAPTER 24

Bath, Richard. "Hulkamania Hits Town," *The Independent*, Oct. 19, 1989.

The Daily News. "Randy's 'Macho' No More," Oct. 27, 1989.

YouTube.com. "Macho Man Announces His Divorce with Elizabeth on Regis & Kathie Lee," November 1992, www.google.com/search?q=Macho+Man+miss+elizabeth+1989+split&rlz=1C5CHFA_enUS717US717&oq=Macho+Man+miss+elizabeth+1989+split&aqs=chrome..69i57j33i160l3.11816j0j7&sourceid=chrome&ie=UTF-8#fpstate=ive&vld=cid:3ddd3f61,vid:bFiDSVoFZqk.

YouTube.com. "Rare Miss Elizabeth Interview — WCW Live Radio," Jan. 20, 2019, www.youtube.com/watch?v=1hfdbTY9MKU.

This book is also available as a Global Certified Accessible™ (GCA) ebook. ECW Press's ebooks are screen reader friendly and are built to meet the needs of those who are unable to read standard print due to blindness, low vision, dyslexia, or a physical disability.

At ECW Press, we want you to enjoy our books in whatever format you like. If you've bought a print copy or an audiobook not purchased with a subscription credit, just send an email to ebook@ecwpress.com and include:

- the book title
- the name of the store where you purchased it
- a screenshot or picture of your order/receipt number and your name

A real person will respond to your email with your ePub attached. If you prefer to receive the ebook in PDF format, please let us know in your email.

Some restrictions apply. This offer is only valid for books already available in the ePub format. Some ECW Press books do not have an ePub format for us to send you. In those cases, we will let you know if a PDF format is available as an alternative. This offer is only valid for books purchased for personal use. At this time, this program is not offered on school or library copies.

Thank you for supporting an independently owned Canadian publisher with your purchase!